OKANAGAN UNIV/COLLEGE LIBRARY

P9-DWF-520

INDIVIDUAL DIFFERENCES IN POSTTRAUMATIC RESPONSE

Problems With the Adversity–Distress Connection

INDIVIDUAL DIFFERENCES IN POSTTRAUMATIC RESPONSE

Problems With the Adversity–Distress Connection

Marilyn Bowman
Simon Fraser University

LEA LAWRENCE ERLBAUM ASSOCIATES, PUBLISHERS
1997 Mahwah, New Jersey   London

Copyright © 1997 by Lawrence Erlbaum Associates, Inc.
All rights reserved. No part of this book may be repro-
duced in any form, by photostat, microfilm, retrieval
system, or any other means, without prior written permis-
sion of the publisher.

Lawrence Erlbaum Associates, Inc., Publishers
10 Industrial Avenue
Mahwah, NJ 07430

Library of Congress Cataloging-in-Publication Data

Bowman, Marilyn (Marilyn L.)
Individual differences in posttraumatic response : problems with the adversity-distress connection / Marilyn
Bowman.
p. cm
Includes bibliographical references and index.
ISBN 0-8058-2713-7 (alk. paper).
1. Post-traumatic stress disorder—Etiology. 2. Individual differences. 3. Distress (Psychology) I. Title.
RC552.P67B69 1997
616.85'21—dc21   97-1892
                                                      CIP

Books published by Lawrence Erlbaum Associates are printed
on acid-free paper, and their bindings are chosen for strength
and durability.

Printed in the United States of America
10 9 8 7 6 5 4 3 2 1

Contents

Preface

This book grew out of my lifelong interest in the ways in which people respond to adversity. This interest has led me to research in coping, clinical work with people who have suffered bad accidents, and an avocational obsession with autobiographical accounts of people who have both suffered and achieved on a scale that seems larger than life. In learning how people respond to nasty and even horrible events I have been struck by the tremendous range of responses. Some individuals become significantly disorganized and distressed by what was a minor event by any objective criterion, while others who experience a vastly more terrible event often show a remarkable resilience. Despite this, the idea that terrible life events have a significant power in affecting mental health has become entrenched in a number of assumptions within professional mental health disciplines and in popular thinking. In particular, the post-traumatic distress disorder diagnosis has served as a prototype for this thinking.

In my attempt to make sense of the diversity of responses that I observed, I studied coping behaviors earlier in my research career, looking at the connections between stress, coping, and distress for evidence concerning the power of life experiences to account for chronic emotional problems that were attributed to life "stressors." The factors that moderate the adversity–distress relationship have been extensively examined in experimental and correlational studies within the fields of stress and coping, in personality studies of emotionality, and in social psychology through studies of attributional processes and their effects on behavior. It became clear that clinical practice is based on an exaggerated idea of the power of life events, and a correspondingly significant inattention to pre-existing factors. Long-standing personality styles and beliefs play a powerful moderating role in the relations between objective adversity and apparent distress responses.

The evidence is so compelling about the power of individual differences in accounting for prolonged distress outcomes after "toxic" life events that I felt compelled to write this book. It represents both a testament to the resilience of those who have been able to surmount horrible experiences, and a different way of thinking about those who find themselves significantly disabled after apparently minor or singular nasty events.

I hope that this way of rethinking prolonged distress syndromes helps direct treatment in ways that will be more helpful than the very event-focused models that are currently used.

ACKNOWLEDGMENTS

I thank my friends and colleagues Charles Crawford and Chris Webster for their support, and Andrew Ross for his calm tolerance of my obsessions. I am grateful to Eve-Marie Lacroix of the National Library of Medicine, who was wonderfully helpful to me for a crucial period, and to Simon Fraser University, which provided me with the time and resources that made this work possible. I would also like to express my appreciation for the pioneers of "the Peace Country" of my northern upbringing; stories of their heroic struggles in a harsh land, and acquaintance with the richness of their responses surely formed a background to my questions.

1

Is There a Problem in Understanding Postevent Distress?

A striking scene was observed on the seashore one August in which men and women wept and lamented loudly. As a result of what had happened, they knew they were forever damned and doomed. In another setting, two little children burst into tears when a man was killed by a gunshot close by. In yet another situation, a man described a certain three decades of his life as having been fun: "I am filled with gratitude for the friends, the adventure, the love, the learning, the excitement, the sheer fun of those years" (Rittenberg & Bennett, 1993, p. 447). Which of these people had been subject to a toxic event, and what was its nature?

The men and women expressing powerful despair had tried to feed themselves to sharks at the mouth of the Hugli river in India in 1640 because they were devout Hindus of a sect who believed this sacrifice was to their spiritual benefit (Manrique, 1927/1967). When they found the already-sated sharks unwilling to eat them, they concluded that they had been found unworthy because they had been too sinful to have their sacrifice accepted, and wailed at their ill luck in not being eaten. In the second case, the children were crying because they had been unable to see a prisoner being executed by soldiers. They became quickly content when their father, a Chinese warlord in Szechuan in the 1920s, held them up so they could see all they wanted of the gory details of the dying man's suffering in the murder (Gervais, 1934). In the final case, the man was Sidney Rittenberg, a young American soldier who stayed in China after World War II. He was describing a period that included two extended imprisonments totaling more than 15 years in solitary confinement in harsh prisons during the turbulent political and military events of the era.

1

Such accounts provide striking examples of the extreme variability of the ways that humans interpret life events. They show how these interpretations have a powerful effect on well-being that can be contrary to common expectations about the power of life events in affecting emotions. Professional mental health activities are increasingly directed to *traumatic* life events as the cause of distress disorders, yet these examples suggest that event characteristics may be much less powerful than is commonly assumed.

This book examines assumptions and evidence about the connections between the experience of an adverse event and reports of distress that are attributed to that adversity. Special attention is given to the power of events in comparison with individual differences in shaping responses to life events. The evidence reviewed shows that acceptance of false assumptions about the significance of events has contributed to ill-directed diagnostic and treatment rhetoric. These errors in understanding the origins of distress have led to professional methods that fail to incorporate important information about individual differences as factors centrally contributing to well-being and distress.

POPULAR ASSUMPTIONS
ABOUT ADVERSITY AND DISTRESS

There are a number of popular and professional assumptions that are currently used to explain human experience following adverse life events. Assumptions related to the nature of events include the following: Acute toxic life events are rare; there is a dose–response relation between toxic life events and postevent distress; toxic events per se account for most postevent distress. There are also assumptions concerning the response to toxic events, including: It is normal to respond to acute toxic life events with significant distress; distress responses diminish with time; distress arises from event characteristics more than from individual factors; distress is validly represented by expressed and reported emotion. Finally, there is the assumption that professional treatment can remedy event-attributed distress.

These assumptions place a major emphasis on external events and on the emotional facets of experience as responses to these, rather than on enduring personal dispositions such as temperament or beliefs. Events are typically given a tautological psychological descriptor that prejudges their assumed subjective effects: they are *traumatic* events. To avoid this over-determined label, for the purposes of this book, significant adverse life events will be termed *toxic events*. This term is used for events that include "violent encounters with nature, technology, or humankind" (Norris, 1992, p. 409). These are acute, objectively observable events intruding on the normal course of life, threatening physical harm or loss of resources, and typically not under the perceived control of individuals. The term *toxic* is chosen to separate the definition from the subjective connotations that the word traumatic provides and to place events in a more objective biological domain in which a high dose exposure may be toxic to an organism even if the object of its effects has no awareness of these.

Event-attributed distress syndromes may include fear and anxiety associated with serious threats to well-being of self or others, as well as depression attributed to losses. In the usage of the popular adversity–distress model, individuals who have encountered a toxic life event are typically described as *victims* and *survivors*, terms that emphasize passivity rather than activity, adaptation, or agency. Individuals are seen as deeply vulnerable to adverse life events that intrude into what would otherwise be a distress-free existence.

These assumptions are related to long-standing issues studied within psychology outside the purely clinical domain. These issues include personality research concerning the relative contributions of person and situation to behavior, the consistency and change in behavior across time within individuals, and the relationships between objective events and subjective experience. The assumptions about adversity and distress support the legitimacy of major professional mental health involvement in the lives of individuals and communities to treat the effects of toxic event exposures on victims.

This book reviews the evidence underlying assumptions supporting the professionalized model of event-attributed distress. Extending work reviewed by Wortman and Silver that focused on coping with the irrevocable losses of bereavement and physical disability (Wortman & Silver, 1987), the book focuses on a broader range of adverse experiences and a more narrow range of outcomes. In particular, outcomes of anxiety and posttraumatic stress disorder (PTSD) frame the examination of the literature.

ASSUMPTIONS OF THE MENTAL HEALTH PROFESSIONS

Toxic events have played a core role in psychological theories of emotional distress syndromes because these derive from the strongly experiential and environmentalist assumptions found in models as different as Freudian and behavioral. The idea that everyday life is full of dangers to long-term emotional well-being represents an update of long-standing 20th-century ideas about emotional pathology that started out in Freudian theory. Trauma (real or imagined) dating to the earliest years of life was asserted to affect all of subsequent emotional life either directly, or indirectly through repression of the conflicts arising from the trauma. A recent review noted explicitly that Freud's original model of neurosis was a posttraumatic paradigm (Wilson, 1994). A book about psychological trauma by psychiatrist Judith Herman (1996) asserted that "everyone is a prisoner of the past" (p. 235). As dynamic models of psychological development expanded to incorporate events across the entire life-span (e.g., Erikson, 1963) , both psychologists and popular culture extended the idea of the power of adverse life events in creating clinically significant emotional disorders from beyond early childhood to across the span of adulthood.

From the ideologically opposite camp of behaviorist theory, there is also an emphasis on specific environmental antecedents to specific emotional experiences and behaviors. This similarly represents a model identifying the powerful factors affecting emotional functioning as being events in the external world. The main difference is that these are restricted to more recent and immediate experiences, rather than sought in remote childhood events. When distress persists long after a toxic event, behaviorists have sought to explain chronicity by invoking mechanisms of conditioning and intrusive images as providing persistent re-exposure experiences (Baum, O'Keefe, & Davidson, 1990).

Despite this common adversity model, there is often little clarity about what specific significant effects adverse events might reliably elicit. Confusion about the consequences of adverse life experiences was exemplified in a newspaper article in which a violence consultant spoke to delegates at a conference concerning children who are exposed to violence. She told them that "while some may respond with shortened attention spans, increasing hostility and aggression, others produce outstanding academic work, standards of perfection (hiding a fear of failure) and overly responsible behavior" (Strachan, 1994, p. B9). Using this reasoning, every kind of behavior has the possibility of being construed as a pathological response to earlier toxic life events.

TOXIC EVENTS CAUSE DISTRESS SYNDROMES
EVEN IF THEY ARE NOT SHOWN

Because mental health (MH) models assert that toxic events create distress, yet data to be reviewed suggest limited emotional distress during or after toxic events, there has been implicit pressure to turn symptomless presentations into pathologies through the use of theoretically derived constructs such as repression and denial, based in psychodynamic theory. The discrepancy between true effects and self-report is explained through the use of these dynamic mechanisms of psychological defense. An individual who fails to show the expected emotional display is seen as *in denial* and at risk of further peril (Shontz, 1975). In a recent study, individuals who reported good mental health on routine questionnaires and showed low neuroticism on formal tests were nevertheless regarded as being in denial by clinicians who decided, instead, that the subjects were not mentally healthy on the basis of a clinical procedure (Shedler, Mayman, & Manis, 1993).

A popular extension of the model assumes that everyone has suffered sufficient adverse life events to have significant emotional disorders, and therefore everyone needs therapy. Self-help 12-step group programs for every kind of troubled behavior, based on the Alcoholics Anonymous program, use such reasoning to assert that people who are not actively in the healing stage are in denial of their emotional problems. This mass-culture model has been critically examined by Wendy Kaminer (1992) in her book *I'm Dysfunctional, You're Dysfunctional.* The model is little different from therapeutic ideas used by most psychodynamic MH professionals. They make use of concepts such as repression, denial, identification with the aggressor, and other defense mechanisms to explain how emotional problems date from early childhood events, even if these are entirely inaccessible to verification or only erratically accessible to memory. A recent example may be seen in a discussion of the "illusion of mental health," in which the argument was put forward that people bias self-reports of mental health, describing themselves as more healthy than judgments made by experienced clinicians (Shedler et al., 1993, p. 1117).

The assumption that an absence of emotional symptoms during or after an event must be pathological leads at times to strange commentary. A recent study relating to the Oakland California fire of 1991, for example, was described in a major newspaper report as showing that heightened emotionality during the disaster was psychologically helpful because this elicited care, whereas calmness during the disaster was followed by a delayed PTSD response seen 7 months later (Goleman, 1994). Closer examination, however, shows that those who had not been highly emotional had not been calm at all during the disaster, but rather had shown dissociation so extreme that they often tried to rush back into their fiery homes (Koopman, Classen, & Spiegel, 1994). This study, therefore, does not provide evidence that pathology is proven by a display of calmness during a disaster.

It has been argued that symptomless presentations are pathological even to the point that a lack of symptoms is taken as proof that pathology is present. In a small study of sexually abused teenage girls, Brooks (1985) failed to find enough evidence of a significant distress syndrome to meet her expectations. She concluded that the failure to show problem or complaints must itself represent behavior pathognomonic of repression and denial. That is, her model of the assumed power and trauma of sexual abuse prevailed over the evidence in front of her.

Because the adversity–distress model is so prevalent, it can contribute to victimization of individuals who fail to conform to expectations after a notable event. There are reports that individuals who violate the expectation that they should show distress after a significant loss are not well received if, instead, they show happiness or well-being (Wortman & Silver, 1987).

Because of the difficulty of verifying hypotheses concerning repression and denial in accounting for symptomless responses as evidence of hidden distress to toxic events, this line of argument is not pursued further in this review.

PTSD: A PROTOTYPE
OF THE ADVERSITY–DISTRESS MODEL

Among the event-attributed distress syndromes where distress is freely reported, posttraumatic stress disorder has become the prototype disorder. Other emotional disorders have also been considered as reactions to adverse life events, including general mood disorders of anxiety, depression, and adjustment disorder. These are all recognized as mental disorders in the latest edition of the American Psychiatric Association's *Diagnostic and Statistical Manual of Mental Disorders* (DSM–IV, American Psychiatric Association, 1994). Although another new event-related disorder, acute stress disorder, was added to DSM–IV, because it is a short-lived condition it is not of as much relevance to study of the main adversity–distress paradigm that underlies the PTSD idea.

The development of the diagnostic category of PTSD represents an attempt to insert consistency into long-lasting distress symptoms attributed specifically to toxic events, and it is the most relevant disorder to a review of the adversity–distress model. Key features include attributing prolonged postevent distress to a specific and extreme external event, emotional symptoms defined as event-specific, and an explicit assumption of an adversity–distress dose–response model. Distress is attributed to the event rather than to pre-existing individual characteristics, and PTSD is considered to be a general trauma-derived syndrome with cross-cultural relevance.

PTSD only entered into the DSM as a formal diagnosis in the third edition (American Psychiatric Association, 1980). Its institutionalization as a formal diagnosis was accompanied by much controversy at the time. There were those who believed it merited representation as a distinct and significant syndrome deriving from events, whereas others were unconvinced of the central power of events in symptoms of distress.

In particular, proponents argued that veterans of the Vietnam war showed a characteristic stress syndrome (Figley, 1978), and this built upon thinking from World War II in which combat neurosis was described (Grinker & Spiegel, 1945).

In subsequent revisions of the DSM, PTSD criteria have been increasingly clarified in response to diagnostic problems and disputes. In particular, event definitions have become broader, starting from the requirement in DSM–III that the event be "outside the range of usual human experience" (p. 236). This was disputed by those who wished to include women and children suffering from family violence, which was not regarded as meeting that criterion. In response, DSM–IV redefined the event characteristics to include events that were not necessarily "outside the range of usual human experience." Further, a person no longer has to experience an event outside the range of usual human experience, but has only to be exposed (defined as experienced, witnessed, or was confronted with) to an event that posed a threat of death or injury. Prior to the 1994 revision of DSM, there was controversy between researchers attempting to field test revised criteria and the governing Task Force, concerning whether an event was even an essential feature of the disorder. Field test workers wanted to ignore stressor event characteristics entirely, while the Task Force refused to accept diagnostic criteria based solely on distress response symptoms (M. First, personal communication, October 27, 1994). This dispute concerns the core problem in the diagnostic formulation: whether or not events have the power over emotional condition that is required in the formal criteria.

As currently defined PTSD has some unusual features, in that its emphasis on self-reported subjective experience and a specific external cause for an emotional disorder is relatively unique within the diagnosable mental disorders. All but 1 of the 20 person-description criteria of PTSD in the latest 1994 version can be provided solely as self-reported symptoms rather than objectively determinable signs. The one objective sign (physiological reactivity on exposure to key cues) is an optional criterion. The other sole criterion is the existence of a threat from an extreme event.

Both popular and professional use of the posttraumatic concept has become increasingly broad. In common parlance, life events ranging from comments heard in childhood to horrendous assault are equally represented as traumatic. A wide range of behavioral aberrations are described as demonstrating the effects of traumatic stress.

The breadth of the event definition and the subjectivity of the symptom definition provide challenges to the validity of the diagnosis in individual cases. Arising from this there are studies attempting to identify more objective biological indices that might provide signs of the syndrome, to remove the subjectivity that is currently at the heart of the diagnosis. There are reports in which objective signs of cortisol and other alarm-system biochemical changes have been seen among combat veterans diagnosed with PTSD in comparison with healthy controls (Morgan, Grillon, Southwick, & Nagy, 1995; Yehuda, Boisoneau, Lowy, & Giller, 1995). A recent report found unusual brain size features, with smaller right hippocampal volumes, in PTSD Vietnam combat veterans compared to matched controls with no psychiatric disorder (Bremner et al., 1995). Reports such as these must be treated with caution, in that it is not established whether abnormal anatomical or physiological features predated or followed the adverse exposures in these subjects, nor is it established how these differentiate between event-attributed distress and other mood disorders, long-standing anxiety, or trait neuroticism. Some authors are circumspect and argue only that psycho-physiological measurement has at least the potential to provide objectivity to PTSD diagnosis (Pitman & Orr, 1993).

The Event is More Important Than Anything Else

A required defining feature of PTSD is an extreme event as the agent of distress, and all symptoms are direct effects of the event. Contemporary models to explain postevent distress syndromes typically pay little attention to the role of individual differences in behavioral history, temperament, personality, and beliefs. The contributions of genetic or long-standing individual differences are usually given only passing attention in considering event-attributed emotionality, even though some biochemical bases of the major mood disorders are now well recognized.

The environmentalist emphasis in psychology, psychiatry, and social work forms an easy blend with long-standing general ideas within U.S. culture in which possibilities for human improvement are seen as almost infinite given the proper environment. The converse is that people are equally strongly vulnerable to bad environments and events. This environmentalist emphasis is also associated with vaguely articulated, although erroneous, beliefs that, if there are significant genetic and evolutionary roots to disordered behavior, then this means we must be powerless to change it, and there is therefore little value in under-standing pre-event individual differences that reflect deeply rooted mechanisms.

Implications of the PTSD Diagnosis for Patients

The diagnosis of PTSD has implications beyond those related to treatment. Because the prolonged disorder is attributed to an external event, it can be the basis for both use and abuse in attempts to blame others and seek financial compensation, and in attempts to avoid the consequences of individual acts. A sizable literature is developing concerning both those problems.

Financial Implications. Inclusion of a condition in the DSM has financial implications because conditions identified as mental disorders in this manual represent officially recognized conditions eligible for compensation in many health insurance systems in the United States. Arising from this, individuals can argue that the agents of an event are legally liable for financial rewards to cover treatment cost, to pay for suffering, and even to be punished through punitive awards. Where financial considerations operate, the question of fraud arises.

The PTSD focus on a specific causal attribution to an event and the diagnosis being based only on self-reported symptoms has contributed to conflicts related to fraud, and credibility problems with the diagnosis in medicolegal situations have been increasingly recognized. Detecting fraudulent PTSD is very difficult as was discovered in a study of 22 survivors of the sinking of a fishing boat in Alaskan waters, where 19 of the 22 eventually provided symptom reports to meet diagnostic criteria for chronic PTSD that would advance their litigation (Rosen, 1995). During independent clinical examinations 9 months later, it became apparent that this 86% incidence rate for chronic PTSD was vastly different from the literature on survival from vessel sinking, and reflected attorney advice and symptom sharing that was explicitly acknowledged in a number of cases.

Even when there is no expert advice, it appears that, if ordinary people are given everyday descriptions of PTSD, they are able to generate biased score profiles on the MMPI–2 personality test showing PTSD that even have good retest stability (Wetter & Deitsch, 1996). Within populations wishing to receive care, on conventional MMPI scales used to detect exaggerated symptom reports, PTSD populations typically show a high level of over-reporting of all kinds of symptoms, leading one researcher to suggest that dissimulation may be a symptom of the disorder (Hyer, Woods, Harrison, & Boudewyns, 1989). An important caution is necessary on the interpretation of this as if it were a deliberate effort to obtain compensation, for Smith and Frueh (1996) found that the high proportion of symptom exaggerators among 145 veterans with PTSD was not associated with those more likely to seek compensation. In addition to these kinds of validity problems, there is evidence that legal judgments concerning PTSD that is attributed to an unwelcome event, may be made on moral or ethical grounds relating to the unfairness of the event, even though these grounds have nothing to do with the psychiatric criteria (Sparr, 1995).

Criminal Responsibility. The diagnosis of PTSD is also being used in defending against charges for criminal activity. Within the criminal courts, PTSD is being used to claim legal insanity in cases where the causal connection between a toxic event and later criminal behavior is highly questionable (Packer, 1983). The diagnosis is also being used in the Balkan War to mitigate against criminal charges on the grounds of diminished responsibility (Goreta, 1994).

Because the credibility problem arising from the self-report nature of the defining symptom criteria affects both civil and criminal cases, there is an increasing literature concerning detection of malingering using traditional and newly devised psychological tests (e.g., Fairbank, McCaffrey, & Keane, 1985).

IMPLICATIONS OF THE ADVERSITY MODEL
FOR PROFESSIONALS

Professional mental health activities expanded significantly in the decades since World War II in the United States (Herman, 1995) and in Europe. In the United Kingdom, the British Association for Counseling has tripled to 11,000 between 1991 and 1996. Mental health professionals see themselves as uniquely capable of redressing the emotional distress or bodily diseases that arise from stressful life events. With the vigorous support of the MH professions, a therapeutic model of human well-being has been widely accepted in the general public as a general way of interpreting well-being. This contrasts with earlier models in which morality, or conformity to hierarchical social norms, represented important ways in which individuals might interpret their experiences. Bliss, self-actualization, self-esteem, and "feeling good about myself" represent the therapeutic comfort language of the current model. The model posits that individuals reporting emotional distress after exposure to a noxious event can be brought to a condition of well-being or happiness if appropriate therapy is provided.

Contemporary popular and professional interest in stress and coping is based on the assumption that life consists of ongoing hassles or traumatic events that are stressful and require coping. A widely used model describes the typical stages of emotional distress responses or "fairly universal conflicts" (Horowitz, 1986, p. 17) to be expected after a stress event. Accidents, difficult child behavior, marital problems, combat or rescue work, assault, illness, bereavement, and community-wide natural disasters have all become defined as the proper domain of professional MH intervention to remedy the clinically significant distress that is assumed must follow the event (Freedy & Donkervoet, 1995). Against this background of event–distress assumptions and their implications, it is useful to consider some specific assumptions and related evidence in more detail.

THE SCOPE OF THE BOOK

Because of the rising popularity of the post-distress syndrome model, the subjectivity of its defining symptoms, its emphasis on external events as the causes of clinical disorder, and the financial and criminal implications arising from this model, it is important to study the power of life events in determining emotional condition.

Typical responses to toxic life events will be studied by looking at evidence concerning the prevalence of toxic events and postevent distress syndromes, the dose–response relationship between toxic events and mental disorder including temporal gradients in the relationship, and the power of individual differences in temperament and beliefs in accounting for clinical responses. Explanations are considered that might account for the popularity of the model in the face of poor evidence, including errors in causal attributions and biased clinical samples.

2

How Prevalent Are Toxic Events and Event-Attributed Clinical Distress Disorders?

If PTSD is to have any meaning as a specific disorder caused by bad experiences, it requires the assumption that toxic events are relatively rare, because most people do not show or report PTSD. To evaluate this background assumption, it is necessary to examine the prevalence rates for toxic events and then to see how these compare to the prevalence rates for event-attributed distress disorders. If toxic events have a powerful role in determining distress disorders, then we should expect rather similar low lifetime prevalence rates for both.

Toxic event rates are higher during wars, and persistent reports of distress from Vietnam veterans were important in the development of the PTSD diagnosis. Despite this assumption of event–distress causation, a psychiatrist working in Vietnam during the war reported in a cautionary note that the vast majority of soldiers were not in combat but were in support roles in which they did not kill anyone and were not themselves exposed to danger of death (Jones, 1967). This suggests that considerable specificity as to events has to be defined in order to assess any connections to distress syndromes, even after war exposure. Aside from such large-scale and potentially lethal events, what about the frequency of toxic events in the general population in peacetime?

PREVALENCE OF TOXIC EVENTS

Evidence suggests that the lifetime occurrence of toxic events is surprisingly high among ordinary citizens in civilian life, even within highly privileged cultures such as the United States where life expectancy is long, and threatened or actual premature deaths of family members from untreated accidents, starvation, disaster, torture, or war are extremely rare.

In one intensive study using detailed clinical interviews with 100 "above average" young men, researchers were surprised at how much pathological family history was uncovered in this superior group (Renaud & Estes, 1961). The family histories were no different from those found in clinical populations receiving treatment. A more formal prevalence study in U.S. university students found that 84% of them reported experiencing at least 1 event out of a list of 11 specific extreme events selected to represent the types of trauma intended to be part of the DSM–III–R conception (American Psychiatric Association, 1987), and one third experienced four or more (Vrana & Lauterbach, 1994). The authors felt it necessary to attempt an explanation for these high rates in this privileged group. In another university sample, 25% reported having experienced at least one of six "extremely negative" life events in their lifetime (Janoff-Bulman, 1989a). Among another group of undergraduates, 80% experienced a highly stressful event (for 49% this was the death of a close friend through drunk driving or suicide), and 34% of all subjects experienced the adverse event within the previous 6 months; 3% reported childhood sexual abuse (Segal & Figley, 1988).

One attempt to estimate the lifetime prevalence of an incident of sexual abuse of children reported a bewildering range from 19% to 54% (Alter-Reid, Gibbs, Lachenmeyer, Sigal, & Massoth, 1986). This is apparently a function of definitional variations; one recent MH professional stated that "most child sexual abuse involves fondling and touching" (Belferman, 1996, p. Md. 2), which may represent a looser definition than most people assume.

Using a broad epidemiological approach, other researchers also reported a high prevalence rate for more general toxic life events. In a random sample of Detroit adults, 39% had at least one traumatic event in their lives (Breslau, Davis, Andreski, & Peterson, 1991). A study of the epidemiology of 10 potentially very traumatic events ("violent encounters marked by sudden and extreme force ... and an external agent," p. 409) in a representative sample of 1,000 adults across four cities in the United States found a lifetime exposure for at least one of these events in 69% of the subjects and exposure of 21% of the subjects within the past year (Norris, 1992). In a probability sample of 4,009 American women, 69% experienced at least one pre-defined toxic event in their lifetimes, and 36% experienced a traumatic criminal event (Resnick, Kilpatrick, Dansky, Saunders, & Best, 1993).

Although these studies show high rates of significantly toxic events, it is possible that they represent underreporting because other evidence exists that people forget even quite striking adverse events, especially if they represent a one-time occurrence. In a study of 200 young women treated for sexual abuse 17 years earlier, 38% of the 129 follow-up cases did not recall the sexual abuse index event although they were willing to talk about other later sexual assault experiences (Williams, 1994), suggesting that the forgetting was not deliberate reticence or active repression about a delicate topic . Other kinds of trauma are similarly often forgotten. More than one fourth of automobile accident participants failed to remember the accident when interviewed 9 to 12 months later, although someone in the car had been injured (Cash & Moss, 1972, cited in Loftus, Garry, & Feldman, 1994). Loftus et al. provided other evidence of similarly high rates of everyday forgetting concerning previous taxing life events such as hospitalizations and medical visits for serious conditions, even within relatively short time spans.

An Australian study found that the reliability of reporting highly distressing experiences is lower than reliability of reporting less distressing events, with considerable neglect in remembering the high-distress events, even comparing reports provided within 7 to 14 days (Steele, Henderson, & Duncan-Jones, 1980). While 78% of low-distress events were reported on both occasions, only 60% concordance was found for high distress events although they were predicted to be more powerful and salient and thus more reliably remembered.

Overall, the evidence suggests that the frequency of toxic events is quite high even among civilian populations living in peace time in one of the most affluent countries in the world. The majority of U.S. respondents experienced several toxic life events, and, for a sizable group, these extreme events were recent. The exposure rates for toxic events among individuals living in countries less well supplied with food and health care and those in the midst of chaos from war, forced migrations, or suffering imprisonment and torture is much greater. If toxic events determine the prevalence of post-event distress syndromes, then these should also be ubiquitous.

PREVALENCE OF EVENT-ATTRIBUTED CLINICAL DISTRESS SYNDROMES

The prevailing clinical model assumes that toxic events "significantly increase the risk of ... serious mental health problems" (Freedy & Hobfoll, 1995, p. ix), and this can occur even if the exposure is second-hand (Beaton & Murphy, 1995). Experiences as proximal as an earthquake or assault, or as distal as long-ago war experiences or childhood events decades earlier, are equally identified as the stressor cause of traumatic distress when it is reported. Clinicians are encouraged to inquire about recent and lifetime histories of unpleasant and unspeakable events as a matter of routine (Davis & Breslau, 1994). The belief is that, when these events do occur, clinical distress is highly predictable and normative. Because it is understood that the definition of PTSD requires that extreme events are relatively rare, for most professionals this means that the overall prevalence of event-attributed distress syndromes at clinically significant levels is expected to be low. In contrast, in the more popular extension of the model to less extreme events, prevalence of PTSD should be expected to be high.

Because it has been established that extreme toxic events show a high prevalence rate in the general United States population, if there is a significant dose–response causal relationship, then there should also be a high lifetime prevalence rate for posttraumatic distress disorders. What is the evidence?

Within the United States, prevalence rates of event-distress syndromes such as PTSD appear to be quite low. In two rural communities in the Pacific Northwest, the community lifetime rate of PTSD was around 3% using DSM–III criteria; if distress was broadened to include anxiety and depression, higher rates were found in the community affected by the eruption of Mount St. Helens (Shore, Vollmer, & Tatum, 1989). In the Epidemiological Catchment Area Survey sampling psychiatric disorder in St. Louis, the lifetime prevalence of PTSD was very low at 1%, rising to 3.5% in those who had experienced physical attack and to 20% in Vietnam veterans who had been wounded (but not in combat veterans of other wars) (Helzer, Robins, & McEvoy, 1987).

More recent studies found higher rates. In the Norris (1992) epidemiological study of 1,000 adults, 6.2% met all the DSM–III–R criteria for current PTSD, even though 21% experienced a severe event within the past 12 months, leading her to comment on the modest scale of trauma effects in comparison with exposures. In a random sample of 1,007 Detroit adults associated with a health maintenance organization, among the 39% who identified a DSM–III–R type of traumatic life event, the rate of PTSD was 24% yielding an estimated lifetime population prevalence of 9.2% PTSD; 76% of those exposed to the event did not show the disorder (Breslau et al., 1991). From a United States national epidemiology sample of 4,008 women, the lifetime prevalence rate for PTSD was 12% (Resnick et al., 1993). The authors noted that they found a higher incidence of sexual assault events than other researchers and suggested this was because they used highly specific questions, although we know that subjects forget adverse events.

In an Icelandic study of the lifetime prevalence of anxiety disorders including PTSD, within a sample that was half the entire cohort of individuals born in 1931 and where the participation rate was 79%, 44% experienced a diagnosable anxiety disorder at some point in their lives, but PTSD was found exclusively in women and was found in only 1.3% of them, or .6% of the total cohort (Lindal & Stefansson, 1993). In a U.S. study, the lifetime prevalence of PTSD among 386 adolescents was almost the least common disorder, at 6.3%; in contrast alcohol and

substance abuse disorders showed a 32% lifetime prevalence rate (Reinherz, Giaconia, Lefkowitz, Pakiz, & Frost, 1993).

Within other populations suffering higher rates of toxic events such
as direct threats of premature death from starvation, illness, war and
other violence we should expect even higher rates of PTSD. Recent
estimates by the Armenian government suggest that 300,000 children
in Armenia have PTSD arising from war, the 1988 earthquake, and
ongoing social instability (Rich, 1994). Across all nations, about 8% of
the Global Burden of Disease represents mental disorder, with higher
levels at about 12% in low-income countries (World Bank, 1993), and
these data conform to a dose–response model. Recently, however, it was
suggested that, despite international gains in life expectancy and infant
mortality reflecting general improvements in environments and well-
being, there are nonetheless hidden increases in mental health disorders including posttraumatic stress disorder arising from general life
conditions in low-income countries (Desjarlais, Eisenberg, Good, &
Kleinman, 1995; Kleinmen & Eisenberg, 1995). If this argument has
merit, it suggests that distress disorders are not, in fact, as tightly
related to objectively toxic circumstances as assumed in the event–distress model, but rather to particular social and individual constructions
of circumstances.

Whatever the true PTSD prevalence rates might be in different
populations, they are vastly lower than the high prevalence of significant traumatic events in the lives of individuals. Toxic events are not
reliably powerful in yielding a chronic, event-focused clinical disorder
such as PTSD. Given this, the next question concerns the incidence of
PTSD and other related clinical disorders after specific toxic exposures
of differing severities.

3

Do More Terrible Events Lead to More Serious Disorders?

The adversity–distress model assumes that there is a dose–response relationship in which a more toxic event will cause greater and longer-lasting distress. If the model is robust in attributing most power to the event, then the incidence of distress disorders should be high after more extreme toxic events. To what extent do the objective characteristics of the event and the objective harm it causes relate to the incidence rates of symptom responses shown and to their duration?

PROBLEMS IN STUDYING DISTRESS THAT IS ATTRIBUTED TO EVENTS

There are two important research methods problems that affect the measurement of events in calculating dose–response relations. Calibrating the severity of events has proved troublesome, and two main approaches have been used. One has been to distinguish qualities of the event that might establish it as a more, or less, toxic type. The other has been to look at different events and estimate the amount of human response that might be predictably required, in other words, defining event toxicity indirectly through judgments of probable responses of physical or emotional illness in the exposed people.

Typing Events Directly by Event Features

Toxic events have been typed in many different ways, for example by event features; comparing natural disasters to man-made disasters, direct experience to secondary awareness, events involving bodily losses to those involving loss of reputation or property, brief or prolonged exposures to horrific materials, and intentional to accidental events. Some kinds of natural disasters, such as earthquakes, lend themselves to objective measures of dose (e.g., distance from epicenter) for dose–distress calculations, and soldiers have had dose evaluated in terms of combat exposure, but many extreme events are not easily quantifiable as to toxicity, as for example, escaping from a sinking ship.

Data concerning the relative toxicity comparing different events are relatively rare, as most research concerns one target event or event type. At the physiological level, there is tentative evidence that different kinds of toxic events have differential effects on parts of the immune system, comparing artificial to natural events, and interpersonal to nonsocial events. According to a meta-analysis of immune responses, these may lead to different cellular responses (Herbert & Cohen, 1993). In terms of psychological functioning, in one attempt to develop a typology, Green reported features of events that increased risks of distress as including threat of death or physical injury, injury, receiving intentional harm, seeing grotesque sights, violent or sudden death of valued people, and receiving information about a toxic exposure (Green, 1990). In a representative sample of 4,008 U.S. women, PTSD incidence rates were found to vary as a function of event characteristics among victims of crime. Crimes that involved injury and life threat were associated with a high case rate of 45%, whereas crimes involving no threat or injury yielded a 19% rate; categories of intermediate harm showed rates in between (Resnick et al., 1993).

More subtle psychological models have also developed in order to predict typologies of events that should be appraised as more distressing, such as Miller and Turnbull's counterfactual fallacy model (Miller & Turnbull, 1992). This model predicts that an event that more easily and strongly evokes a counterfactual image ("if only x had not happened then there would have been a far better outcome") will elicit less acknowledgment that it should have a negative impact. "If only you hadn't gone to buy lottery tickets you wouldn't have been hit by the bus" (meaning you were doing something that was not important, therefore your suffering does not require as much sympathy). This counterfactual image is, in essence a confusion of what might have been and what ought to have been, and has mostly been studied in laboratory research. Events that are not routine and not necessary more readily elicit counterfactual thinking and less acknowledgment of victimization and justified distress.

To date, there is no standard system for toxic event classification through objective qualities. What about indirect classification of toxic event severity based on psychological responses to it?

Typing Events Indirectly by Response Features

In most studies, the toxicity of different types of events is approached more indirectly in a method that is tautological, through comparisons of distress response rates to varying events across studies. The quantified literature on significant life events started with the method pioneered by Holmes and Rahe (1967), judging the magnitude of events in terms of the demand for change that they represented, in studies attempting to predict health from life stress. It was shown that people reliably differentiate events as more or less powerful in the effects they are expected to elicit, and reliably agree on the identification of events as being negative or positive in their main effects.

A recent examination of different weighting schemes for different events concluded that differential weighting of items in terms of either judged or statistically generated values was no better than simple equal unit weight for extremely different events in predicting physical health outcomes (Crandall, 1992). This is consistent with a long history of similar results. This suggests that different events may not represent reliably different toxic levels even though judges will reliably believe that they do. Further, it suggests that dose–response relationships are weak within the range of normal human life events and illness. The dimensions of events that might account for different levels of toxicity however is an empirical matter that requires evidence beyond those interrater opinion agreements on probable responses. This has been studied looking at two broad kinds of possible distress outcomes: physical illness and emotional distress.

Physical Illness as Response.   Despite widespread interest in the dose–response model of Holmes and Rahe and three decades of research attempting to establish the power of a link between adversity or stress with physical illness, reviews of the evidence generally fail to support the model at any level of robustness. Early studies concluded that psychosocial stress accounted for up to 9% of variance in physical illness (Rabkin & Struening, 1976). A recent review concluded that there is still is no conclusive evidence of a stress–infection link (Cohen & Williamson, 1991). A review of the interactions of brain, immune system, behavior, and stressors concluded that, despite some specific connections, there is no general, reliable effect of a stressor challenge on the immune system that is known to have an effect on disease (Maier, Watkins, & Fleschner, 1994). Negative, stressful life events have been found to show no effects on the disease progression of HIV (Patterson et al., 1996). A recent study of the factors that contribute to physical health found that stressful life events accounted for only something like 2% of variance in post-event physical illness, which instead is far more strongly predicted (12% of variance) by specific medical features (Miranda, Perez-Stable, Munoz, Hargreaves, & Henke, 1991).

In a review of the role of psychosocial factors in cancer incidence and prognosis, Fox (1995) recently concluded that the data do not support psychological stress or emotional variables as being significant factors whose effects can be predicted. Attempts to link social or psychological state to cancer progression or survival have not been successful (Cassileth, Lusk, Miller, Brown, & Miller, 1985; Greenwald, 1995; Spiegel & Sands, 1989). A formal meta-analysis of the effects of psychosocial treatments with cancer patients found that there was no significant medical effect for these (Meyer & Mark, 1995). To the extent that abnormal emotional states are found in cancer patients, it appears that these are a result of the disease rather than a prediagnosis characteristic. Additionally, although psychological therapies may provide relief from emotional distress, they do not affect individual disease outcome. In sum, psychosocial events (toxic or enhancing) appear to play only a very limited role in determining the outcome of serious bodily illness which, instead, is affected far more by physical disease features.

One of the few compelling data sets showing some effects of life events on survival within a specific population was a careful analysis of deaths from cardiovascular disease on the day of a major earthquake north of Los Angeles in 1994 (Leor, Poole, & Kloner, 1996). In comparison with a number of control periods, there was a clear rise in deaths in the hours immediately following the earthquake "in people who are predisposed to such events" (p. 413). That is, preexisting vulnerabilities were a necessary feature for the event to have significant impact. To date, it appears probable that only a small proportion of variance in disease will be accounted for by psychosocial stress factors.

Emotional Distress as Response.   When significant emotional distress, rather than bodily illness, is the outcome of interest, how strong are stress dose–response relations? If the experience of distress is strongly a function of the objective toxicity of an intrusive event, then the currently popular model and the DSM focus on event characteristics in the definition of PTSD is justified. This is the central question of this book, and it is complicated by an additional research method problem.

Measuring Responses: Biased Samples.   The measurement of distress responses presents a problem in studying dose–response relations, particularly in determining incidence rates of disorder after an event. Many incidence rates reported in the literature are based on highly biased samples consisting of persons presenting for treatment rather than being based on the population experiencing the event. As a result, distress syndrome rates often appear very high; these, however, do not represent true incidence rates. Goenjian (1993) for example, reported that 74% of 582 children and adults showed posttraumatic stress disorder, and 22% showed major depressive disorder after the 1988 earthquake in Armenia. These percentages, however, were calculated on a base that consisted only of the people who presented themselves for treatment from 3 to 6 months after the event, and no estimate of true overall incidence in the population was attempted in this report. Similarly, although Lima and Pai (1993) reported a very high incidence (40% to 55%) of distress among the survivors of a Colombian volcanic eruption in the late 1980s, with many showing PTSD, in fact, the sample of 300 was but a small fraction of the affected population of 6,000 survivors and was biased, in part, through being selected from individuals attending clinics.

EVIDENCE CONCERNING THE DOSE–RESPONSE MODEL

From research in personality and social psychology looking at person and situation effects on behavior, there is evidence that intrusive and powerful situational characteristics exert stronger and more universal effects on behavior, whereas objectively trivial, routine, or ambiguous situational features more reliably elicit more individual differences in behavior. We should expect this general rule to apply to the effects of toxic events intended in the event-defined model of PTSD. By definition, these events are extreme and intrusive, and thus represent a higher dose event. Within a given type of event, one that provides a range of severity of objective threat, a dose–response relationship should emerge. Greater distress should be expected where the toxic exposure is direct rather than indirect and prolonged rather than brief. Prolonged disruption of life circumstances after a direct but brief exposure should provide intermediate toxicity. In addition, there should be declines across time in the distress responses as more routine events accumulate with the passage of time since the toxic exposure.

In the review that follows, *direct* is used to describe events in which there is significant personal threat directly experienced by the individual, and *indirect* is used to describe events in which there is exposure to the threats or harms directly experienced by others either through physical exposure or verbal accounts.

4

What Are Typical Responses to Direct Exposure to Toxic Life Events?

DIRECT AND PROLONGED EXPOSURE

Distinguished developmental psychologist Michael Rutter (1994) criticized the entire body of research in child psychopathology for failing to meet a basic criterion when studying putative life event risk or recovery factors. Studies nearly always fail to examine systematic dose–response relationships between the alleged factors and outcome, but instead just measure child characteristics before and after. This yields completely uninterpretable results in which "utterly different mechanisms (treatments) all carry some worthwhile therapeutic benefit" (p. 936) without giving any hint at all about the mechanisms that are at work in contributing to normalcy or disorder. His view is relevant to studies of the connection of toxic life events with distress, although such research more frequently examines these phenomena in ways that can yield dose–response relationships.

If the nature of the event is a key factor in post-event distress, then toxic events delivered in terms of direct, prolonged high-dose exposures should elicit the highest incidence rates of distress and PTSD. Events that have a particularly horrific physical involvement with direct threat to survival or other physical harm should be most reliably followed by distress responses. Combat experience represents this, and U.S. veterans of World War II, the Vietnam War, and the Persian Gulf War represent one of the most widely studied toxic exposure groups. They account for a significant body of research and clinical work concerning

PTSD evidence pertaining to dose–response relations. Childhood abuse is another example of a direct, prolonged high-dose toxic exposure.

War and Combat

It is extremely hard to find evidence that supports the model in any clear, powerful manner showing dose–response effects, for most studies instead show that only a small minority of individuals respond to drastic toxic experiences such as war with persisting clinical distress. One study found that greater combat exposure in the Persian Gulf War correlated with symptom reports, although full diagnostic criteria for PTSD were rarely met in the sample of 84 National Guard reservists (Southwick et al., 1993). Most studies provide mixed and even contradictory evidence of dose-dependent effects, suggesting there are powerful moderator variables of several kinds.

A prospective study of Harvard University men later exposed to combat in World War II found that 17 out of 152 reported two or more distress symptoms immediately after the war, but only 1 met PTSD criteria (Lee, Vaillant, Torrey, & Elder, 1995). Another study described long-lasting PTSD among Australian soldiers from World War II receiving ongoing psychiatric care (Kidson, 1993). Among the agreeable 109 out of 120 seen during a 3-month period in the clinic, 45% still met criteria for PTSD 45 years after the war. Because this rate is not based on the total pool of soldiers but upon an extremely small clinical population and no estimate is provided of the true population size of the veteran pool served by the clinic, this cannot be considered an incidence rate.

A huge study of more than 92,000 U.S. Navy men who enlisted in 1966 and were followed through to 1977 for hospitalizations, found that highest hospitalization rates for stress-related disorders were in the group not exposed to combat (Hoiberg, 1980). A small 1991 study of World War II veterans who were repatriated prisoners of war compared those with and without ongoing PTSD and found there were no differences between these two groups in terms of the traumatic memories of the war that they reported (Fairbank, Fitterling, & Hansen, 1991). Vietnam combat veterans who had either high or low combat experience showed no differences on overall stress or on current stress (Cordray, Polk, & Britton, 1992). In a study comparing Vietnam veterans seeking treatment for PTSD with those seeking medical treatments, rates of reported childhood physical abuse were much higher (27%:7%) in the group seeking PTSD treatment, and these significant differences persisted even after controlling for combat experience (Bremner, Southwick, Johnson, Yehuda, & Charney, 1993). The PTSD group also showed a significantly higher number of total traumatic events prior to joining the military. Another study of combat-attributed PTSD similarly found a strong correlation between experience of physical abuse early in life and adult PTSD reports in veterans (Zaidi & Foy, 1994).

In a study of veterans of the Persian Gulf War, severity of stressor was not a significant variable in classifying those 97 who were diagnosed with PTSD and those 484 without any psychological distress (Sutker, Davis, Uddo, & Ditta, 1995). Instead, personal characteristics (hardiness, commitment, avoidance coping, and perceived family cohesion) were powerful, and 87% could be accurately classified using these variables. Among 62 veterans of the Gulf War who showed a small but detectable increase in symptoms on the Mississippi Scale for combat-related PTSD, scores on a symptom scale based on the DSM–III–R criteria for PTSD did not increase (Southwick et al., 1993).

Studies of children in wartime have similarly failed to find support for a dose–response model. Israeli children living in kibbutzim near the Jordan border and subject to frequent bombardments were compared with children living in more distant areas not shelled; contrary to expectations, there were no differences in anxiety symptoms (Ziv & Israeli, 1973).

In times of great communal adversity, at least in some cultures, psychiatric admissions actually fall even when treatment facilities are readily available. Data from Northern Ireland show that psychiatric admissions remained stable despite twenty years of terrorist violence (Curran, 1988). These findings draw our attention to the impact of individual and group differences as factors that may influence reports of emotional distress and claims for damages or treatment after war exposure.

Garmezy (1993) argued that the presence of both resilient behavior and emotional distress is to be expected during adversity, pointing out that war provides a particularly strong example of the copresence of fear and functional behavior. He and others noted the adaptability that was shown by children and adults during the Blitz in wartime London during World War II. Ziegler's (1995) book on London at war reports that the psychiatric clinics set up to handle wartime neurosis were barely used, with actual incidence rates lower during the war. In a study after the bombing of Hiroshima, survivors reported that they felt great community spirit and pride for the way they had responded to the horrific events (Hersey, 1980). A recent book of studies of bereaved American parents who had lost a child noted that reactions among parents varied significantly. One father observed that child deaths were a common experience for parents of earlier generations, who had learned that such things happen (Finkbeiner, 1996).

Torture and Brutal Imprisonment

Long-term torment of civilians through torture or brutal imprisonment represents a similar direct and prolonged exposure, and here too evidence fai: to support PTSD as a major phenomenon. Among 55 victims of torture in Turkey, severity as measured by number of torture experiences (a total of 291 events) was not predictive of post-torture psychological problems, which instead were best predicted by self-reports of (subjective) distress during the experiences (Basoglu & Paker, 1995). Studies of Jewish survivors of the Holocaust found that mental illness symptom rates, income, family cohesion, physical health, and general satisfaction were no different from matched controls when community epidemiological data were used, rather than clinical samples (Sigal & Weinfeld, 1989).

Childhood Abuse

In the case of child abuse, there appears to be no reliable level of distress or disorder arising from abuse. Among 95 sexually abused children, abuse and social variables did not predict psychiatric diagnosis 12 months after disclosure, but mothers' mental status did (Merry & Andrews, 1994). Within a group of 19 of sexually abused adolescents living in a group home in New York, none showed symptoms meeting PTSD criteria or more general symptom patterns on the MMPI associated with PTSD in adults, although they showed moderate elevations of anxiety and depression (Hillary & Schare, 1993). A study of 41 children who had been repeatedly physically or sexually abused found that PTSD was predicted by number of stressors, but these were stressors other than abuse; other conditions such as conduct disorders were more powerfully predicted by demographic variables (male sex and increasing age) rather than by abuse events (Livingston, Lawson, & Jones, 1993).

Adult Reports of Childhood Abuse

The vast literature concerned with the possible recovery of memories of early adverse events in association with adult therapy for syndromes of emotional distress will not be examined in this review, mostly because the validity of the accounts of the early events is usually impossible to establish. This means dose is usually unknown, and any ascription of adult distress symptoms to an early event is usually only speculative.

Even if early events are verified, studies of distressed adults who long ago suffered a toxic event can provide little good evidence concerning long-term effects of that event, because of severe subject selection bias and the complications from multiple intervening events. In view of the rather weak evidence of dose–response relations for more contiguous toxic events, it is probable that factors other than childhood events may better account for symptoms first reported or shown only many years later.

The best way to study long-term effects of early toxic events is through longitudinal studies, and, because these are expensive and time-consuming, they are relatively rare. Although important psychological theories of development and of psychopathology posit that early adverse experiences occur at a critical period and are therefore especially harmful in ways that will affect all subsequent life, the actual evidence suggests that long-term outcomes after early toxic experiences are remarkably diverse (Rutter, 1989). Evidence of this diversity in responses weakens the notion that childhood represents a critical period for experience that will permanently affect all of life.

Being the child of alcoholic parents, for example, is not associated with any increased risk of emotional pathology in adulthood (D'Andrea, 1994). The incidence levels of experienced early abuse within adult patients with acute mental disorders is relatively low; data suggest perhaps 9% of such patients had experienced early sexual abuse, 10% physical abuse, and 3% combined abuse (Brown & Anderson, 1991). Skuse (1984) reviewed the evidence concerning the effects of extreme deprivation in early childhood and found that, even with extreme conditions of environmental adversity, there can be surprisingly substantial recovery when children experience an environmental change into good rearing circumstances. This recovery becomes visible even within a matter of months.

Norman Garmezy (1993) worked over two decades to identify the ways in which children reared in very difficult circumstances may nevertheless show resilience, adaptability, and competence. In a recent review, he summarized considerable evidence that "there are children who, despite their exposure to multiple risk factors, do not show the dire consequences" (p. 129). Despite much current public and therapist concern about the sexual abuse of young children and a general belief that there is currently a rise in incidence, evidence suggests that abuse of children was much higher in the years immediately following World War II, affecting more of the cohort of adults now 40–49 than of younger groups (Finkelhor, 1990).

Any student of biography knows of hundreds of individual life histories that show that early adversity does not set fixed determining limits on adult well-being and accomplishment; individual differences are powerful mediators of life events. In a review of formal research on human resilience, Cicchetti and Garmezy (1993) detailed a significant body of evidence showing positive life outcomes in individuals who have grown up under very difficult conditions, both economic and social. Groups mentioned in their review included the children of the great depression, children reared in foster homes and institutional settings, severely economically disadvantaged children, delinquents, and children of severely criminal fathers. In addition, they noted that similar evidence of human resilience and adaptive coping has been found in children exposed to more acute kinds of adversity such as the civil unrest in Northern Ireland, the Holocaust, and natural disasters.

Summary: Behavior After Direct, Prolonged Toxic Exposure

In sum, there are striking individual differences in distress responses following direct and prolonged exposures to serious threats. Toxic events contribute to chronic post-event clinical distress syndromes in a small minority of adults. The evidence provides only limited support as to the power of extreme and prolonged exposure to toxic events in determining chronic distress syndromes. When event outcome is studied in a way that includes dimensions of functioning that go beyond pathology, direct, prolonged exposures are associated with mixed effects that include both harm and benefits, whether the exposure is involuntary or planned.

In light of these findings, what are the effects of toxic exposures that are direct, but only brief, followed by prolonged physical disruption?

DIRECT BRIEF EXPOSURE
WITH PROLONGED PHYSICAL DISRUPTION

When exposure to a toxic event is direct, but brief, with prolonged physical disruption of life circumstances, the adversity–distress model predicts there should be a more rapid decrease in symptoms across time than if direct toxic exposure is prolonged. Natural disasters and prolonged medical treatment following a bad burn or accident provide examples of this kind of toxic event.

Evidence Supporting the Model

Some studies suggest dose is an important determinant of response when the stressor consists of a large, acute public event such as an earthquake, flood, or hurricane. For those who do respond with general emotional distress, their distress shows a temporal gradient, with initial symptoms diminishing across time.

A small study of 22 U.S. children 6 to 8 months after they had been affected by an earthquake found that the children who lived closer to a heavily damaged area were more likely to report distress (Bradburn, 1991). Among 162 young children in Bangladesh who experienced the most severe flood disaster ever recorded in their country in 1988, data were available concerning the pre- and post-flood incidence rates of aggression and enuresis, and these showed significant increases following the flood (Durkin, Khan, Davidson, Zaman, & Stein, 1993). Five months after the flood, the incidence of aggressive behavior changed from 0% to 10%, and enuresis in previously continent children rose to 34%. Among college students who responded with distress to Hurricane Andrew in Florida, symptoms showed a dose–response effect, with those who reported having the greatest impact of the event also showing more symptoms (Pickens, Field, Prodromidis, & Pelaez-Nogueras, 1995).

A controlled study of Puerto Rican adults comparing those who had or had not experienced serious flooding in 1985, found that flood-exposed individuals had more diagnosable mental disorders than those who were not exposed (Canino, Bravo, Rubio-Stipec, & Woodbury, 1990). Freedy, Shaw, Jarrell, and Masters (1992) studied 418 faculty and staff of a medical university after Hurricane Hugo and found a dose–response relationship, where dose was measured as resource-loss. This objective risk factor contributed relatively more to psychological distress than did more personal characteristics and coping behavior.

Within those who report distress, time since event then affects the average symptom level in some studies, although there is often a failure to differentiate subjects who did not show clinical symptoms as an initial response, and thus group mean values for symptoms obscure important individual variation. Among 300 elementary school children in six Italian villages after an earthquake, reductions in emotional risk factors were significantly related to time since the disaster, and this temporal effect was stronger than treatment provision (Galante & Foa, 1987). A 14-year follow-up of 120 survivors of a dam collapse in the United States found that symptoms decreased on all aspects measured by the Psychiatric Evaluation Form (Green, Lindy, Grace, & Gleser, 1990). Adults in two communities who had been forced to move following a disaster showed significant reductions in stress symptoms at 4 and 16 months after the disaster, although direct dose–response relations were significantly moderated by community differences as well as by sex (Steinglass & Gerrity, 1990).

The experience of being seriously burned is another horrific event with prolonged, painful, and often incomplete recovery. It results in very high rates of initial distress that may persist in some survivors even long after discharge from hospital. Five severely burned football fans who survived the Bradford (United Kingdom) Stadium fire of 1985 showed changes in their distress levels as their physical recovery progressed, with clinical levels during the first four weeks of their hospitalization that were transient, a period of recovery followed by another transient loss of well-being at the time of discharge from the hospital, followed by significant recovery such that neither anxiety nor depression were found at 12 months (Khoosal, Broad, & Smith, 1987).

For the more specific clinical disorder of PTSD, there is limited evidence of dose–response relations to this kind of brief, direct exposure. The rate of PTSD among presenting patients following the 1988 Armenian earthquake was higher in the town closer to the epicenter (Goenjian, 1993). Among 231 children randomly screened from their schools, the rate correlated with distance from the epicenter (Pynoos et al., 1993).

Mixed Evidence

There is also evidence that responses to direct, but brief, exposures with prolonged physical aftermath are much more variable than is predicted from the event-focused model of PTSD.

Disaster responses often show a mixed pattern. In a study of U.S. children after Hurricane Hugo, although the majority of children were significantly distressed five months after it happened, overall, the global adjustment of the children was not largely affected (Belter, Dunn, & Jeney, 1991). A study of adults in South Africa subjected to repeated floods showed evidence they had learned from their experience and thereby increased their external coping with the disaster, although internal coping mechanisms were judged as depleted (Burger, 1992). Among 39 burn patients seen 1 year after hospital discharge in Florida, 38% met DSM–III–R criteria for PTSD and 43% met the criteria proposed for DSM–IV; there were no differences in PTSD rates whether or not the patients had burns they could have prevented (Powers, Cruse, Daniels, & Stevens, 1994).

Evidence Against the Model

Raising problems for the model, however, is the considerable evidence that dose alone accounts quite poorly for post-event distress effects after direct brief exposure and that there are significant individual variations both in general distress and in PTSD. Since the time of Charcot (Micale, 1994), there have been reports of some individuals who are exposed to distressing events with little immediate evidence of harmful effects who eventually show distress long after events. Contrary to the assumptions of the model, their symptoms are slow to appear and gradually increase across time. Charcot concluded that this represented an interaction of constitutional predisposition with environmentally provocative agents. This phenomenon points to the role of individual factors more powerful than event characteristics, and there are many modern studies that contradict predictions arising from the dose–response model.

Serious Accidents. Across a period of recovery among 188 consecutive hospitalized victims of serious car accidents, specific posttraumatic symptoms were associated with intrusive horrific memories of the accident in the one tenth who showed PTSD at 12 months, but post-event emotional disorder was more strongly associated with having pre-event psychological and social problems (Mayou, Bryant, & Duthie, 1993).

Among Dutch adults who had been in serious motor vehicle accidents, after 6 months about 90% did not suffer PTSD (Brom, Kleber, & Hofman, 1993). In a Norwegian study to follow the long-term psychiatric consequences of 107 people physically injured in accidents, there was only one case of PTSD at 6 months and at 2 years there was not one (Malt, 1988). Among 31 burned adults, only 2 showed PTSD at discharge, yet seven met PTSD criteria after 4 months (Roca, Spence, & Munster, 1992), contrary to what would be expected from a dose–response model.

Intrusive Illness.   Intrusive illness with prolonged physical disruption appears to elicit relatively low rates of event-attributed clinically significant distress. Of 18 survivors of a first heart attack, after 2 years only one showed some PTSD symptoms (van Driel & Op den Velde, 1995). Although cancer is commonly considered to be a highly stress-laden disease, depression and hopelessness are not common among cancer patients and should not be considered a normal response to the disease (Grassi, Rosti, LaSalvia, & Marangolo, 1993). Studies of individuals infected with the fatal illness of HIV similarly show that neither the stress of the diagnosis nor of disease progression was reliably associated with any increase in psychopathology symptoms (Rabkin, Wagner, & Rabkin, 1996).

Natural Disasters.   A large study of elementary school children in six Italian villages following an earthquake found that there was no relationship between the amount of destruction in a village and the number of children at risk for developing emotional or antisocial behavior problems (Galante & Foa, 1987). In a follow-up study of 195 adolescents who had been severely exposed to Hurricane Hugo 15 months earlier, not 1 of the 207 different stressors spontaneously listed by the children referred to the hurricane event (Hardin, Carbaugh, Weinrich, Pesut, & Carbaugh, 1992). Instead, stressors focused heavily on current dating issues (36% of subjects) and social relations with classmates (26%).

Even at the height of a disastrous event such as an earthquake or hurricane, most people respond with resignation rather than with panic, excessive rationality, or emotional display, until the unanticipated event has completed its course (Fogelman & Parenton, 1959). Following a tornado in Nebraska, even older people, for whom theories predict a more disabling emotional response, were found to show relatively little anxiety and stress and considerable interpersonal stability (Bell, Kara, & Batterson, 1978). In a study of 42 survivors of another tornado, rates of psychiatric disorder were low and even rates of symptoms were low, with subjects turning to family and friends for support as the most frequent coping method (North, Smith, McCool, & Lightcap, 1989). The vast majority of adults do not require mental health services for any extended period following natural disasters despite the general disruption and major losses (Summers & Cowan, 1991).

In studies of Australian children whose lives were thrown into upheaval by massive bush fires in 1983, McFarlane, Policansky, and Irwin (1987) reported that, after 2 months, the children showed less distress than a nonexposed comparison group as well as more compliant and obedient behavior at home and school. Instead of showing further reductions in symptoms, they then showed increases in symptoms or *caseness* at 8 and 26 months, which were associated with school underachievement problems and absenteeism. The authors decided that this unusual longitudinal trend reflected genuine increases in distress, after examining and rejecting the possibility that the symptoms reported by parents and teachers might have represented a sensitization of the adults or children by the repeated measures procedures. Apart from this unusual temporal pattern, the authors noted that the magnitude of the increase in morbidity during the event exposure was smaller than expected, and that most of the children did not decompensate even under these life-threatening circumstances.

A series of studies followed 469 firefighters who experienced a particularly intense exposure to a huge bushfire in southeastern Australia. From these, a subgroup of 130 agreeable subjects was selected for detailed study after being identified as being most at risk (Spurrell & McFarlane, 1993), and 70 were diagnosed with PTSD at 42 months, representing about 15% of the full sample. In an earlier study of these men, severity variables related to this adverse event and other recent life events accounted for only 9% of the variance on the General Health Questionnaire (GHQ) of psychiatric caseness or distress symptoms despite significant correlations among GHQ scores and fire-related variables (McFarlane, 1987). Although these correlations were statistically significant, the actual differences in mean scores were not clinically meaningful. McFarlane concluded by noting that the majority of the fire-fighters "did not become cases, despite experiencing prolonged life-threatening stress, frequent injury, and property loss" (p. 366).

An associated study found that acute distress appeared to be independent of psychiatric impairment and that psychiatric impairment was more affected by an acute intervening subjective variable (distress) than by exposure severity or losses (McFarlane, 1988b). Of further interest, it was found that some men were extremely distressed in the acute aftermath but did not go on to become psychiatrically impaired, again raising the question of pre-existing vulnerabilities in accounting for chronic distress such as PTSD. These findings raise the possibility that psychiatric morbidity after a disaster could be more accurately modeled if pre-existing individual differences in vulnerability were included, and the life event construed only as one variable among many.

Among survivors after the eruption of Mount St. Helens in Washington state, those with higher levels of disaster losses reported higher levels of health symptoms (although these were not objectively assessed), with greatest emotional distress including anger found among those with property losses rather than among those suffering bereavement (Murphy, 1984). Nondose factors other than bereavement contributed to delayed recovery according to the bereaved, who reported that media intrusions and errors inhibited their recovery. Another researcher reporting on hostage victims similarly reported that media intrusions can increase the level of traumatization (Allodi, 1994). Although the Puerto Rican floods of 1985 contributed to a rise in the level of some mental symptoms, particularly depressive and somatic, there were no differences in the occurrence of PTSD symptoms among exposed and non-exposed subjects (Canino et al., 1990). A group of miners trapped for 7 days without knowing if they would be rescued maintained emotional control throughout the period and later explained that it was the influence of group standards of behavior that had the most powerful effect on their individual behavior (Lucas, 1969).

A study of children who had experienced the Buffalo Creek dam collapse and flood disaster in West Virginia in 1972 showed that contextual and interpersonal factors were far more important than the objective threat factor (Green, Grace, Lindy, Grace, & Gleser, 1990). Some children appeared to show a high rate of PTSD (37%) in a study done 2 years later on a subsample, but the detailed multiple regressions show that life threat accounted for only 4.4% of variance, while irritable atmosphere in the home contributed 6.4%, mother severity accounted for 6.3%, and sex of child accounted for 3.6% (Green, Korol, Grace, & Vary, 1991). Of further relevance, these 179 children represented only a subsample in that they were members of a group of 118 families that had decided to sue for psychic impairment following a disaster that led to 125 deaths and left thousands homeless. The apparent occurrence rate of PTSD, therefore, in no way represents a true incidence rate. In a 17-year follow-up, 7% of those who had been assessed in the earlier work showed PTSD, all of whom were women (Green et al., 1994). In comparison with a control group from a similar community, there were no significant differences on any of the seven measures of current emotional distress and no differences in lifetime prevalence rates of major depression and alcohol abuse. The only variable showing a statistically significant difference was lifetime prevalence of PTSD. (Additional findings with significant treatment implications were those that showed significant symptom decreases across time for both children and adults despite the absence of treatment. These findings conform to the dose–response model among the subset of those affected.)

Complex Disasters. Complex disasters include war, famine, civil strife, and forced migrations that lead to massive public health problems. A recent review noted that although the acute emergency stage is followed by increasingly successful remedies for feeding and health care with significant decreases in mortality and significant increases in personal safety, there is a paradoxical increase in anxiety about personal safety (Burkholder & Toole, 1995).

Representative Samples. When data are reported from representative samples or total populations rather than from more selective samples of individuals presenting for treatment services, most data suggest that the rates of observed significant or chronic post-event distress syndromes are typically quite low following disasters. De la Fuente (1990) found that, of 208 women housed in shelters after the Mexican earthquake of 1985, more than 72% showed no psychopathological symptoms, whereas 9% showed significant decompensation. In another sample of 573 earthquake refugees housed in shelters, he reported that 32% reported PTSD symptoms, but only 4% required special care, and only .3% required psychiatric hospitalization. "Most of the victims displayed a notable capacity to adapt" (p. 25). Natural disaster was not associated with any PTSD effects in the large epidemiological study of lifetime prevalence of PTSD in the United States (Helzer, Robins, & McEvoy, 1987).

Prospective Studies. In three studies that were able to use a prospective research design, no dose–response relationships were found. Among Bangladeshi children assessed before and after the flood of 1988, there was no correlation between the severity of the flood experiences of the children and the development of behavioral problems (Durkin et al., 1993). A similar absence of dose–response effects was found in two other studies of children: measures were obtained both before and, in one case, during a war (Milgram & Milgram, 1976), and in the other, after a disastrous storm (Burke, Borus, Burns, Millstein, & Beasley, 1982) .

Summary: Direct, Brief Exposures
With Prolonged Physical Disruption

Taken as a whole, the evidence suggests that dose–response relationships for events that consist of a brief, direct exposure to an extreme event followed by prolonged physical disruption of life circumstances are only weak, unreliable, and subject to many moderating factors whenever these factors are directly measured. Most evidence suggests that a disaster syndrome may not be a significant phenomenon. Dynes and Quarantelli (1976) concluded that to the extent that it appears in extreme and sudden catastrophes, it is apparently confined to the post-impact period, lasts only a short time, and does not occur on a large scale. In 1987 Breslau and Davis reviewed studies of types of posttraumatic stress disorder and not only concluded that the evidence did not support the dose–response model, but noted that disasters in general do not "produce psychopathology in the majority of individuals" (p. 259). More recent data appear to continue supporting this conclusion.

DIRECT, BRIEF EXPOSURE

What is the evidence of dose–response relations where there is direct but brief toxic exposure with no prolonged physical aftermath? The model predicts limited distress effects, with a relatively rapid decline across time; in particular, PTSD rates should be low.

There is evidence showing that direct brief exposure to toxic events can elicit emotional distress including PTSD. About 45% of the variance in long-term emotional impairment in survivors of the Beverly Hills Supper Club fire of 1977 at 1 year could be accounted for by the individual's fire-stress experiences, while intervening variables such as the use of social supports, coping tactics, and education were quite modest in impact (Green, Grace, & Gleser, 1985).

In addition, more variable results have been documented concerning the effects of direct, brief toxic exposures, including results that contradict the standard MH model. Many studies show that other factors are more important than dose in determining the report of post-event distress or PTSD.

In an early review, Burstein (1985) studied 120 consecutive case records of PTSD where a well-identified stressor was known, and concluded that distress was typically immediate and diminishing. Of note however, delayed PTSD appeared in two cases up to 4 and 12 months after the event, showing the variability of responses. In a large Detroit random sample studying uncategorized, but relatively domestic, toxic events and PTSD, the PTSD rate varied significantly across types of events. There were lower rates following sudden personal injury or serious accident whereas higher rates were associated with seeing someone hurt or killed and for hearing news of the accident or sudden death of a friend (Breslau et al., 1991). That is, proximity to a toxic event directly experienced by another was more distressing than direct personal experience.

Among a group of 100 elementary school children exposed to a sniper who killed one child and injured 14 other people, evidence of distress was mixed 14 months later in that stress symptom reports correlated with exposure, whereas grief reactions were independent of degree of exposure (Nader, Pynoos, Fairbanks, & Frederick, 1990). In a U.S. of 60 deputy sheriffs involved in shooting incidents, 30% reported the event had affected them greatly, 33% reported only moderate effects, and 35% reported none at all, leading the researchers to note that it is inappropriate for mental health professionals to expect that significant emotional disability always follows events of this sort (Stratton, Parker, & Snibbe, 1984).

Although elderly people surviving in the village of Lockerbie Scotland after the well-known airplane explosion disaster showed a pattern of decreasing PTSD symptoms over a 3-year period, symptoms at Year 3 were not correlated with any specific event characteristics, that is, not with witnessing gruesome sights, experiencing the loss of a partner, or property destruction (Livingston, Livingston, & Fell, 1994).

Motor vehicle accident victims showed a statistically significant relation between the extent of physical injuries and the report of PTSD symptoms, but this accounted for only 12% of the variance in their distress (Blanchard, Hickling, Mitnick, & Taylor, 1995). Similarly, there was little support for the dose–response model for PTSD from a study of 48 people exposed to physical trauma with fractures severe enough to require surgery (Feinstein & Dolan, 1991). Although PTSD declined and was not shown in three fourths of the subjects at Week 6 and not shown in six sevenths of the subjects by 6 months, two measures of trauma severity were not correlated with outcome at either 6 weeks or 6 months. What was highly predictive of PTSD was mean usual levels of alcohol use and subjective emotionality recorded within days of hospital admission on the Impact of Events Scale. Violation of the dose–response model was also shown in a study that found persistent significant losses in well-being and high symptom reports in some people as long as 4 to 7 years after accidental bereavement (Lehman, Wortman, & Williams, 1987). Among 120 victims of crime, there were no differences in PTSD symptoms or depression whether they had experienced one or multiple criminal events, although symptom rates were higher in comparison to nonvictims (Falsetti & Resick, 1995).

Among the small fraction of individuals who do report PTSD after an accident, data suggest a temporal decline in caseness in most but not all cases. In a study of 98 victims of recent motor vehicle accidents, 30 showed PTSD symptoms at 4 months compared with 40 immediately following the event. At 6 months only 20 continued to meet PTSD criteria (Blanchard, Hickling, Mitnick, & Taylor, 1995). Among 84 volunteer subjects who had experienced a nonsexual assault within the previous 30 days, there was a steady decline across time in the percentage who met criteria for PTSD, starting with 71% of the women and 50% of the men and declining to 21% of the women and none of the men at 3 months (Riggs, Rothman, & Foa, 1995); these values cannot be treated as incidence rates because of the nature of the sample.

Prospective Studies

Prospective studies involving time-limited highly toxic events are rare, but they suggest that the incidence of PTSD is very much a minority phenomenon. Saigh (1988) reported on a group of 12 university students before and after the militia bombardment of their university in Beirut in 1984. It was found that self-reported anxiety and depression levels measured 63 days before the event were followed by increases 8 days post-bombardment, but that by Days 37 and 316 these values were no different from pre-event. Only one student developed PTSD. When a broader criterion of outcome is considered, such as need for rehospitalization following intrusive life events, the classic studies by Leff and Vaughn (1985) of the expressed emotion in family environments and life events within psychiatric patients at home found that the occurrence of an independent stressful life event was not reliably followed by rehospitalization across a 3-month period. Other factors were more important.

CHRONIC, LOW-DOSE EVENTS

Many people believe that any one of an extensive range of small magnitude experiences that individuals do not like (e.g., "hassles"), can be traumatic and function as toxic experience sufficient to account for clinically significant distress that deserves compensation and requires treatment. If this exposure is persistent, it is believed to have an even greater effect. Verbal interactions which an individual interprets as making him or her feel uncomfortable are held to contribute to losses in self-esteem. Self-esteem is construed as a fragile but extremely important individual characteristic whose variations have major effects on life achievement and happiness (Brandon, 1969; Mecca, Smelser, & Vasconsellos, 1989). Such a claim does not relate to PTSD specifically because in the self-esteem model there is no definable event that meets the required criterion of the DSM–IV, but the self-esteem model does form part of the thinking implicit in much psychotherapy for emotional disarray. This conception stretches the idea of adverse events from those that are objectively toxic and represent a high dose to those that depend entirely on the subjective constructions of the individual. It, thus, in effect, undercuts an event-oriented model in favor of one that is person oriented.

A classic study comparing the effects of daily hassles on emotional symptoms found that minor domestic adversities accounted for distress symptoms equally as well as the larger life events measured using scales derived from the earlier Holmes and Rahe research (Kanner, Coyne,

Schaefer, & Lazarus, 1981). This does not illuminate our understanding of PTSD, but it does suggest that emotional distress may not be a good index of broader well-being.

In the case of the adversity associated with a troubled family life, it is interesting to note, as one recent historian did, that across the history of the British monarchy "all the heirs-apparent who had 'normal' childhoods turned out losers" as monarchs (P. Johnson, 1995, p. 34), whereas all those who had very disturbed and even dangerous childhoods turned out to be exemplary rulers. Apart from this unique observation, there is little evidence to support a claim of a lasting traumatic distress syndrome arising from low-dose, but persistent, adverse exposures to dysfunctional family life. In view of the huge biographical literature of accomplished adults who show early chronic adversity overcome, event-related distress disorders are unlikely to be found among individuals with chronic exposure to low-toxicity events unless there are additional long-standing individual factors.

When toxic events are direct, chronic, and high dose, they have been described as chronic strains. Ongoing evidence does suggest that these have a generally debilitating effect on well-being since a classic study (Pearlin & Schooler, 1978), although these effects do not speak directly to the issue of PTSD.

REVIEWS: EVENTS AND PSYCHOLOGICAL WELL-BEING

Broad reviews examining many similar studies have concluded that exposure to life stress does not account for any significant proportion of psychological illness. An early review of large-scale prospective studies did not find a significant correlation between life events, stress, and psychological illness (Andrews, Tennant, Hewson & Vaillant, 1978). More recently Rubonis and Bickman (1991) did a meta-analysis of the power of objective dose variables relating disasters to psychological impairment, finding a small overall effect size of .17. Larger effects were found when the event was of a more drastic nature (e.g., nuclear or nature-caused) and when the harm level of the dose was more striking (greater number of deaths, closeness to the disaster). Meta-analyses are very sensitive to the rules for inclusion and the quality of the studies included. A meta-analysis of the psychological effects of military service in Vietnam, for example, found that effect sizes were larger if a study had no control group, if it were more recent and part of the Veterans Administration, and if actual combat history were documented providing objective dose variables (Kaylor, King, & King, 1987). These results show that intrusions from contextual and group factors reflecting popu-

lar beliefs and compensation-oriented behavior all significantly contributed to the distress emotions reported.

Although case reports cannot provide evidence supporting the validity of a model, they can provide evidence challenging it. There are
countless case reports and biographical accounts of individuals suffering
extremely horrific events such as politically motivated torture and
mutilation, yet not reporting any symptoms of PTSD and continuing to
live productively and with every evidence of well-being. In many cases,
it appears that this adjustment is associated with personal interpretations of the meaning of the experience (e.g., Bracken, Giller, & Summerfield, 1995). These reports suggest there are powerful individual factors
that affect the meaning individuals place on events. These interpretations are crucial in the question of forming a clinical distress syndrome.

OBJECTIVE DAMAGE AND SUBJECTIVE DISTRESS

The objective damage done to an individual in a toxic event does not
show a significant correlation with distress reports when both kinds of
measures are taken. Objective–subjective discrepancies are found in
both directions. Charcot saw this dissociation of objective and subjective
effects in his early studies of traumatic neuroses from the late 1870s
onward (Micale, 1994). In more recent evidence, among 54 children who
suffered closed head injury and were re-examined after 2 years, reports
of subjective distress did not correlate with objective variables describing neurological, behavioral or intellectual functioning, although these
latter signs did correlate with original measures of trauma severity
(Ruijs, Gabreels, & Keyser, 1993). Similar results were found with 124
adults who suffered head injury, in that normal and abnormal profiles
on the MMPI were not associated with injury-related neurological
characteristics (Bornstein, Miller, & van Schoor, 1988). A study of the
effects of a motor vehicle accident on PTSD found that 18 months after
the event there was no association between physical outcome and the
diagnosis of PTSD (Green, McFarlane, Hunter, & Griggs, 1993). In a
study of whistle-blowers who complained about scientific misconduct of
researchers to the Office of Research Integrity of the U.S. Department
of Health and Human Services, fully two thirds had suffered negative
consequences of their actions and one fourth had even lost their jobs, yet
80% reported they would do it again (Holden, 1996). Overall, then,
subjective distress reports do not represent any valid reflection of
objective harm suffered; in particular, high distress cannot be taken as
an index of objective damage.

SUMMARY: DOSE–RESPONSE EFFECTS
WITH DIRECT EXPOSURE

Most people do not develop PTSD from direct exposure to toxic events whether acute or chronic, accidental or deliberate. Nor do most people develop other distress syndromes of clinical significance. The dose–response model represented by the PTSD diagnosis where the event is a central factor, does not provide a good fit for the data whenever representative samples are studied (rather than clinical or litigation samples) and when individuals are followed in a prospective way starting before toxic events. While most people respond with some emotional distress to a powerful and sustained toxic event, even under these conditions most do not develop clinically significant disorders, and most recover their pre-event emotional condition within a relatively short time. Among that minority of exposed people who do respond with clinical distress, there is modest support for time-related aspects of the dose–response model, although some individuals actually get worse across time. In general, however, objective dose characteristics of toxic events do not provide any reliable predictive power in determining the incidence or duration of PTSD.

Taken overall, this means that event-related factors do not represent the most important component in any useful conceptualization of event-attributed clinical distress. The findings fail to provide support for the more general dose–response environmental model in which a toxic event plays a necessary and powerful role. Despite this, the power of individual differences in determining outcome has made little impact on the event-oriented model used by clinicians. In his examination of the nosology of PTSD for example, March (1990) strongly endorsed the dose/exposure–distress model based on his literature review yet soon noted "While these findings generally support the importance of fear conditioning, most individuals exposed to PTSD qualifying stressors do not develop a psychiatric disturbance, suggesting that cognitive and/or neurobiological vulnerabilities are also important if ill-understood" (p. 67).

Against this background of evidence, what are the effects of toxic events when they are learned of indirectly through either physical exposure to the harms that others have suffered or through psychological exposure to the stories of harms they have suffered?

5

What Are the Effects of Indirect Toxic Exposures?

The previous chapter examined the effects of the most extreme toxic exposures, those in which physical threat or harm was directly experienced. This chapter looks at toxic events that are not experienced as direct physical threats. If the event-oriented model of PTSD is robust and events are the crucial feature accounting for distress that is later reported, then toxic events that are not experienced directly as personal threats should have no clinical impact on well-being.

Indirect exposure to the trauma of others can be experienced in two ways. People can work in physical settings in which direct trauma has been experienced by others, such as in the experience of rescue workers. At a more remote distance from the event, indirect psychological exposure can be described as learning about toxic events from those directly affected, whether family members, acquaintances, strangers, or clients. What do the data reveal about these two different levels of indirect exposure to toxic events that were directly experienced by others?

PHYSICAL EXPOSURE TO TOXIC EVENTS EXPERIENCED BY OTHERS

Popular lore predicts that rescue and clean-up workers who have to deal with the aftermath of a disaster should show moderately high rates of emotional distress after repeatedly participating in gory and tragic scenes. Having to handle injured and dead people and destroyed human body parts represents no direct personal threat of harm but may provide prolonged exposure, so this vivid sensory experience should be expected to yield intermediate rates of distress compared to that expected from directly receiving personal threat.

There is evidence that direct physical exposure to toxic events suffered by others can be followed by clinically significant distress in some individuals. Almost half of a sample of 24 U.S. army reservists who had handled human remains while serving during the Persian Gulf War met PTSD criteria eight months after return home. These soldiers specifically referred to the gruesome aspects of this work as factors in their distress (Sutker, Uddo, Brailey, Allain, & Errera, 1994). Another Gulf War study of soldiers whose job was recovering human remains found that they were more likely to report PTSD symptoms a year after their return home than those who did not handle remains (McCarroll, Ursano, & Fullerton, 1995).

In contrast, along a stretch of the cliffs of Dover that is famous for attracting suicides, a group of volunteers routinely retrieve damaged dead bodies and do not regard it is traumatic or as something that contributes to emotional distress. They regard it as a useful public duty: "How else do you think people survived the war?" (de Berniéres, 1996). In the United States, membership in the Crime Scene Unit of the New York police is regarded as a prize assignment even though the work consists almost exclusively of handling all the frequently gruesome physical evidence at the scene of violent crimes (Pogrebin, 1996). In both of these examples, the individuals volunteering for the job represent a self-selected group and may represent certain characteristic personality features reflecting individual differences that allow them to handle their tasks without clinical distress.

Studies of individuals accidentally confronted with a horrific event suffered by others also suggest that these experiences are not necessarily trauma inducing. In a study of 76 subway train drivers in London who had witnessed bloody suicides in front of their moving trains, at one month post-event, 17% met PTSD criteria which resolved rapidly (Tranah & Farmer, 1994). Of the 56 reinterviewed after 6 months, none met the PTSD criteria, and only two drivers showed any diagnosable disorder (neurotic depression and phobic state). Police rescue workers in Scotland who had to find body parts of those who died after the Lockerbie air terrorism disaster did not suffer high rates of PTSD (M. Mitchell, personal communication, August 24, 1995). Contrary to a dose-focused model, Mitchell found that prolonged and repeated exposure was even more beneficial than brief, which was more frequently associated with distress sequelae of longer duration.

A study of 48 Scottish police officers who worked to retrieve the scattered remaining body parts of 105 people in a burnt oil platform in the North Sea found at 3 months and at 3 years that, although the experience was very distasteful and often dangerous, it did not result in substantial adverse reactions in comparison with control policemen

(Alexander, 1993). Anxiety scores actually fell below pre-event baseline levels at 3 months, leading Alexander to conclude that the results "counter the concern that psychiatric morbidity after such duties is an almost inevitable consequence" (p. 808). Nearly all the officers judged the experience as positive, recorded their interest in doing such work again in the future, and reported they had been glad to be part of the body-handling work team. The relatively straightforward passage of the body handlers through such a difficult experience was attributed to good organization and preparation prior to the task, good management practices, debriefing, good group cohesion and support, and the acquisition of new coping skills as the events unfolded. In an English abstract of a Russian publication, Deryugin (1989) reported that the soldiers who worked to rescue people during the emergency of the Armenian earthquake showed more emotional stability than the civilian helpers.

When the evidence is taken as a whole, among those professionals or volunteers with brief or prolonged exposure to physical settings where toxic events have harmed others, these indirect exposures do not appear to represent much significant or lasting psychological threat. The evidence raises the question of whether the high rate reported by the military personnel in the Gulf War, who were not necessarily volunteers in their military duties, is mainly a function of horrific exposures, or if it is more well understood as a reflection of specific beliefs, values, and other contextual features about the events and expected responses.

PSYCHOLOGICAL EXPOSURE TO A TOXIC EVENT EXPERIENCED BY OTHERS

If an event-focused model of traumatic distress is a strong model, psychological exposures to the stories of events directly experienced by others should not be expected to lead to distress responses because, in effect, there is no objective dose. The idea that a story provides a traumatic dose means that trauma is a subjective construction determined entirely by individual characteristics of the listener. The event-focused PTSD model would predict no clinical distress attributable to such a vicarious exposure. Because the PTSD criteria do not include such secondary, metaexposures as traumatic events, the strict case of PTSD is not at issue in this examination. Instead, the more general adversity–distress model is assessed in terms of more loosely defined reports of anxiety and distress attributed to stories heard of the toxic events experienced by others. To the extent that distress is reported following hearing of events suffered by others, it disconfirms the event-focused model. What does the evidence suggest?

Virtually all humans hear about bad things that happen to others. Among health and social service professionals, hearing these stories represents a daily experience across a lifetime. Because the majority of people do not suffer chronic distress disorders from this indirect exposure to the stories of adversity even if they feel touched and sympathy is elicited, the event-focused model of distress is supported in a general way. The more interesting data concern those individuals who do report significant distress under these conditions, in contradiction to the event/dose–response model.

There are emerging claims that individuals can suffer PTSD symptoms following an event that was neither experienced nor witnessed, but experienced by another person and learned about secondhand. Some reports concern events that trigger personal memories, or individuals whose lives are intimately bound up with the victim in a long-term relationship. In a case report, the murder of a colleague triggered secondhand PTSD in a woman (Bledin, 1994). Brief therapy revealed that she had construed events early in her childhood in a way that linked them with the adult event. There is a report of vicarious PTSD symptoms in the wives of men where the men, but not their wives, had suffered a frightening accident (Slagle, Reichman, Rodenhauser, Knoedler, & Davis, 1990). More remotely, in the United Kingdom, a series of ferry workers who had no direct contact with a major ferry disaster either as survivors, bereaved relatives, or as helpers presented themselves for professional treatment of PTSD during 3 years following the event (Dixon, Rehling, & Shiwach, 1993).

A recent stream of reports concerns the distress reported by professionals who provide MH services to clients who describe their experiences of adverse life events (Lyon, 1993; Schauben & Frazier, 1995). A book was recently devoted to what was called compassion fatigue among those who learn of adverse events secondhand in the course of their work (Figley, 1995). This was defined as a secondary traumatic stress disorder. According to the author of one chapter, this group of vicarious trauma victims includes lawyers, judges, physicians, and applied researchers, among others of those who associate with either crime perpetrators or victims (Dutton & Rubenstein, 1995). Authors of another chapter (Munroe et al., 1995) even argued that there is a dose–response relationship in which MH workers are at risk of PTSD proportional to the severity of the objective events suffered by their clients. Case examples they provided, however, often included directly abusive client behavior rather than secondary exposure.

This type of indirect, vicarious relationship to an event means that such professionals cannot fully meet the diagnostic criteria for PTSD; however, to the extent that more cases and reliable incidence rates of secondary significant and chronic distress disorders become established, these data will speak to the limitations of the event-oriented model.

SUMMARY: EFFECTS OF INDIRECT EXPOSURES

The evidence shows that the indirect toxic exposure represented by direct physical experience with a setting where others have been harmed is followed by diverse responses in different people. These mixed responses reflect an intermediate outcome zone where predictions according to either a dose–response model or a competing individual differences model cannot be differentiated, and neither model can be rejected. These variations have to be accounted for by other factors.

In contrast, the event/dose–response model cannot account for distress reported after only secondary exposure to stories about the toxic events that others have experienced, because there is no dose. Nevertheless, case studies and reports from groups suggest that some individuals do respond with significant distress to such indirect exposures. Cases of this type require an explanation of distress in which individual differences in psychological qualities including emotionality and beliefs are more powerful in accounting for traumatic distress reports.

The data force us to consider a more complex model incorporating individual differences arising from both nature and nurture. Elements important in this model are found from within the literatures on stress and coping, clinical and experimental studies of neuroticism and temperament, and attribution studies in social psychology. Thus, one of the important questions concerns the role of pre-existing individual differences in past behavior, emotionality, cognitive competency, beliefs, and values.

6

How Much Do Individual Differences in Pre-Event Competencies Affect Responses to a Toxic Event?

Because the dose–response data show poor support for the singular emphasis on the event that defines PTSD, the reasons behind the striking differences in the impact of risk experiences on different individuals are important. This question of individual differences in interaction with environmental factors is an enduring issue in several domains of applied psychology. Long ago it was strongly articulated by psychologist Lee Cronbach (1957) in his call for more Aptitude × Treatment interaction research to study both individual differences and events in interaction, rather than having them studied by separate clusters of researchers working in isolation. This interactional approach has also been stressed as important in trying to understand causes and consequences of pathologies during the developmental period (Rutter, 1994), where researchers of development are often heavily focused on environmental events as the major determinants of behavioral problems.

This chapter reviews some of the pre-event factors that have been shown to influence the responses people make when they are confronted with toxic events. The factors include individual differences in pre-event history, acts, disorders, and cognitive competency. Subsequent chapters examine pre-event temperament, personality, and beliefs.

PRE-EVENT HISTORY

Life history events prior to a specific adverse exposure may contribute to the range of responses that individuals show after a new toxic event. In general, this longer-term approach has not been closely studied in PTSD research, but it has been more intensively studied in the looser context of stress and coping. In these studies, a typical method is simply to count the number of significant life events that occurred within a given period of time. Predictions of well-being are then made on these general accumulations, rather than in terms of response to one key event. In studies where a specified event is also set as a marker, there is some evidence that events prior to the marker toxic exposure do interact with it in accounting for differences in distress reports.

A study of adolescents who experienced Hurricane Hugo in South Carolina found that the strongest predictor of distress sufficient to meet PTSD criteria was previous experience with violent events, not the hurricane experience (Garrison, Weinrich, Hardin, Weinrich, & Wang, 1993). The odds ratio of meeting PTSD criteria in those adolescents with prehurricane violent experiences was 2.5, whereas the experience of the hurricane contributed to an odds ratio about half that, of 1.3. The meaning of this value is that it is quite low in terms of weights used to measure risk factors (Team, 1995). Anything lower than 3 for example, is considered not worth pursuing in epidemiological studies (Taubes, 1995). In another study of the acute effects of losses, injuries, or life threats from Hurricane Hugo, distress reactions were powerfully mediated by long-standing financial, marital, filial, and physical strains (Norris & Gary, 1993). Among 118 trauma therapists, the 60% who had personal trauma histories were more distressed by their professional work with post-event distressed subjects than the therapists without such personal trauma experiences (Pearlman & MacIan, 1995). In a complex study of 1,632 Vietnam veterans with PTSD, prewar factors, including trauma histories, family instability, childhood antisocial behavior, and age, all had significant direct or indirect effects on PTSD in men with combat experience (King, King, Foy, & Gudanowski, 1996).

PRE-EVENT ACTS

The distressed-victim model assumes that distressed individuals are recipients of events not in their control, yet events of another nature have also been found to contribute to post-event distress. Individual acts of initiative may begin a chain of events that leads to a toxic event that is then followed by distress, or some acts alone may lead directly to a distress response.

With children, acts often lead to toxic events such as poisonings and other injuries that are then experienced as distressing. There is evidence that these acts and toxic exposures are not randomly distributed across all children, but occur with much greater frequency among children with traits of high risk taking, hyperactivity, and little general concern about safety (Farmer & Peterson, 1995; Flagler, 1987). Among Vietnam veterans, similar findings showed that those with PTSD were more disposed to behave and think in ways that led them to experiences of pain, punishment, and risk compared with controls (Kuhne, Orr, & Barage, 1993). On the other hand, long-standing positive attitudes towards the self, family, and community were associated with fewer posttraumatic symptoms among 24 school staff at 6 and 18 months following a shooting in the school (Schwarz & Kowalski, 1993).

Individual acts of deliberate harm to another person prior to a marker toxic event, or prior to post-event distress reports, also contribute significantly to a later PTSD syndrome. For example, although dose–response relationships were found among Kuwaiti children who experienced the war in the Persian Gulf and a high percentage reported posttraumatic distress symptoms, the highest mean distress score was found in children who reported hurting someone, rather than in those who had been passive victims of the harmful actions of others (Nader, Pynoos, Fairbanks, al Ajeel, & al Asfour, 1993). Similar results were found in 43 Vietnam veterans who sought help and whose combat experiences were obtained. Investigators found that a reliable assessment of war "trauma" could be made using seven dichotomous questions concerning very specific experiences; two of these were acts of deliberate harm to others, while a third was a mixed active/passive event: "firing a weapon or being fired upon" (Lund, Foy, Sipprelle, & Strachan, 1984). In another study of 350 Vietnam veterans, participation in abusive violence was associated with later reports of distress symptoms (Laufer, Gallops, & Frey-Wouters, 1984). Among 1,632 Vietnam veterans who were diagnosed with PTSD, participation in atrocities or abusive violence, in interaction with combat experience, played a significant role in predicting PTSD (King et al., 1996). Complementing these findings in another sample, a lack of participation in excessive violence was typical of Vietnam combat veterans who did not show PTSD (Hendin & Haas, 1984).

On a more domestic scale, in a 20-year follow-up of 228 London school children, antisocial behavior at age 10 was followed by a marked increase in the rate of severely toxic life events over the next two decades (Champion, Goodall, & Rutter, 1995). Within the families of abused elders, the only three stressor events that could be identified in the year prior to the abuse incident that differed from family stressor events in matched nonabusive households, were all related to initiatives of the abuser. These included being in activities that led to arrest, leaving the household, or joining the household, rather than intruding stressor events acting on a passive recipient (Pillemer, 1986).

PRE-EVENT ACUTE CLINICAL DISORDERS

There is good evidence of high levels of comorbidity of PTSD with other acute mental disorders, long-standing personality disorders, and substance abuse (Keane & Wolfe, 1990). This appears to be equally true for people after disasters and after combat (Green, Lindy, Grace, & Leonard, 1992).

If adversity plays a powerful role in triggering the distress behavior of the PTSD, we should expect that the addition of a disastrous event should trigger even higher levels of distress among people already identified as mentally disordered and receiving protective care because of their significant problems in adapting to the changing demands of everyday life. Contrary to this expectation, Stout and Knight (1990) found that 2 months after a huge flood and the chaos of evacuation of psychiatric inpatients, the event was no longer even being discussed by the patients. In particular, there was no evidence of PTSD.

Within the general population, however, there is evidence that previous mental disorders represent a risk factor for distress after a toxic event. In a major review of the effects of disasters on people living regularly in the community, Smith et al. concluded that the best predictors of post-disaster disorders were pre-disaster diagnostic and symptom levels relating both to mental and physical health (Smith, Robins, Przubeck, Goldrig, & Solomon, 1986). Among a small subset of survivors of the Lockerbie, Scotland air disaster who had settled claims for posttraumatic distress, 12 of 25 had a previous psychiatric history (Scott, Brooks, & McKinlay, 1995). Further to the issue of individual differences in comparison to dose exposure, of those who met a caseness definition according to questionnaire cutoff scores, caseness was higher among those who had little or no property damage than it was among those who had such resource losses. There was also no relationship between caseness and being a witness to gruesome sights or suffering the death or injury of a close friend.

In a study within a general sample of 179 Vietnam War veterans, of the 29% with PTSD, premilitary and postmilitary factors contributed as much (21% of variance in total) to PTSD as did military factors (19%). Most of the premilitary factor was a prewar Axis I diagnosis of a clinical mental disorder (Green et al., 1990). When 135 Vietnam veterans with combat-attributed PTSD were studied for comorbidity, all had at least one other diagnosable major mental disorder (Talbert et al., 1994).

Studies also examined the pre-event mental disorder histories of those reporting distress after a more individual event such as a motor vehicle accident (MVA). Among MVA survivors with PTSD, a prior history of depression has been identified as a risk factor for development of the PTSD syndrome (Blanchard, Hickling, Taylor & Loos, 1995). Although a study of 50 victims of recent motor vehicle accidents who sought medical attention found a high figure of 46% who met the criteria for PTSD and an additional 20% who showed some symptoms, this group of 66% of the patients was significantly more likely to have experienced previous trauma other than a serious MVA. Furthermore, patients were much more likely to have met PTSD criteria previously (Blanchard, Hickling, Taylor, Loos, & Gerardi, 1994). Among a group of patients reporting chronic headache after MVAs, those with concurrent PTSD were significantly more likely to have suffered headaches prior to the accident (Chibnall & Duckro, 1994).

LONG-STANDING PERSONALITY DISORDERS

Personality disorders (PD) are long-standing syndromes in which there is a problem with character. Behavior is difficult, and this affects personal relationships. There is considerable evidence that personality disorders are found in an increased frequency among people diagnosed with PTSD. Among combat veterans seeking treatment for PTSD, for example, it is common to find a high rate of character pathology (Southwick, Yehuda, & Giller, 1993). To what extent does PTSD reflect long-standing behavioral problems, including those severe enough to meet DSM criteria for personality disorders?

There is some controversy among researchers as to whether or not an individual can be diagnosed with both an acute clinical disorder representing a currently disturbed *state* (Axis I disorders on the DSM) and long-standing *trait* patterns such as found in the personality disorders (Axis II disorders on the DSM). In particular, there is controversy about what DSM–III–R called Borderline Personality Disorder, and PTSD. Some have argued that Borderline PD is a posttraumatic stress disorder itself, or a frequent precursor to PTSD, with both viewed as a response to trauma (Famularo, Kinscherff, & Fenton, 1991). Others have disputed this (Silk, Westen, Lohr, & Ogata, 1991), while still others have argued that an individual can have one or the other but probably not both (Gunderson & Sabo, 1993). Generally, it appears that clinicians find it helpful to diagnose both conditions when they find an adult patient meeting criteria for both, and it has been argued that the PTSD represents a complex mixture of both current state and long-standing personality disorder trait features (Kudler, 1993; Watson, 1989).

At the level of individual cases, there are reports of men presenting with PTSD complaints in whom it is soon determined that personality disorder was the only disorder. One case was of a soldier who, 9 years after the Vietnam experience, reported persistent stress symptoms and fugue states that he attributed to his work as a "super soldier" (Silsby & Jones, 1985). It was eventually determined that his combat history and symptom reports were fantasy. The authors concluded, "it is our opinion that ... the initial stressor was not an actual traumatic combat experience. We believe that what the soldier took to the war (in the form of personality, family, marital, or other problems), coupled with social neglect and dissatisfaction, compounded with current ongoing environmental stress to produce the clinical syndrome we are seeing and often diagnosing as PTSD" (p. 522). There are other similar cases in the literature, with antisocial personality disorder (Weston & Dalby, 1991) and long-standing narcissistic personality disorder (W. B. Johnson, 1995).

On a more general level, a history of behavioral problems before the age of 15 contributed significantly to the probability of future PTSD in a large representative study (Helzer et al., 1987). In another study, personality disorders (e.g., passive-aggressive, schizoid, avoidant, and borderline) were so strikingly associated with PTSD among 189 Vietnam veterans that the researchers recommended that treatment should focus as much on these character problems as on PTSD symptoms (Sherwood, Funari, & Piekarski, 1990). Therapy transcripts from 60 Vietnam veterans with PTSD were examined using an Adlerian perspective and showed that early recollections involved less social interest (a positive attribute in the Adlerian system), as well as pursuit of goals in a more devious social manner (Hyer, Woods, & Boudewyns, 1989).

Substance abuse disorders are also frequently associated with PTSD, raising the question as to which diagnosis more reliably comes first. Within the general population, there is evidence that, for substance abusers with PTSD, the onset of substance abuse typically precedes the onset of PTSD symptoms rather than the converse (Cottler, Compton, Mager, Spitznagel, & Janca, 1992). There is at least one case study in which the full symptoms of PTSD were entirely attributable to alcohol abuse, clearing when the patient abstained (Cohen, 1994). Multiple personality disorder (now named dissociative identity disorder in DSM–IV) is often understood as a disorder arising from early toxic experience, although it has been noted that attempts are very rarely made to corroborate claims of early trauma in these cases (Frankel, 1993).

In summary, it appears that PTSD is more likely to be reported by individuals who had a pre-existing mental disorder, and personality disorders are especially well represented in the list of pre-existing conditions.

SENSATION-SEEKING

Because the adversity–distress model has high risk exposure as a defining characteristic, it is worth considering individual differences in the disposition to experience risk. This can be one of the facets of emotional regulation, for high-risk activities provide emotional arousal. Antisocial personality disorder carries with it a willingness to engage in risky activities without consideration of the consequences, and this general disposition has been subject to research attention. Long ago, Zuckerman (Zuckerman, 1971; Zuckerman, Kolin, Price, & Zoob, 1964) articulated a sensation-seeking disposition in which individuals characteristically seek out preferred levels of sensation and risk. A related version of this risk homeostasis model has been used in studies of driving behavior, providing at least some evidence that drivers respond with increases in risky behavior if vehicle or highway regulations or design apparently lower risk (Wilde, 1982). This change in behavior is done in order to reduce the discrepancy between perceived external risk and individually preferred risk levels.

When individuals who enjoy high levels of risk act so as to satisfy this disposition, exposure to risk events increases. If this is then followed by toxic events and post-event distress, it is clear that the distress arises out of a longer chain of causal factors than the event itself. This can be seen in populations that are more general, in addition to those in personality disorder groups in which it is more expected. In a study of college-educated adults, Arnett (1991) found that 50% had performed risky behaviors within the last year. Sensation-seeking scores were correlated with risky driving behaviors, such as speeding and driving while under the influence of alcohol, which increased the probability of harm events.

INTELLIGENCE

Individual differences in general cognitive competence appear to account for part of the post-event distress syndrome. In theory, if intelligence as measured by IQ tests does represent a measure, however imperfect, of ability to learn and to adapt to new information and experience, then IQ should have a modest positive correlation to general well-being. This might operate through providing more competent individuals with a broader perspective from which they can understand events. There is some evidence that this is the case.

Studies of the factors associated with resilience in children exposed to high-risk environments with high levels of toxic events, have generally found that intellectual competence is an important factor in eventual adult well-being. One exception is a study of 144 adolescents in a high-risk urban setting in the United States where higher intelligence was associated with greater vulnerability to negative life events (Luthar, 1991). In contrast, most evidence shows that intelligence works as a compensatory factor to toxic events, whether the childhood competency is defined as problem-solving (Masten & Best, 1990), intellectual capacity (Cederblad & Dahlin, 1994), cognitive skills (Garmezy, 1991), or in terms of formal academic achievement and verbal skills (Bland & Sowa, 1994). Those with higher IQs respond more adaptively to stress when this is studied over a long term (Garmezy & Masten, 1986).

Among 105 combat-exposed Vietnam veterans with chronic PTSD, intelligence predicted a significant amount of the variation in PTSD symptoms, with lower intelligence predicting more severe symptoms (McNally & Shin, 1995). All the cases of resilient adults who had suffered highly toxic childhoods, described by Gina Higgins (1994) in her book, had average or better intelligence. Higher educational achievement and rank (both correlates of IQ) were associated with different rates of PTSD among World War II veterans who had been prisoners of war, with those who were aviators (who had more education and higher rank) showing lower rates of distress (Sutker & Allain, 1995).

SUMMARY: PRE-EVENT HISTORY
AND COGNITIVE COMPETENCE

Taken as a whole, there is modest evidence that individual differences in pre-event factors including general reasoning ability, long-standing personality styles, acute mental disorders, and individual actions of a harmful nature, each contribute to variations in distress that are reported after toxic exposures. What about the general emotionality of individuals? Do differences in usual emotional condition affect the way that individuals respond when they are confronted with a toxic event? The next chapter considers the evidence.

7

How Powerful Are Individual Differences in Emotionality?

In summing up the effects of life events on individuals, the grand old man of personality theory, Gordon Allport, is reported to have said, "The same fire that melts the butter, hardens the egg." This statement puts individual differences in temperament at the center of any attempts to understand the behavior of an individual who is confronted with adversity. For many decades, this approach was attacked both from psychodynamic and behaviorist positions as being excessively particular. It was seen as unhelpful in the development of a general, scientific understanding of behavior.

Interest in individual personality differences in distress responses became rejuvenated with the experimental studies of stress and coping described in Richard Lazarus' classic book on stress (Lazarus, 1966). Modern studies have continued to show that life experiences are not in themselves unfailingly endowed with a fixed affective meaning for all people, but acquire emotional significance after a process of interpretation within the personal cognitive framework of the individual. A study of 30 survivors of an airplane crash landing for example, found significant individual differences in the experience of stress reported by the men (Sloan, 1988). When Foa and Riggs (1995) studied post-assault cases, they found that there were significant individual differences in symptom levels measurable within 10 days, and these differentiated those who eventually showed persistent PTSD after 3 months in comparison with those who showed a steady decrease in symptoms. Foa and Riggs attributed these to individual differences in emotional processing during the first month post-assault.

The sources of such individual differences, and their stability within individuals, have been studied within personality psychology with renewed vigor in recent years. One approach has been to examine temperament reactivity to determine its predictability within individuals across time (Block, 1993; Kagan, 1994). Another approach has been to examine the genetics of temperament and personality through the study of increasingly large twin and adoption samples followed across time (e.g., Bouchard, Lykken, McGue, Segal, & Tellegen, 1990). Temperament is usually construed as basic stable traits of emotional responsivity that are present from early childhood and primarily determined by biological factors, although in one recent conceptualization it has been regarded as a cluster of risk factors that may operate differently under different environmental conditions (Strelau, 1995).

Despite these efforts, most of this research has not been well incorporated into the thinking of researchers working in the general area of stress and coping. It has been used even less in the framework ideas of clinicians who work with patients reporting post-event distress. In 1986, Depue and Monroe reviewed the best evidence then concerning the contributions of life stress to clinical disorder by concluding "stable attributes of the individual are equal to, or more powerful than, socioenvironmental factors in predicting human disorder" (p. 48). Has subsequent evidence challenged this conclusion?

Within studies of the stability of temperament, the terms *neuroticism, emotional instability,* and *negative affect* have often been used interchangeably to refer to a general propensity to experience and report distress emotions such as anxiety and depression, because there is good evidence of a general personality factor of negative affectivity (Tellegen et al., 1988; Watson & Tellegen, 1985). These terms are used interchangeably in this section. The opposite emotional tendency, to respond with optimism, resilience, and sustained well-being despite taxing events, has been studied under the rubric of *hardiness* (Kobasa, Hilker, & Maddi, 1979), *happiness* (Diener & Diener, 1996; Lykken & Tellegen, 1996; Myers, 1993; Myers & Diener, 1995), and *resilience* (Garmezy, 1993). Both kinds of temperament have become increasingly documented as enduring and stable individual characteristics, and both are relevant to the chronic negative emotionality that is characteristic of PTSD.

LIFESPAN STABILITY OF NEGATIVE EMOTIONALITY

Neuroticism is an important general trait in adults, one of the *Big Five* personality descriptors that identifies key features in personality (McCrae & Costa, 1987). Because of its importance, it is relevant to review evidence concerning the stability of neuroticism within individuals across time. This evidence can provide a context for understanding the pre-event temperaments of those who provide significant distress reports after a toxic event. Studies of negative emotionality have often used different terms in considering the behavior in children or in adults, but the construct of fearful emotionality across the lifespan has consistently been of interest.

One important research effort has considered individual differences in temperament enduring across childhood, considering qualities such as irritability, sociability, and adaptability to new situations. The tendency to show emotional disarray and fear has been studied in longitudinal studies of children, and clinical research suggests that the helpful qualities that permit some children to navigate perilous lives without destruction include personality characteristics that are equally as durable as the distressed emotionality of those who do not manage these difficulties well.

Early classic work by psychiatrist Thomas Chess (1977) reported that behavioral disorders in children could not be explained solely on the basis of adverse environmental factors but were, in part, a function of temperament style. More recently, Jerome Kagan (1989) wrote extensively, summarizing evidence of enduring individual differences in temperamental reactivity from an early age, particularly as it relates to the display of shyness and fearfulness. Fearfulness is a key feature of adult PTSD, so the consistency with which fear is reported or shown from early life onward is relevant to understanding reports of fears that are attributed to specific events in adulthood.

From his and others' work, Kagan (1989) concluded that behavioral inhibition appears to be a style some individuals show as a consistent attribute. He viewed this nervous inhibition more in terms of the biological idea of a genetic strain within a species rather than seeing it as simply representing one end of a continuous personality dimension, even though one could theoretically place all individuals at some point along such a continuum. Kagan concluded that this quality has genetic origins because the behavior correlates with both physical and psychophysical characteristics such as low arousal thresholds and high sympathetic nervous system reactivity. A composite index of this inhibited and fearful style measured in infancy shows a substantial positive correlation ($r = .64$) with similar behavior at age 7½. Such a correlation still allows for environmental interactions as contributing to behaviors shown at school age, even as it reveals significant long-term stability of the style.

Enduring temperamental styles have similarly been found with increasing age across childhood. There is evidence that extreme temperaments measured in children at age 7 correlate with levels of psychiatric symptoms at ages 12 and 16 (Maziade et al., 1990). Children high on "difficult" temperament at age 7 showed significantly higher rates of clinical disorder as teenagers than those classed as showing "easy" temperaments at the earlier age.

Within adults, a parallel examination of enduring characteristics, such as neuroticism and other traits, has been undertaken in studies of the Big Five basic dimensions of personality (Costa & McCrae, 1986). Across adult life, the tendency to report negative emotional reactions that represents the core feature of neuroticism has been studied in personality research for a very long time, and evidence is consistent that this disposition shows great stability.

The greatest part of personality variance is stable from age 30 onward for neuroticism and for the other four factors of the Big Five major dimensions of personality (Costa & McCrae, 1986; Costa & Metter, 1994). Long-standing neuroticism acts as a powerful moderator variable that accounts for virtually all of the effects found in studies of the relationships between poor coping strategies and well-being (Costa & Metter, 1994). Using even very different kinds of measures, there is evidence that long-standing emotional difficulties in managing stress, including personality features of guilt, resentment, and insecurity, are characteristic of people who later seek treatment for PTSD after a toxic exposure (Schwarz & Kowalski, 1992; Swanson & Blount, 1990).

Across 30 years of the adult lifespan, neuroticism, as shown on the negative affectivity factor of the MMPI, shows solid test–retest stability averaging around .53 (Finn, 1986). In studies of a volunteer sample of engaged couples across a longer 45-year span, Conley (1984) found stability correlations ranging from .3 to .4 for neuroticism variables.

Anxiety is often considered as a specific aspect of neuroticism, being a particular type of negative emotionality. Evidence suggests that trait anxiety levels in adults are also highly stable within individuals, with an average 2-year longitudinal stability of .91, contrasting with the predictably lower state anxiety stability of .57 (Usala & Hertzog, 1991). Among Vietnam veterans, those with PTSD had higher trait anxiety in comparison with those without the disorder (Kuhne et al., 1993). At the other end of the affective dimension, self-reports of well-being and happiness are also very stable and independent of significant life events (Costa, McCrae, & Zonderman, 1987; Diener & Diener, 1996; Myers & Diener, 1995).

GENETIC CONTRIBUTIONS
TO NEGATIVE EMOTIONALITY

Evidence increasingly suggests there is a substantial genetic component for neuroticism which contributes to its longitudinal stability (Costa & McCrae, 1986; Costa & Metter, 1994; Plomin, 1989). The physiological mechanisms have been suggested in studies that have found individual differences in the amount of activation of frontal brain areas which are important in the regulation of emotion (Fox, 1994). When more than 25,000 pairs of twins were studied across different data sets, the proportion of variance for neuroticism arising from all genetic sources ranged upward from 65% (Henderson, 1982). More recently in a four-country study of 30,000 twin pairs, heritability for neuroticism was calculated at 50% (Loehlin, 1989). There are significant genetic components not only for negative emotionality, but also for self-reported well-being (Tellegen et al., 1988).

Concerning genetic research on PTSD as a specific expression of negative emotionality, neuroticism has been shown to account for the majority of the variance of measures of PTSD symptoms (Hyer et al., 1994). In addition, research in Norway has suggested that the more specific features of PTSD also represent a genetic component in that there was a higher prevalence rate for PTSD in monozygotic (MZ) co-twins compared to dizygotic (DZ) co-twins, when MZ and DZ twins with anxiety disorder were examined (Skre, Onstad, Torgersen, Lygren, & Kringlen, 1993).

Other post-event distress syndromes show a similar role for genetic contributions. In a population-based twin study of 2,164 female twins followed across a year, genetic liability was found to account for significant differences in the probability of onset of major depression following a severely stressful life event (Kendler et al., 1995). The research showed that, for a low-risk MZ twin (co-twin unaffected) exposed to a toxic event, the probability of onset was 6.2%, whereas for an MZ twin with an affected twin and thus at greater genetic risk, the probability of depression was 14.6%. The increased risk was 2.4 times greater in those at high genetic risk, although "Even in the presence of high genetic risk and severe stressful life events, the majority of individuals do not develop an episode...." (p. 837). The authors concluded that genetic factors alter the sensitivity of individuals to adverse life events and that this interaction changes the probability of becoming depressed as a response. A study of 345 MZ and 100 DZ twins from the California twin registry included a measure of stress reaction as part of a larger study and found MZ correlations of .40 and DZ correlations of .08 on the measure (Waller & Shaver, 1994), again demonstrating a significant genetic component.

Negative Emotionality and PTSD

Distress is a condition of unstable negative emotions which may include anxiety, depression, anger, and embarrassment. Negative emotionality is the central, defining characteristic of neuroticism (McCrae & Costa,

1987). Trait neuroticism early in life has a direct effect on later reports of distress, as shown in a large British study that followed 296 people over a 7-year period (Ormel & Wohlfarth, 1991). The direct effect of neuroticism was strikingly stronger than the effects of long-term difficulties and life situation changes. To what extent do long-standing individual differences in neuroticism levels help explain why most individuals do not develop a clinical distress disorder such as PTSD following a significant adverse event?

There is evidence that elevated levels of trait neuroticism contribute significantly if a prolonged distress syndrome is shown after a toxic event. In a deadly 1987 fire in the King's Cross underground station in London, the correlation between scores of acute distress on the General Health Questionnaire and scores on a trait measure of neuroticism was significant at $r = .46$ among those who came forward to receive psychological assistance (Rosser, Dewar, & Thompson, 1991). Among children who experienced Hurricane Hugo in the United States, long-standing trait anxiety, and reactivity during a hurricane, was more predictive of PTSD symptoms later than was actual exposure (Lonigan, Shannon, Taylor, Finch, & Sallee, 1994). Among a small group of schoolchildren studied after experiencing the Loma Prieta earthquake in California, there were significant individual differences in baseline emotional reactivity measured at the time of school entry that contributed to patterns of change in respiratory illnesses (defined as a distress response to the event) seen in individuals following the earthquake (Boyce, Chesterman, Martin, & Folkman, 1993). Interestingly, these illness responses showed high variability, with 6 of 20 children showing increases in illness and 5 of 20 showing decreases. In a study of 80 Vietnam veterans with PTSD, a trait measure of neuroticism accounted for the majority of the variance of PTSD as measured on PTSD and combat scales (Hyer, Broswell, Albrecht, Boyd, Boudewyns, & Talbert, 1994).

Among men who volunteered to fight huge bushfires in Australia, those who were diagnosed solely with PTSD showed greater property loss and a less chronic outcome in comparison with those diagnosed with PTSD and additional diagnoses of other emotional disorders (77% of those who met PTSD criteria; McFarlane & Papay, 1992). These disorders did not show any dose–response relations but instead suggested an important role for pre-existing vulnerabilities. Overall, the incidence rate for PTSD was estimated at 12.5% if the DSM–III criterion of severity was respected for subjects who reported they did not see their symptoms as "interfering with their life a lot" (p. 500).

Concerning a more constrained and individual event, among 31 litigants seeking damage awards following a motor vehicle accident, MMPI profiles for those diagnosed with PTSD were notable for showing consistently low scores on the Ego Strength scale, which is regarded as an index of long-standing general adjustment level. Also notable was a normal-range mean score on the Anxiety content scale, which is sensitive to both state and trait anxiety (Platt & Husband, 1986). This pattern undermined the claim of acute anxiety while at the same time suggesting that pre-event functioning was poor and may have contributed to the attempt to receive compensation.

It is also of interest to examine individuals exposed to toxic events who do not report emotional distress. Hendin and Hass (1984) studied 10 combat veterans who had no lasting distress effects and found that they shared five features in common, including the ability to function calmly under pressure and acceptance of fear in themselves and others, both of which appear to represent low neuroticism.

Negative Emotionality and Coping Styles

Coping styles appear to modulate the emotional effects of events. Although the traditional mental health model argues in favor of open discussion and confrontation of feelings as a beneficial way of achieving emotional health, and much therapy is based on this assumption, there is evidence that normal individuals often make use of denial and avoidance to deal with toxic exposures, with good effect.

Early research with surgery patients showed that denial was an adaptive coping strategy for individuals who were *repressors* (Cohen & Lazarus, 1973), contrary to predictions from the psychodynamic model but consistent with a model that takes individual differences into account. Among 492 Israeli schoolchildren subjected to SCUD missile bombardment during the Persian Gulf War and kept in a room sealed against biological or chemical agents, the dominant stance of the children was detached optimism and denial, which was associated with the least postwar stress reactions (Weisenberg, Schwarzwald, Waysman, Solomon, & Klingman, 1993).

If individual differences in coping style interact with toxic life events in affecting responses, to what extent are coping styles an expression of enduring individual features? There is evidence that coping styles show longitudinal stability, although research progress has been hampered by a lack of agreement on the major dimensions of coping and on how coping styles might differ from personality dimensions.

Concerning the stability of coping style, avoidant or confrontational coping styles to extreme stress represent a stable response predisposition over many decades. Sigal and Weinfeld (1985) found this in studies of Jewish survivors of the Holocaust 33 years later, when a new communal stressor arose. A study of 152 Vietnam combat veterans reported that those who showed good postwar adjustment were notably different in coping styles from those who showed PTSD symptoms in that the thriving veterans used significantly less externalizing coping tactics and less behavioral avoidance (Wolfe, Keane, Kaloupek, Mora, & Wine,

1993). The greatest proportion (26%) of variance in PTSD symptoms came from this externalization factor, whereas only 9% was predictable from the toxic event of combat exposure.

PROBLEMS IN IDENTIFYING
A PROTECTIVE EMOTIONAL STANCE

A specific understanding of the kind of personality or coping style that should be protective against toxic events is far from established. It appears that popular and national personality style preferences may interfere with a clear examination of the evidence. It has long been recognized in the personality literature, for example, that British and U.S. researchers endow the terms extraversion and introversion with affective and preferential interpretations in opposition to each other. For British researchers, the introverted person is one who is calm and reflective as well as capable of sustained individual effort. For U.S. researchers, introversion represents a more seclusive, unsociable style. Similarly, British personality researchers view extraversion as shallow and transient emotionality, while U.S. researchers view extraversion as a desirable style of openness and sociability. Against this background, what have we learned about personality traits that might contribute to general or physical well-being in the face of life's general adversities?

Popular treatment programs intended to increase both subjective well-being as well as physical survival typically include relaxation exercises and other techniques such as visualization and hypnotic induction directly intended to reduce anxiety and negative emotions and implicitly intended to enhance positive emotional experience. A popular literature has developed describing various treatment programs aimed at making patients feel positive emotions rather than bad old anxiety, anger, or depression. Author Norman Cousins (1979) became a temporary folk hero of the middle class after publishing an account of his recovery from a rheumatoid condition. He ascribed his recovery to a self-directed treatment regimen using laughter, in his book *Anatomy of an Illness*. In a similar vein, physician Elizabeth Kübler-Ross (1969) wrote of the necessity of helping dying people to get rid of their negativity before death.

Such an emphasis on positive emotions has also come from a more research-based position. Friedman and VandenBos (1992) argued that a *self-healing* personality is characterized by being enthusiastic, contrasting this style with personality features such as chronic hostility and depression which apparently negatively influence recovery from illness. These findings are similar to the identification of optimism as a positive factor in general well-being reported in a review (Scheier & Carver,

1992), the studies of the beneficial effects of the optimism of *positive illusions* (Taylor & Brown, 1988), and research in the beneficial effects of training pessimistic individuals in coping tactics of learned optimism (Seligman & Buchanan, 1995).

In a controlled study of breast cancer patients in London, there were better breast cancer survival rates among patients with either a spirit of optimism or an attitude of denial, compared to those who showed a stoic acceptance or a depressed and helpless response (Greer, Morris, & Pettingale, 1979). That is, repression of anger did not shorten cancer survival time, and full emotional expression of anger did not prolong survival. In contrast to these upbeat reports arguing the psychological and physical benefits of positive emotionality in short-term studies, some studies of patients with breast cancer have found better immune activity in those expressing anger more openly, although the effect was weak (Levy, Herberman, Maluish, Schlien, & Lippman, 1985).

Evidence concerning the dangerous role of the expression of anger in contributing to fatal heart disease is becoming increasingly clear. An experimental study at Stanford found that people who are, by nature, irritable and hostile are five times more likely to die of heart disease than their even-tempered peers. The experimental Stanford study found that even remembering a past incident in which anger was experienced led to a loss in heart pumping efficiency in patients with heart disease (Ironson et al., 1992). This cardiac effect was significantly greater for heart patients than the effects of performing vigorous exercise, doing mental arithmetic, or giving a speech defending themselves against an accusation of shoplifting. Personality researcher Hans Eysenck (1994) considered the evidence clear that the high negative emotionality of neuroticism is positively associated with heart disease but negatively associated with cancer. This view contrasts with a much larger review and meta-analysis of studies relating personality style to five major disorders often considered to be stress sensitive (asthma, arthritis, ulcers, headaches, and coronary heart disease). Although a generic disease-related personality style of general depression, anger, and anxiety was found, the evidence was weak concerning any causal relationship (Friedman & Booth-Kewley, 1987) .

Perhaps in an attempt to resolve these contradictions, over time the aggressive and angry style earlier favored in studies of cancer survival has become sanitized, described more positively as a fighting spirit. In turn, the definition of a fighting spirit has been further shifted to mean being optimistic, contrasting with the undesirable tactic of being depressed or stoic.

Despite the popularity of the optimism model of general health and well-being, a recent long-term follow-up of the 1921 Terman sample of high-IQ Californians found that childhood cheerfulness (rated optimism and sense of humor) was inversely associated with longevity (Friedman

& Tucker, 1993; Friedman et al., 1995). Individuals in the Terman sample were school children in the top 1% IQ in the California school system in 1921. They have been followed for 7 decades in what is probably the most long-lasting longitudinal study in the history of psychology, described in a series of publications over this period. In a similar vein, self-reports of well-being among elderly nursing-home residents were associated with a higher death rate over the ensuing 30 months (Janoff-Bulman & Marshall, 1982). Increasingly, studies are failing to support any specific model relating emotional condition to health and general well-being (Friedman, 1991).

NEGATIVE EMOTIONALITY REPORTS
AND OBJECTIVE FUNCTIONING

A further question concerns the relation of subjective distress reports as found in PTSD to objective performance in daily functioning. There is evidence that productive daily functioning may be present even in individuals with PTSD, although impairment in some of the activities of daily living is required to meet the full criteria for the diagnosis.

A study of personality change from adolescence to mid-life in men who were veterans of the Korean War and World War II found that veterans with the greatest combat exposure showed the most emotional distress in the short-term after the war, but also made the greatest gains in resilience and the greatest decreases in helplessness over time in comparison with low-combat men (Elder & Clipp, 1989). A 6-year follow-up of 46 Cambodian refugee youth found that they were functioning well despite their PTSD profiles (Sack et al., 1993). A large study of Vietnam veteran identical twins found that, within twins discordant for PTSD and controlled for premilitary and military service factors, most socio-economic indicators of functioning (e.g., income, education, marital status, educational level, occupational group, and years employed at current job), were not significantly affected by PTSD, although current employment was, when scores were adjusted for premilitary service factors (McCarren et al., 1995).

SUMMARY: INDIVIDUAL DIFFERENCES
IN NEGATIVE EMOTIONALITY

The negative emotionality that is the key feature of reports of chronic postevent distress represents a long-standing personality trait that shows stability across childhood and adulthood. Genetic research shows that this general trait of neuroticism has a sizable genetic component.

In addition, the trait of risk-taking represents a stable personality disposition through which high-trait individuals selectively act to encounter risk, thus exposing themselves to an increased probability of being part of toxic events. These long-standing individual differences in the self-report of emotional disarray and in the tendency to seek risky situations thus represent important pre-event risk factors. These contribute to the probability that an event-attributed distress disorder will be reported, even though the PTSD criteria do not apply to them. Further, when symptoms characteristic of PTSD are reported, evidence suggests that, even with some impairment in some aspect of daily functioning, there can be substantially effective performance in important life domains and that the disorder may not be a source of significant objective impairment in functioning. Long-standing emotional instability may coexist with competent participation in daily life.

8

Do Beliefs Affect Individual Reactions to Toxic Events?

Another aspect of differences between individuals concerns the role of beliefs or attributions about the way the world works, about sources of danger, and about one's efficacy in the world. Beliefs that might contribute to heightened distress reports or experiences can include attributions that one is being deliberately harmed, attributions arising out of long-standing individual beliefs about emotionality, and attributions arising out of cognitive limitations, memory impairments, or mental disorders such as delusions. Other attributions may be generated out of the normal efforts of the brain to bring order out of chaos even in an absence of important information, or out of beliefs about personal control or the general benevolence of the world. In addition, some deliberately false attributions are made out of an attempt to defraud others. There is evidence that PTSD is associated with a high frequency of irrational beliefs in general (Hyer, Woods, & Boudewyns, 1991). What is the evidence about the relations between more specific beliefs and PTSD?

BELIEFS ABOUT THE WORLD

Beliefs about the world have been studied to see how they affect responses to life events, and to consider how stable these beliefs are when individuals are confronted with experiences that challenge them. Antonovsky (1987) argued that worldviews are long-standing dispositions that function as stable predictors of responses to life events, in his model describing the *sense of coherence*. He showed that it was a contributing factor in well-being and thought of it as a stable tendency to interpret taxing or tension-creating life stimuli as being within one's capacity to create order through the flexible use of varying coping strategies.

When people have experiences of toxic events that violate long-held benevolent expectancies or justice-based worldviews, there is evidence that they report different beliefs than nonvictims (Janoff-Bulman, 1989; Lehman et al., 1987). Wortman and Silver (1992) provided further examinations of this way of construing the world in relation to vulnerability to distress following irrevocable loss. They observed that anywhere from 25% to 75% of individuals confronted with an irrevocable loss do not show intense distress and concluded that three popular adversity–distress models (the learned helplessness model, stage models, and the stress and coping model) do not account well for this wide variability in response. They then considered evidence that a world view in which good behavior and hard work are linked with expectations that fate will be just is associated with greater distress when circumstances violate this expectation. Whether or not this specific "world-view" model is crucial in the development of distress will be determined by further research. Overall however, the kinds of meaning that individuals place on events do appear to contribute to post-event reports of well-being or distress.

Although Antonovsky considered sense of coherence to be an enduring trait, others see comparable worldviews as developing out of life events. Janoff-Bulman's (1989a) model considers general life assumptions or life-schemas as important features of victim experience and construes these as being changeable in response to toxic life events rather than as being enduring expectancies. Others proposed that adverse life events such as bereavement are more likely to result in significant losses in well-being to the extent that they shatter people's long-held assumptions and beliefs about the world, suggesting that these beliefs are mostly enduring but are susceptible to change with sufficiently toxic experience (Wortman, Silver, & Kessler, 1993).

Another line of research examined the role of optimism or *positive illusions* as an important feature contributing to a positive response to crisis events (Taylor & Brown, 1988), although the limitations of positive illusions as a correlate of mental health have been identified (Colvin & Block, 1994; Janoff-Bulman, 1989b). Janoff-Bulman proposed a hierarchical model to differentiate levels of illusions, in which accuracy at highly particular levels of self-descriptors in combination with illusions at more general levels of world view, are construed as hallmarks of mental health. These different beliefs play a role in the experience of postevent distress, and evidence suggests that beliefs that construct meaning about life events are powerful in determining emotion reports and displays. Some current approaches to psychotherapy research focus on the meaning of events to a patient; critical therapy events where a change in the meaning of an emotional event is created are argued as being at the heart of effective treatment (Clarke, 1996).

Beliefs About Sources of Danger

In addition to general worldviews, more specific beliefs about sources of danger can lead to individual differences in emotional distress. In some cases, these beliefs may not provide an accurate risk assessment of objective danger yet may contribute to highly distressed responses. Such dissociations between the dose of the event and the emotional response can be seen at a group level in the numerous studies of mass delusions and hysterical contagion. Historical investigations have suggested that the outbursts of uncontrolled dancing that occurred during the Middle Ages were hysterical epidemics similar to the mass fainting observed in modern rock concerts (Morens, 1995). Some of the hysterical epidemics reported in very recent times continue to provide examples of what might be called empty-calorie emotions—emotional distress that is entirely attributed to a specific cause despite being entirely dissociated from it on objective criteria of toxic exposure.

One study described an epidemic of hysterical distress attributed to so called "mysterious gas poisoning" that affected more than 9,000 people, primarily schoolgirls, in the Jordan West Bank regions (Hefez, 1985). There was no actual toxic substance and no demonstrable medical pathology, yet the hospitals were deluged by hysterical crowds of patients and their parents, fanned by newspaper reports and interviews with traumatized girls in distress. In 1989 in Santa Monica, California, 247 student performers in a high school auditorium became supposedly ill in an episode that was eventually described as hysterical contagion in newspaper reports (Scott, 1991): 16 sopranos fainted, and 19 students were taken to hospital emergency rooms. The spreading contagion, later likened to the frenzied outbreaks of the Middle Ages, resulted in the largest evacuation in the city's history. After the event, it was speculated that perhaps the emotional experience of performance stress was the trigger factor (Small & Propper, 1991). The symptoms were rapidly spread merely by visual contact, with those who observed a symptomatic friend soon showing the same symptoms.

In Malaysia, young female factory workers earning good incomes in the production lines of high technology products were prone to flamboyant hysterical states with seizures whenever one of them concluded that there were evil demon spirits at her work station or inside her microscope (Chew, Phoon, & Mae-Lim, 1976; Newman, 1980). The speed of contagion to those nearby was rapid. Employers found it necessary to keep special staff on watch to be able to rush in and remove a girl as soon as she went into a fit in order to prevent the entire work floor from erupting into mass screaming and convulsions.

The phenomenon of *koro* provides another example of hysterical contagion in which extreme distress is attributed to a cause (an event) that is not actually happening. *Koro* is a disorder found in Chinese societies, particularly in South China, in which a man believes that his penis is retracting into his abdomen and that death is inevitable (Mo, Chen, Li, & Tseng, 1995). When in this frame of mind, the man becomes terrorized, and the typically nighttime event quickly creates panic in the entire family. Extreme measures are taken to grab the organ at risk, and to tie it to heavy weights or to stick pins through it or the nipples, which are similarly believed to be at risk. The treatments occasionally lead to serious results, including death. The entire episode is based on a set of faulty beliefs that started with ideas in the classic textbook of Chinese medicine, the Yellow Emperor's book of internal medicine, dated about 200 BC. This book, still the basis of Chinese traditional medicine, argues that the shrinking of protruding (yang) organs can occur if too much semen is wasted and that death is inevitable. Over time, this has been interpreted to mean that masturbation is a serious source of this loss and that ghosts will come in the night to take away the penis of a man who has not heeded these warnings. Whereas individual cases may occur at any time, whole epidemics of *koro* have affected huge numbers of the population, including five major waves since World War II. In the epidemic on Hainan Island in 1984, there were more than 3,000 victims showing this extreme distress syndrome.

These syndromes represent purely emotional manifestations of distress with no causal connection to life-threatening toxic features in the objective situation. Nor do they arise out of individual psychopathology. Wessely (1987) reviewed the typical circumstances under which mass outbursts of emotional distress develop, noting that visual contact is important. Even more importantly, these cases show the importance of shared but entirely mistaken beliefs about sources of danger. They are a function of shared belief systems that provide constructed interpretations about danger. These examples show how emotional displays of distress that is attributed to a situation do not necessarily provide evidence of the occurrence of a toxic event, even if there is no deliberate attempt to deceive.

In addition to acutely triggered or long-standing beliefs about sources of danger that may lead to acute emotional distress, more recently induced beliefs can also play a role in determining emotional distress (Henderson, Byrne, & Duncan-Jones, 1981). This was shown in a study of the effects of predicting an earthquake on 314 schoolchildren in the United States. Measurements taken before the predicted date of the event and 6 to 8 weeks later found that mild PTSD-like anticipatory distress was created in the children through the disaster warning alone, even though the earthquake never occurred (Kiser, Heston, Hickerson, & Millsap, 1993). Among workers referred to a clinic for PTSD following a toxic chemical exposure, 20% had symptoms that could not be explained by the established effects of the exposure or any other detectable injury or disease (Schottenfield & Cullen, 1995). Careful histories revealed that most of them had histories of previous distress syndromes such as pain, conversion disorder, and other inexplicable somatic disorders. In a study of emotional distress levels of Vietnam veterans attributing their distress to Agent Orange, those who believed they had been exposed had higher MMPI distress scores than those who were actually closer to the spraying but may have had no knowledge of their exposure (Korgeski & Leon, 1983).

BELIEFS ABOUT THE SELF

In addition to individual differences in beliefs about the world and its sources of danger, there are other individual differences in beliefs about the self that are important in affecting well-being. Antonovsky (1979, 1987) observed that many individuals experiencing high levels of stressors do not become distressed or ill and argued that events that challenged an individual's sense of coherence (SoC) were more likely to result in reduced well-being. He showed that there was a modest positive correlation between sense of coherence and self-reported health status, describing this sense as a constant, pervasive, and enduring dispositional orientation. In a recent laboratory study, low SoC subjects showed greater physiological signs of anticipatory and postevent distress (McSherry & Holm, 1994).

A religion-associated sense of meaning to life has also been correlated with less distress. Following the loss of an infant, parents with greater participation in religion reported a greater sense of meaning and less distress (McIntosh, Cohen, & Wortman, 1993). Bereaved individuals who were able to find meaning in the death showed less intense grief (Schwartzberg & Janoff-Bulman, 1991). The complexity of self-beliefs has been found to differentiate undergraduates who suffered high or low trauma after toxic life events, with those who reported more complexity on positive self-attributes showing least distress (Morgan & Janoff-Bulman, 1994). Complexity of self-view was largely irrelevant to the adjustment of subjects who had not experienced a stressor event. Evidence from addicted veterans suggests that a style of attributing helplessness to one's own efforts is significantly associated with PTSD (McCormick, Taber, & Kruedelback, 1989). Consistent with this, longitudinal studies of children within a high-stress urban environment have shown that early optimism and positive expectations are associated with more successful navigation of toxic events and better school adjustment (Wyman & Cowen, 1993).

Attributional Styles and Events

There is a well-established general law deriving from studies in social psychology, called the fundamental error of attribution. This refers to the general human tendency to overly attribute the causes of the behavior of other people to their long-standing personality traits, yet to attribute one's personal behavior to situational factors. People reporting an event-attributed distress syndrome provide an example of this general tendency to attribute their own condition to situational factors. Because this is a general tendency known to represent a bias, there is the risk that the specific situational attribution is also biased.

Because emotional instability is the core concept underlying the personality trait of neuroticism and states of negative emotionality such as PTSD, it is of interest to consider attributional styles associated with neuroticism. Neuroticism may express itself through characteristic ways of interpreting objectively toxic life events, and these attributional styles may directly increase distress or other features of impaired well-being. For example, the explanations that individuals make of bad events at age 25 have been shown to predict poor health at ages 45 through 60 when baseline health is controlled (Peterson, Seligman, & Vaillant, 1988). The kind of explanations that predicted poor health explained bad events in term of factors that were stable over time, pervasive in impact, and internal in origin.

Similarly, among 282 persons who considered themselves to be suffering from chronic fatigue syndrome, those who considered that they would have a catastrophic response to a stressful situation were far more disabled in their daily life than those who predicted a less dramatic response, even though these groups were matched on length of illness and general psychological well-being (Petrie, Moss-Morris, & Weinman, 1995). The researchers concluded that personal beliefs played a significant role in maintaining the illness. A study of the way in which the focus of attention is associated with selectively more recall of personal negative events in depressed subjects found that depressed people, in comparison with non-depressed, recalled significantly more negative events if asked to focus on themselves (Pyszczynski, 1989). In contrast, if asked to focus on external topics, they showed no differences in recalling positive or negative events in comparison with non-depressed individuals.

Beliefs About Agency and Emotional Regulation

Positive and negative emotions are a product of life events in combination with individual factors including beliefs about personal agency or power and about self-regulation of emotion.

Gross and Munoz (1995) have reviewed the ways in which people actively regulate the emotions they experience. These start out with active choices affecting the antecedent physical and mental environments that can trigger emotion, and include the way attention is directed and the way events are appraised. All of these factors contribute to experienced emotion. Following these antecedent stages, emotional responses are further actively regulated through the use of active masking of feelings in circumstances that require this, such as through reframing or taking other points of view. In describing emotions across the lifespan, these authors noted how adults vary in emotional experience and expression depending on circumstances. Professionals who work with individuals actively suffering from some acute harm, for example, typically control emotional expression as a part of being professional and accomplishing the tasks at hand. Emotional regulation is seen as a necessary competence in the world of work, in friendships, in intimate relationships, and in managing inner life. Poor emotional regulation is seen as contributing to mental illness. As discussed earlier, the key aspect of neuroticism is excessive, poorly regulated emotionality, which by necessity includes negative emotions. It has been suggested that the capacity to control displays of negative emotionality may confer an evolutionary advantage to individuals (Harkness, Tellegen, & Waller, 1995).

Taken as a whole, individual beliefs about the possibilities and the appropriateness of emotional regulation can contribute to greater or lesser displays of distress following participation in a toxic event. An airplane attendant who pulls a young woman passenger from a burning airplane may soothe her and then rush on to help others, controlling her own fears and focusing on the task. The flight attendant may or may not experience or display a more vivid emotional reaction some time later, depending on her own unique combination of reactivity and beliefs. The passenger's attention may focus on her own brush with death. If the passenger releases a dramatic emotional display it will be regarded as a natural display attributable to the circumstances, but so will the controlled presentation of the flight attendant, even though both have experienced the same event from an objective perspective. They will have shown very different emotional responses in accordance with beliefs about what kind of emotional display is appropriate.

BELIEFS ABOUT THE LOCUS OF CONTROL
OF EXPERIENCE: WORLD VERSUS SELF

Because the belief that an external adverse event has caused distress is a core feature of PTSD, it is of interest to know if external or internal attributions of causality for life events are reliably associated with greater or lesser well-being. Beliefs about causation are powerful in predicting distress levels, for example, following experimental pain relief procedures using acupuncture. Beliefs alone accounted for 85% of pain relief in one study (Kreitler, Kreitler, & Carasso, 1987) and were similarly significant in reports of pain relief in another (Norton, Goszer, Strub, & Man, 1984).

One way of thinking about a disposition to make certain attributions of cause or control has been through the idea of generalized expectancies of internal or external control of reinforcement (later referred to as Locus of Control or LoC). This is a model proposed by Rotter in 1966 and studied extensively since then by many others. It appears that expectancies of the locus of control are stable, habitual ways of construing experience; recent work has shown high stability ($r = .46$) from age 17 across 25 years (Frenkel, Kugelmass, Nathan, & Ingraham, 1995).

Evidence suggests that these expectancies have an effect on emotional condition. Since the time of Rotter's work, a major literature developed that appeared to relate internal LoC with greater well-being. Internal LoC is the disposition to believe that one has agency and control over important experiences in life, whereas external locus of control refers to the belief that forces external to oneself and beyond personal control are more powerful. Concerning the experience of distress, for example, Vietnam veteran inpatients with PTSD showed external LoC, and reported high numbers of perceived and experienced current stressors (Hyer, Boudewyns, O'Leary, & Harrison, 1987).

More recent examinations, however, have cast increasing doubt on the power of the general LoC idea. Reviews have noted that internal control is mostly related to well-being within carefully selected and insulated populations in which circumstances are truly mostly under individual control (Dawes, 1994). The construct has not been as well examined in populations with a wider range of intrusive toxic events. Others have found that, when undesirable events occur, individuals with internal attributions are more likely to suffer greater losses of well-being (Janoff-Bulman & Brickman, 1982).

Empirical evidence from a prospective study of a large representative sample suggests that those who believe they have great control over life events have worse psychological responses when unexpectedly confronted with a toxic event such as bereavement (Wortman, Sheedy, Gluhoski, & Kessler, 1992). Thus locus of control may not account for the consistent finding that individuals differ in the ways they respond to adverse events. One theorist suggested that it may not matter whether beliefs about causation are consistently internal or external. Rather, it may be that individuals are most distressed if an event violates their beliefs about where control should reside in that kind of situation (Antonovsky, 1979). In this view, greater losses to well-being will occur when control is apparently not functioning as expected.

BELIEFS ASSIGNING CAUSAL RESPONSIBILITY
AFTER A TOXIC EVENT

Evidence is contradictory as to whether blaming oneself or blaming another yields greater distress after a toxic event. Beliefs about blame add a moralistic dimension to the experience. Both blaming others and feeling that one could have avoided an accident (a counterfactual interpretation of self-blame) were predictors of poor functioning in 29 paralyzed accident victims in one early study (Bulman & Wortman, 1977). Other research suggests that a possible reason that behavioral self-blame has been found to be adaptive, is that it represents an attempt to understand an adverse event as something under control rather than entirely random (Janoff-Bulman, 1989; Wortman, 1976).

In contrast to these findings, causal attributions that identified the causes of negative events as being enduring personal characteristics eliciting self-blame increased the symptoms of PTSD or decreased well-being in other studies. For example, adolescent survivors who blamed themselves for uncontrollable negative events arising out of the sinking of the Jupiter cruise ship showed more posttraumatic symptoms 1 year later (Joseph, Brewin, Yule, & Williams, 1993). Similarly, the studies of the pessimistic explanatory style, in which responsibility for bad events is attributed to enduring personal characteristics, have shown it to be an enduring disposition associated with higher risk for depression and other illness (Burns & Seligman, 1989; Kamen & Seligman, 1987; Peterson et al., 1988).

The resolution to this contradiction may lie in evidence that prolonged attention to any kind of attributions of blame may have negative consequences for recovery. This was suggested in a study that found that attending to attributions of the cause of Sudden Infant Death Syndrome deaths among 124 bereaved parents was more strongly associated with symptoms (Downey, Silver, & Wortman, 1990). In contrast, there was less distress among the 45% of parents who were no longer concerned with attributional issues by week three. Other evidence suggests that those who report more distress even years after the loss of a close family member to sudden death characteristically spend more time on counterfactual ideas to try to "undo" the actual causal relations (Davis, Lehman, Wortman, Silver, & Thompson, 1995): "If only I had done that differently, my sister would not have died."

Intentional or Accidental Causes

Do adverse events that are accidental have less power in contributing to postevent distress? If the objective qualities of the event represent its most important feature, then this distinction should make no difference, because the dose–response model will not distinguish between experiences that represent human agency from those that are entirely accidental. If subjective interpretations of the meaning of an event are important human additions to experience, then this distinction should be more important.

Long ago, Goldsteen and Schorr (1982) concluded that natural disasters often result in minimal or no long-term effects, whereas the response to disasters caused by humans may have long-term negative effects, such as they found in the community around Three-Mile Island following the nuclear accident of 1979. In that event, there was little direct physical harm associated with the accident, but immense media attention was given to the vast potential threats arising out of human actions. More recently, a large population prevalence study found that natural disaster was not associated with one case of PTSD (Helzer et al., 1987). Similarly, a large randomized study in Los Angeles, California found that core symptoms of PTSD were more associated with adverse experiences that included a broad range of physical assaults (ranging from war to rape) while national disasters and accidents were significantly less associated with symptoms (Ullman, 1995). In a U.S. study of nationally representative sample of 12,500 adults comparing those who had lost a family member to criminal homicide or to alcohol-related vehicular homicide, neither group was found more likely than the other to develop either lifetime or current PTSD (Amick-McMullan, Kilpatrick, & Resnick, 1991). These conflicting findings may in part arise because the causes of toxic events are not always clear.

When the cause of a toxic event is unclear, as in the case of many accidents that combine human acts with accidental conditions, individual differences in assigning causation may affect emotional distress. Death of a family member has been studied in terms of the relative role of different causes of death on the distress of family members. In a study in the Netherlands, it was found that there were no differences in PTSD symptoms when comparing people who lost a family member to an unnatural death, such as suicide or traffic accident, with those who lost a family member to a "natural" death from illness, some 14 months after the loss (Cleiren, Diekstra, Kerkhof, & van der Wal, 1994). In contrast, a recent study in Honduras looked at the levels of distress among families who lost a member through so-called political disappearance in comparison with those who lost someone due to illness or accident, as well as with others who had not lost a family member (Quirk & Casco, 1994). The families of those who lost their member through disappearance were twice as likely to suffer PTSD and other anxiety disorders, suggesting that awareness of the deliberate, evil human intentions that led to the loss were more important in contributing to distress than the loss itself.

Although the intentionally inflicted horrors of war contribute to the experience of distress and PTSD, the way in which constructed interpretations of experience interact with the war events was shown in a study of U.S. Air Force nurses who served in the Vietnam War (Ravella, 1995). Although 25% of the sample reported symptoms of PTSD, all the nurses also reported that serving in the war had been their most rewarding professional experience and reported frustration with the slow pace and constraints they faced in returning to nursing practice in the United States.

THE STABILITY OF CAUSAL ATTRIBUTIONS

Is the attribution of the cause of a toxic event variable depending upon circumstances, or are such beliefs stable and characteristic dispositions within individuals across time? In Rotter's original monograph (1966) and in most subsequent research, it appears these attribution beliefs are stable. Evidence from related work evolving from Martin Seligman and colleagues' learned helplessness model of the late 1970s suggests that a pessimistic explanatory style for negative life events is associated with impaired well-being (Kamen & Seligman, 1987; Peterson & Seligman, 1983, 1984). This style shows remarkable stability across the life-span. In another study, a pessimistic explanatory style showed clinically and statistically significant long-term stability ($r = .54$) across a 50-year span (Burns & Seligman, 1989). This style consists of making internal, stable, and global explanations for negative events ("I always mess everything up"). In other studies reviewed in Seligman, Kamen, and Nolen-Hoekema (1988), it correlated with long-term distress symptoms including depression, low achievement, and physical illness. In contrast, there was no comparable stability for interpretations of positive events. Notably, the life events to which these explanations were directed covered a wide range of human events because of the long time-span. Equally notably, the attributional style most associated with poor well-being was internal rather than the external LoC that was earlier considered characteristic of poor well-being.

COGNITIVE PROCESSES:
ASSUMPTIONS ABOUT THE WORLD

Other researchers considered ongoing cognitive processes as mechanisms accounting for the apparently constrained effects of extreme life experiences whether they are extremely good or bad. In early work of this type, Brickman, Coates, and Janoff-Bulman (1978) attempted to use adaptation level theory to explain empirical findings in which lottery winners did not show major elevations in happiness. The theory was less clearly useful in explaining the persistence of unhappiness in paralyzed accident victims, although more recent studies of subjective well-being have found that emotion is more positive than negative among people with disabilities and many other groups perceived to be disadvantaged by others (summarized in Diener & Diener, 1996). The interest in cognitive processes has evolved in the work of Janoff-Bulman (1992) into examinations of the ways in which basic assumptions about the world, especially assumptions concerning the meaningfulness of the world, account for differences in the ways people respond to bereavement. In particular, self-blame after an adverse event has the potentially beneficial effect of restoring some sense of order, predictability, and control into a person's assumptions about the world.

VALUES AND MORAL DEVELOPMENT

Long-standing individual differences in moral values in which more self-interest and less altruism are characteristic appear to be pre-event predictors of postevent distress. Such antisocial values are associated with psychopathic behavior and personality disorder and represent a general tendency to attribute responsibility to others when bad events occur. Premilitary score elevations on Scale 4 (originally named "psychopathic deviate") of the MMPI personality test were significantly associated with PTSD symptoms after combat in one study (Schnurr, Friedman, & Rosenberg, 1993). In another, among Vietnam veterans with PTSD, combat intensity contributed to PTSD symptoms only in those who scored low on a moral development scale (Berg, Watson, Nugent, Gearhart, & Juba, 1994). These results make sense conceptually in that a core feature of PTSD is the attribution of responsibility for current status to an external event, and externalizing responsibility is a core aspect of both high Scale 4 and low levels of moral development.

SUMMARY: BELIEFS, VALUES, AND POSTEVENT DISTRESS

Postevent reports and displays of distress to some degree reflect long-standing beliefs about the world, sources of danger in the world, the self and the amount of power the self possesses, and the suitability of emotional displays, as well as values typical of a general moral style. These beliefs and values are relatively stable individual differences that are brought into extreme events and help individuals structure the meaning of the event. They provide a framework for attributions of responsibility or blame and help shape the kind of emotional response the individual shows. Individuals normally constrain emotional displays even in extreme situations when they believe that such constraint is required of them. In parallel fashion, individuals may also provide vivid release of emotions such as distress when they believe that such displays are expected, are appropriate, or may bring resources.

9

Do Groups Differ in Postevent Reactions?

Wherever detailed recording of demographic characteristics is done, these are found to contribute to variations in the incidence rates of postevent distress, although results are not consistent. A study of 1,264 adolescents who experienced Hurricane Hugo in 1989 found that one year later, the incidence rates of PTSD varied from 1.5% to 6.2% depending on which demographic group was studied; rates were lowest in Black males (1.5%) but the differences were not significant (Garrison et al., 1993). When odds ratios were calculated for the relative risk of each of several stressor variables, the highest relative risk for PTSD was found in children who had experienced other violent events (odds ratio = 2.46), whereas exposure to the hurricane alone only raised the odds ratio of reporting distress to 1.26. This increased odds ratio for risk is still at very modest levels. Because individuals can be put into groupings in many different ways that overlap, rather broad clusters are used to frame this review.

BIOLOGICAL GROUPINGS: SEX, RACE, AND AGE

When people are grouped into clusters that share some common biological features such as sex, race, or age, these groups often show variations in response to toxic events that differentiate them from other clusters. A study of 5,687 U.S. schoolchildren after Hurricane Hugo found that about 5% met criteria for PTSD; it was noted that there were significant variations in the incidence rates depending on race, sex, and age (Shan-

non, Lonigan, Finch, & Taylor, 1994). Some of the demographic variations in incidence were also linked with differential risk of exposure
and reporting bias.

In U.S. studies that compare Black/White exposures and responses
to toxic events, there are mixed results. Black children responded with
more PTSD symptoms in a study of 5,687 schoolchildren's responses to
a devastating hurricane (Lonigan, Shannon, Finch, & Daugherty, 1991).
Black men reported higher perceived stress in an epidemiological study,
but Whites appeared to have higher lifetime exposure to traumatic
events (Norris, 1992). In the Epidemiologic Catchment Area study of
PTSD prevalence in the general U.S. population sampled in St. Louis,
Missouri there were no significant variations associated with race, sex,
or age (Helzer et al., 1987).

Evidence about sex differences is also mixed. In a prevalence study
of PTSD and anxiety disorders studying half of the whole cohort of
individuals born in Iceland in 1931, women were the only subjects
reporting PTSD, at the very low rate of 1.3% (Lindal & Stefansson,
1993). Females have been found to report higher levels of subjective
distress than males in many studies of responses to specific toxic events.
Among White survivors of a major flood disaster in South Africa, women
reported more stress (Burger, Van-Staden, & Nieuwoudt, 1989). Women
outnumbered men at a ratio of more than 2 to 1 in terms of diagnosable
disorder among the homeless sheltered after the 1985 Mexican earthquakes (de la Fuente, 1990). A similar sex ratio for PTSD rates was found
in a large random U.S. sample of young adults in relation to a broadly
defined traumatic event (Breslau et al., 1991). Women showed substantially higher levels of stress symptoms and diagnosable PTSD than men
in a study of two communities after disaster-triggered family relocation
(Steinglass & Gerrity, 1990).

When exposure to the Armenian earthquake was controlled for among
schoolchildren, girls were more likely than boys to report persistent
fears (Pynoos et al., 1993). In a large study of 5,687 children ages 9
through 19 assessed 3 months after Hurricane Hugo in South Carolina,
girls and younger children reported most PTSD symptoms and anxiety
(Lonigan et al., 1991; Shannon et al., 1994); a similar age effect was
found in male Vietnam veterans diagnosed with PTSD after combat
experience (King et al., 1996). Among 1,264 adolescents studied after
Hurricane Hugo, females showed an odds ratio of 2.17 times that of
males in terms of meeting DSM criteria for PTSD, a ratio of distress
that was almost double the 1.26 that was associated with hurricane
exposure alone (Garrison et al., 1993). In contrast, there were neither
sex nor age differences in a study of psychological distress among
survivors of a ferry that capsized off Belgium in 1987 (Joseph, Yule,
Williams, & Hodgkinson, 1994).

There is some evidence of sex differences in other factors that predict the occurrence of PTSD. In a large study of Vietnam veterans with PTSD, men showed evidence of many prewar factors directly and indirectly affecting the incidence of PTSD. In women, the main factors were not prewar, but actual battlefield, experiences (King et al., 1996).

CULTURAL GROUPINGS: BELIEFS AND CUSTOMS

Beyond these universal biological variables, cultural factors such as group beliefs and customs may affect the responses of individuals faced with an adverse event. Stress measurement research was forced to incorporate ways of assessing group differences because, for example, evidence based on the Psychiatric Epidemiological Research Interview –Life Events Scale (Dohrenwend & Dohrenwend, 1978) suggested ethnic-based group differences in responses to adverse life events among U.S. samples.

Demographic factors including sex, age, income, and ethnicity were all significantly associated with emotional distress following an earthquake in Los Angeles county in 1991. Of these factors, the strongest was Hispanic ethnicity which was more significant than other substantial correlations with dose-type variables such as resource loss (Freedy, Saladin, Kilpatrick, Resnick, & Saunders, 1994). Aptaker (1990) compared the responses to community disasters of people in California and in McClellanville, South Carolina; the Californians were mostly Mexican-American, while the South Carolinians were predominantly African-American. He found group differences in presentations of anger and anger resolution that he attributed to differences in political history. Similarly, significant differences were found in two different communities in response to forced relocation after a disaster (Steinglass & Gerrity, 1990).

On a more international scale, the Armenian earthquake of 1988 revealed cultural beliefs that acted to style behavior after the disastrous event. Cultural values of "overcoming at any price," and a face-saving ethic that required individuals to maintain an outward show of prosperity, both contributed to a style that took precedence over any intrapsychic comfort values among adults (Konkov, 1991). Instead, they focused their discussions with MH professionals on the well-being of their children. There is also evidence that individuals in different cultures show significant variability in the form of postevent distress syndromes such as those arising from torture (Basoglu, 1992).

Although it is usually difficult to compare toxic exposures in different countries because of cultural differences, occasionally naturally occurring events take place that invite such comparisons. There were two events of this type occurring separately in the United States and in Israel. In both these events, children were kept isolated under conditions of high perceived threat that led to no objective harm. In the U.S. case, 23 schoolchildren were kidnapped in their school bus, driven around for 11 hours, and driven into a trailer truck that (unknown to them) was then buried for 16 hours before the strongest boys dug their way out (Terr, 1981). In a rough observational account based on assessments 5 to 13 months later, it was concluded that all of the children suffered postevent trauma. The parents were angry that they had not been offered professional help after the event and spoke to mass media to express their bitterness. In contrast, Israeli children forced into hermetically sealed rooms to protect them from biological and chemical weapons during the SCUD missile bombardments of the Gulf War showed mostly optimism and little evidence of any postevent disorder (Weisenberg et al., 1993). Although these situations were clearly not identical, it is hard to argue that the Israeli event was objectively less full of threat. It is possible that differing interpretations of the events (exposure to an unknown threat, vs. attempted protection from exposure to an unpredictable threat), and possibly differing cultural expectations contributed to the behavior reported and displayed by children.

Generational Differences in the Display of Distress

In light of some evidence that younger people report more postevent distress, is it possible that these age differences reflect cohort differences of generational culture rather than biological factors of aging? If distress responses are significantly affected by the expectations people have about what kind of emotional response is considered normal, and if cultural beliefs shift across time, then we can expect cohort differences. There is little controlled evidence concerning this because of the formidable research method problems posed in such a study, but there is some observational material.

One generation ago, a famous descriptive study often included in introductory psychology texts reported on the levels of emotional display in different U.S. ethnic groups during pain (Zborowski, 1969). Old-stock "Yankees" were generally observed to be more stoic and quiet, whereas immigrants from more extraverted cultures showed more vivid emotional displays. Based on current observations of popular culture, including television newscasts, there is some reason to think that the old modal Yankee style is no longer the norm and that the amount of emotion expected and displayed now is greater than in earlier generations.

Popular thought has gone even farther. With the explosion of television and of the therapeutic culture since the 1970s, it seems there is now a general belief that a vivid emotional display is the expected expression of inner experience in crisis situations. Not only are vivid emotional displays now regarded as a normative response, there is a popular belief that failure to show emotions is an actively harmful process called *repression*. This cathartic, Freudian model of our present cohort has treatment implications. The current model of adversity–distress relations is mostly based on an assumption that free emotional expression is beneficial in achieving personal resolution after a toxic experience. In earlier times, however, our grandparents were reared to believe that stoicism in the face of adversity was a mark of mature, formed character.

As a consequence of this shift in beliefs about emotional expression, when the expected emotional display is not provided by people after a toxic event, observers may become annoyed or even offended that the exposed individual is not behaving "appropriately." In the aftermath of the murder of 16 kindergarten children in Scotland in April 1996, for example, television news anchors from the United States were frustrated by the constraint of the stricken parents, expecting television-ready displays (Fraser, 1996). Instead, the devastated Scots simply repeated over and over "We're totally devastated, totally numb," and could not be successfully encouraged to provide more colorful language or emotional displays in order to meet the standard 7-second sound-bites allotted. Visiting reporters agreed that responses typical of U.S. television news were more readily elicited at home from participants following a sudden tragic event.

SOCIAL CONTEXT

There is a large literature on social support as a moderator variable in the adversity–distress relationship (e.g., Sarason, Sarason, & Pierce, 1990), which I will not review here. In general, there is evidence of some amelioration of the effects of toxic exposure if the individuals perceive that they have social support from others. It also appears that such support is most likely to be shown toward individuals who display balanced coping rather than toward those who appear excessively needy (Silver, Wortman, & Crofton, 1990). Social support may account for more of the variation in individual distress responses than more objective measures of dose toxicity, even with a drastic event such as unexpected bereavement. In a study of survivors of a huge ferry sinking off Belgium in 1987 in which 193 of 600 died, 17% of the variance in symptoms reported was accounted for by crisis support. Being bereaved in the event did not account for symptom scores of general distress or avoidance symptoms, and contributed only 4% of the variance on intrusion symptoms (Joseph et al., 1994).

Money and Other Resources

People's financial security contributes to the way in which they respond to acute toxic events, with individuals who are more prosperous not reporting postevent distress at rates as high as those who are less prosperous. Among U.S. civilian internees of the Japanese during World War II, for example, incidence of PTSD within a recent 6-month period was lower among those with higher incomes (Potts, 1994). In general, it appears that although money does not ensure well-being, congruence between individual goals with financial resources does predict subjective well-being (Diener & Fujita, 1995), and, logically, the prosperous have greater congruence.

The money that people wish to have may contribute to reports of postevent distress, when these reports can be used to seek financial benefits such as in veterans benefits, damage lawsuits, and workers' compensation systems, because the disorder is so clearly defined in terms of an external event for which others might be held liable. There is evidence that a desire for money plays a role in fraudulent claims of posttraumatic disorders in civilians (Burgess & Dworkin, 1993) and among combat veterans (Atkinson, Henderson, Sparr, & Deale, 1982). In one instance, a number of Vietnam veterans who presented to the Reno Veterans Administration hospital reporting PTSD, were found not to have been either in Vietnam or in combat (Lynn & Belze, 1984).

As noted earlier, fraudulent claims are relatively easy to put forward because PTSD criteria are entirely symptom based and without any objective signs. It is been shown, for example, that 86% of untrained subjects who are given a symptom checklist and instructed to respond as if they suffered from PTSD are able to check sufficient correct symptoms to meet the official DSM–III–R criteria for the disorder (Lees-Haley & Dunn, 1994). There is no single method for detecting fraud in claims of posttraumatic distress and, therefore, no clear data on the proportion of fraudulent claims in different populations.

SUMMARY: GROUP FACTORS
IN POSTEVENT DISTRESS

In 1985, Quarantelli noted that factors other than the event alone are substantially involved in a distress response. These additional factors included group characteristics, such as age, race, and sex, along with individual factors relating to previous behavior, long-standing personality, and previous life events.

More recent evidence continues to suggest that demographic groupings clustered by both biological and cultural variables contribute to the distress shown after a toxic event. Recent evidence from meta-analytic studies, however, suggests that these group characteristics play a relatively slight role in altering the core dose–response relationship in comparison with the power of more individual differences. In their meta-analysis, Weaver and Clum (1995) found most demographic variables, other than female sex, of insignificant power, and they cautioned about problems in interpreting even that exception.

10

Which Has More Power in Determining Distress, the Event or the Person?

The most powerful and clear data concerning the origins of posttraumatic distress come from studies that look directly at the objective stressor characteristics, at pre-event individual differences, and at postevent factors. What is the relative power of these families of variables when both individual differences and event characteristics are included in the analysis? To what extent do these variables interact in accounting for variations in event-attributed chronic distress?

COMPARISONS OF DOSE AND INDIVIDUAL DIFFERENCES

Recent empirical data have provided direct comparisons of the contributions of dose and individual differences variables. In the studies of the Australian bush fires of 1983 which were so thoroughly documented by McFarlane and others, fire exposure and other life events accounted for only about 9% of symptom reports after 4 months (McFarlane, 1987). Long-term psychiatric morbidity seen in a small proportion of men after the fires was predicted better by pre-event individual differences than by exposure to the fires or losses from them (McFarlane, 1990). In particular, family histories of psychiatric illness and neuroticism accounted for the progression from acute distress to psychiatric disorder in two thirds of the cases (McFarlane, 1992). Another study of posttraumatic stress among the volunteer firefighters in Australia, examined the 751 who responded to a survey request sent to 3,000. The Impact Events Scale reflected 23% of the variance in PTSD symptoms. Of this 23%, 11% represented subjective, perceived characteristics of the event or self, 6% represented after-fire stressful events, while only 5% came from the objective proximity-to-death variable (McFarlane, 1988a). A study of the responses of 5,687 U.S. schoolchildren to a hurricane 3 months earlier found that anxiety and PTSD symptoms were correlated with degree of exposure to the hurricane (measured on the basis of objective harms and losses), with demographic differences as moderating variables (Lonigan et al., 1991). Later, when the relative power of different types of risk factors was directly compared, trait anxiety and in-event emotional response contributed more to PTSD symptoms than exposure factors (Lonigan et al., 1994). Trait anxiety was the single strongest risk for the development of severe posttraumatic stress reactions.

Although war experience in general contributes to risk of developing PTSD, combat experience can sometimes have salutary effects on personality and overall function; the risk of PTSD becoming chronic is highly dependent on pre- and postmilitary factors (Friedman, Schnurr, & McDonagh, 1994). A study of 152 Vietnam combat veterans found that the greatest proportion (26%) of variance in PTSD symptoms came from an externalization coping style factor, while only 9% was predictable from combat exposure (Wolfe et al., 1993).

Of 107 Harvard men followed from 1939 through World War II to 1988, the 16 men with high combat exposure and prewar mature defenses reported significantly fewer PTSD symptoms in 1988 compared to the 17 men with high combat exposure but less mature prewar defenses (Lee et al., 1995). Croatian soldiers serving on the war front showed a 13% incidence of PTSD which was somewhat associated with duration on the front. In addition, unstable family situation and a disposition to psychotraumatic experiences were equally identified as contributors to symptom reports of the disorder, in a descriptive study (Pozgain, Filakovic, & Perekovic, 1992). In a large study of U.S. soldiers in the Persian Gulf War, 97 of 775 were identified as meeting PTSD criteria and were compared with 484 who had no distress. Personality variables were importantly present in the prediction equation that correctly classified 87% of the subjects, and demographic and stress severity variables did not alter this (Sutker et al., 1995).

The role of individual interpretations of life events was powerfully demonstrated among Jewish Holocaust survivors living in Montreal during contemporary unrest arising from Quebec separatism. There was a dramatic interaction effect in which long-standing symptom levels were exacerbated among survivors who perceived an increase in antisemitism as part of that nationalism, with 48% showing significant increases in symptoms. Importantly, however, among survivors who did not perceive or interpret these events as representing an increase in antisemitism, there was no increase in symptom levels, with symptom levels matching the much lower levels found in matched controls (Eaton, Sigal, & Weinfeld, 1982).

The ways in which personality characteristics affect how ways individuals select and construct their environments is also relevant to this problem, because some environments provide higher risk levels than others. In the Kaui Longitudinal Study of children raised in high-risk environments, Werner (1993) found that the children's individual dispositions led to significant differences in the environments they sought out and that these differences were important in contributing to later adult well-being.

In studying noxious events of a smaller magnitude, such as daily hassles, trait anxiety has similarly been found to be a more powerful predictor of perceived stress than hassle events. In combination, trait anxiety and hassles accounted for 67% of the variance of psychiatric symptom levels (Kohn, Lafreniere, & Gurevich, 1991). In attempting to account for high correlations among anxiety, reactivity, and hassles, the researchers raised the possibility that individuals high in trait anxiety subjectively overestimate their exposure to hassles. Similar data were reported in the much larger study of 1,159 older men in the Normative Aging Study (Aldwin, Levenson, Spiro, & Bossé, 1989). The personality variable emotionality had a greater effect on mental health symptoms than did two families of stressor variables. Analysis showed that the personality variable of emotionality had a total effect on mental health of .47, whereas hassles had an effect of .19 and life events, .38. Because reports of hassles show high reliability across time (an average correlation of .77; DeLongis, Folkman, & Lazarus, 1988), perceived hassles may reflect long-standing personality predispositions more than objective events.

Few adversity–distress studies are prospective in nature, but both objective and subjective features were included in a prospective study of college students before and at two time points after a California earthquake (Nolen-Hoeksema & Morrow, 1991). It found that students with pre-event elevations in emotional distress showed additional elevations following the earthquake and that students who were exposed to more severe circumstances during the earthquake (a higher dose) also showed elevations of distress measures following the event.

Finally, Weaver and Clum (1995) reported a meta-analysis of studies examining the relative magnitude of objective violence and subjective factors on distress. They found that objective factors were much more likely to have been studied. Despite this imbalance, they found that subjective factors contributed twice as much to the magnitude of distress as did objective characteristics of the violence.

INTERACTIONS OF DOSE
WITH INDIVIDUAL DIFFERENCES

A more comprehensive way of construing life events requires considering behavior and events as interactional. It has been argued that individual differences are less important, depending on event characteristics. If an event is very important, if feedback about it is objective, and if the situation demands action, then individual differences are less important in determining response (Frese, 1992). The literature on PTSD that studies interactional effects of toxic exposures with individual difference variables is relatively limited but shows that pre-event personality traits interact significantly with toxic event experiences in determining distress levels.

Suzanne Miller (1992) studied two contrasting attentional styles (monitoring vs. blunting) as an individual differences variable and found interactions with stressor toxicity account for variations in distress. High monitoring is associated with greater distress if stressors are minor, whereas high blunting is associated with greater distress if stressors are highly traumatic. In a study of 295 female victims of crime, precrime depression interacted with crime stressor level in predicting PTSD (Resnick, Kilpatrick, Best, & Kramer, 1992). Among 107 Vietnam veterans, those with high combat experience yet no PTSD showed lower trait neuroticism scores than those with low combat experience and PTSD (Casella & Motta, 1990). Among a different group of 100 Vietnam veterans with combat-attributed PTSD, who were classified into three levels of combat exposure, the most striking finding was an extremely high trait Neuroticism score (Talbert, Braswell, Albrecht, Hyer, & Boudewyns, 1993). This was characteristic of all groups, independent of combat exposure.

Because of significant variations in the occurrence of postevent distress syndromes, research has also looked the ways in which people behave with resilience despite toxic life experiences, in addition to studying the factors that contribute to reports of distress. Developmental studies of children resilient to environments of abuse and severe disadvantage have been expanding since the mid-1970s, starting with important work by Norman Garmezy (1971) and Michael Rutter (1989). Gina Higgins' (1994) book *Resilient Adults: Overcoming a Cruel Past* provides many case examples of adults who endured brutal childhoods yet were able to create lives of "hope and happiness." She focused on the origins of mental health rather than the origins of mental illness. Another recent book reporting on *Urban Children in Distress* (Blanc, 1994) in five nations documents both the toxic environments as well as the resilience of street children and their families (Blanc, 1994). These books add to the large biographical literature describing the lives of individuals overcoming significant adversity and reaching outstanding levels of achievement. They inform us in a way that is often hard to see in the shorter time span of epidemiological studies of segments of lives in progress or in the biased samples of those who seek help.

Suzanne Kobasa studied the ways in which personal resilience or hardiness may interact with different kinds of social support to contribute to varying outcomes after stressful life events. In one study of 170 successful executives she and a colleague found that, for those low in hardiness, perceived family support led to poorer health outcomes, while perceived supervisor support contributed to well-being (Kobasa & Puccetti, 1983). That is, there was an interaction in which people with differing levels of hardiness were differentially helped or harmed by different kinds of social support after encountering stressful life events. In comparing the relative power of hardiness with other factors implicated in resistance to stressful life events, hardiness was more important than exercise or social support in reducing subsequent illness (Kobasa, Maddi, Puccetti, & Zola, 1985).

A series of studies that look at both genetics and toxic life events as they interact in contributing to clinical distress has been reported using data from the Virginia Twin Registry. Recent findings concerning these factors in contributing to depression, for example, show that, even in the presence of high genetic risk and severely stressful life events, most individuals do not develop an episode of major depression (Kendler et al., 1995). The impact of toxic events as a risk factor was substantially greater on those people who were at greater genetic risk

SUMMARY: EVENTS OR PERSONAL QUALITIES?

Although evidence concerning the relative power of event characteristics in comparison with personal qualities in accounting for postevent distress does not constitute a large quantity of work, the direction of findings is consistent. Whenever data are collected that include individual qualities (pre- and post-event) as well as event characteristics so these can be directly compared, individual qualities are more powerful in accounting for distress. Most people do not respond to even highly toxic events with persistent diagnosable mental disorders such as PTSD, and those who do respond with reports of serious deterioration in personal functioning and distress represent a small minority. The evidence shows that these people have a combination of individual factors that contribute significantly to their distress. These factors include cognitive competence, previous history of acts and experiences, and long-standing personality traits of emotionality and attraction to risk, as well as beliefs about the self, the world, sources of danger, and the appropriateness of emotional displays. Overall, these pre-event factors contribute more to serious distress disorders than does the toxic event. Given that this evidence is clear and striking, why is it that clinicians have increasingly placed toxic events at the heart of the explanation for distress disorders? This question is investigated in the following chapter.

11

Why Are Clinicians Reluctant to Look for Causes Beyond the Event?

Understanding the origins of human behavior is difficult, and the diversity of theories is a reflection of this. In the specific case of event-attributed distress, although the evidence shows that events do not account for the major part of the disorder, the DSM and popular and clinical thinking continue to view the disorder as if the event caused it. Why does this error of attribution continue?

In the PTSD paradigm the condition is defined in terms of the event, and treatment methods are often centered around the idea that the distress response is an entirely natural, predictable response given the awful event. There is resistance to attending to long-standing individual difference variables such as premorbid personality and emotionality or the social constructions of experience made by individuals reporting distress after an adverse event. This reluctance is often justified on the grounds that such person-oriented explanations blame the victim, and are therefore morally reprehensible.

Brickman for example, took this approach in his attempt to develop a model of attributions for causes and solutions in remedying human problems (Brickman et al., 1982). He concluded that, of four possible models, the compensatory one was the best because it did not blame the victim. This model does not attribute any responsibility to individuals for their problems but does assign individuals responsibility for solving these. In recent research reviews on responses to toxic life events, the very environment-oriented stress–distress model continues to dominate. In one such review of the impact of disasters, only a small section was allocated for personal characteristics, and these consisted entirely of group demographic characteristics rather than individual differences (Green & Solomon, 1995).

One reason for the persistent ignoring of individual differences is probably that it seems transparently logical and reasonable to attribute distress symptoms to a recent event when it is something obviously harmful, such as a motor vehicle accident. The attribution seems even more justifiable if images of the event are reported as symptoms of the emotional disorder. Both sets of reasoning in fact do account for accurate explanations in some cases but fail to provide an explanation for the symptom-free behavior of those who do not show persisting significant distress after a comparable exposure. Nor does this reasoning account for the cases that show event-attributed distress where this cannot possibly be true. For cases where toxic exposure and distress are discordant, and where most people with a similar exposure do not show distress that one person reports, other sources of errors in understanding the origins of distress must be considered.

The way in which life events are identified and extracted from the flow of a life can contribute to mistaken notions about causes of distress. In order to be compatible with popular and therapeutic models that assume that distress is caused by adverse life events, an ongoing life is sliced into a specific segment of cause and effect that starts with the event and ends with the distress response.

Life is more complicated, however, and a specific toxic event is not simply an intrusive stimulus that starts an isolated segment of life that then ends with distress. A toxic event can be a stimulus that elicits a reaction, an outcome of previous acts, or a moderator of the effects of other personal or situational factors. Life events occur as part of a continuous stream of interactions in which acts, thoughts, and emotions are also events that can function in ongoing life simultaneously as stimulus, personal interpretation, and result.

Causal explanations of distress try to pull out meaningful event–response segments that can be understood in a unidirectional way. If a larger perspective is taken, however, evidence suggests that focusing on a short segment of dose–response distorts the meaning of the segment. The capacity to initiate actions and to show agency is a general human quality which is not limited to those with visible physical or social power, yet agency is largely ignored in the adversity–distress thinking. Instead, there is a general assumption that we can best understand distress by breaking life's segments into patterns that start with a toxic event and end with an emotion. Although this reasoning is readily accepted in the immediate aftermath of a toxic event when distress is reported by some people, it does not account well for the reports from the many people who do not report clinical distress after toxic events. Why should such an interpretive pattern persist in the face of our recognition that causes of human behavior cannot be understood in terms of such isolated packages? There are several sources of errors in building up causal explanations in attempting to understand lives in progress.

OUR BRAINS CAN FOOL US
WHEN WE TRY TO UNDERSTAND
WHY WE DO THINGS

Unusual Biological Conditions

Some errors in causal reasoning about distress may arise out of universal biological features of the human brain. Working brains operate so as to allow an individual to make sense of ongoing events. The effort is continuous in the waking brain, whether it is fully conscious or otherwise and whether the results are rational, misguided, fanciful, or completely delusional. Humans have a striking capacity to provide plausible explanations of their behavior even when it is clear to an observer that the explanation is completely without merit. The faulty explanation does not always imply deception or delusion, and at least part of the origin of faulty explanations lies in the way that the brain is organized.

Reports of phantom pain in body parts that have been amputated provide an obvious example of an honest but incorrect attribution. While it seems logical that a toe cannot hurt if it no longer exists, implying that the report of pain is false, research has established that the experience of pain can still be real because it is still being generated by neuronal activity within the central nervous system rather than within the now-gone periphery of a limb. It is the brain that assesses a certain pattern of neural activation as representing pain, whether that activation comes from a limb or arises spontaneously in neural circuits that had previously been active when the limb was still present.

Other evidence of the biological pressure to generate a coherent, meaningful explanation of experience, even when this is an impossible task, comes from some famous experiments with split-brain patients. These are patients whose corpus callosum was surgically severed to limit disability from epilepsy. The corpus callosum is a band of tissue that connects the right and left cerebral hemispheres and allows the passage of neural messages between the two hemispheres. In some cases of epilepsy, the neural messages across the corpus callosum include pathological excitations that result in seizures.

The patients who had surgical separation of the hemispheres were capable of quickly and easily generating honest but completely false explanations of the causes of their actions under certain conditions (Gazzaniga & LeDoux, 1978). Patient P. S., for example, had been given instructions to do certain actions with his left hand. These instructions were given solely to his low-verbal right hemisphere through special stimulus–display procedures, and these instructions could not be transferred to the left hemisphere because of the surgical disconnection. Normally the left hemisphere operates to construct causal, sequential meanings out of ongoing events, but P. S. had no conscious awareness of the instructions that had been directed to the right hemisphere, even though he acted as instructed. When asked to explain his actions, which required using his verbal left hemisphere, which "knew" nothing of the instruction because of the severed corpus callosum, he readily put forward well-intentioned but incorrect and fanciful explanations of his actions. His perfectly fluent explanation attributed a cause to his actions in a plausible but entirely invented scenario, and he fully believed that his explanation was accurate and honest although it was arbitrary and untrue.

Gazzaniga's findings show that, under some conditions, honest individuals can and will quickly provide a plausible explanation for their actions that is entirely constructed on the moment, believing it to be an accurate account. It seems an inherent quality of the human brain that causal explanations are constructed when needed; there are undoubtedly powerful reasons why our brains should have evolved to do this. Of course, Gazzaniga's patients differed from most people in having had a special surgical procedure that altered the connections within the brain. What about the construction of false but plausible attributions of cause in people who have not had any surgical changes to their brains?

Psychological Operations

One way in which normal people with intact brains can grossly misunderstand the causes of their actions can be seen in the special condition created by hypnosis. We can observe entirely incorrect explanations of behavior provided by subjects justifying acts they performed in response to posthypnotic suggestion.

On a more hypothetical level, the entire body of psychoanalytic theory consists of arguments claiming that much significant behavior arises from irrational motives whose sources are not available in consciousness. In this model, it is assumed that people will give plausible accounts for their actions that will be interpreted as seriously in error by the clinician. The model asserts that less obvious but more powerful unconscious memories and emotional conflicts are the true source of motives for actions.

HOW DO WE MISUNDERSTAND
THE CAUSES OF EMOTIONAL AROUSAL?

If acts can be mistakenly explained by people who are attempting to give an honest account of their behavior, what of attempts to describe and explain emotional condition? Interpretations of the nature and causes of emotion may also be completely wrong, even in the absence of any attempt to deceive. In particular, attributions of the origins of distress can be entirely invalid. This can be seen most strikingly in the cases of people with certain major mental disorders where we can observe actively delusional explanations of distress. In the case of paranoid and other thought disorders, an affected person may identify the cause of his distress as the workings of enemies, an evil conspiracy, or alien invasions. These distressing thoughts provide vivid imagery experienced as frightening. Antipsychotic medications usually stop these images, delusional ideas, and the distress that is attributed to them without the need for any psychological treatment directed at the thought content. The persistent and intrusive frightening mental images that reflect the disturbed brain chemistry of the disorder are correctly interpreted by the clinician as correlates of distress but not the cause. It would be considered grossly inappropriate for a therapist to treat a delusional patient by requiring him to focus on the frightening delusional images as a therapeutic measure to remedy the disorder, because the thought content is a by-product of more basic physiological disturbances that can be dealt with more directly.

What about individuals who have a normally integrated functioning brain and no major thought disorder? Other kinds of errors in attributing the causes of distress can be found in populations that do not have any obvious structural or chemical problems in their brains. Studies in neuropsychology, psychopathology, and social psychology have shown that errors in interpreting the causes and meanings of emotional arousal operate in ordinary people, and there are mechanisms that contribute in predictable ways to these errors in explanations.

Experimental Studies of Attributing Meaning To Emotions

Long ago, psychologists Schachter and Singer (1962) showed that individuals search the environment for emotionally meaningful stimuli when they experience arousal for which they do not otherwise have an available explanation. In a classic study they administered the stimulant epinephrine or a placebo to subjects, half of whom had the drug's effects explained. They then exposed half of each group to either a happy or angry confederate, following which they obtained descriptions of their subjects' experienced emotion. They found that emotional reports were consistent with the emotional style of the confederate, among the subjects who had no explanation for their arousal. For the nonaroused placebo subjects, there were no reports of significant emotion. That is, emotionally neutral physiological arousal was interpreted through the exposure to emotionally toned stimuli by subjects when they were asked about their emotional state and had no other information about their condition.

Evidence has mostly supported this basic model across more than three decades of continuing studies of misattributions of emotional arousal. A recent experimental study discovered that there are additional sources of misattributions of the meaning of arousal. It showed that when there is no immediate environmental stimulus to which unexplained arousal can be attributed, individuals will then search memory for recent ideas and will quickly make use of emotionally loaded but completely irrelevant information in memory in order to present a meaningful report of their emotional state (Sinclair, Hoffman, Mark, Martin, & Pickering, 1994). People even do this under conditions when the remembered material is arbitrary and of no meaningful personal import, without realizing that this is what they are doing.

These and many other related studies show that raw arousal, immediate environmental stimuli, and recent thoughts can all be the sources of misattributions of the nature of emotional arousal. These factors can all result in reports of emotional condition that do not reflect any meaningful inner state or any meaningful explanation of any cause. These mistaken attributions do, nevertheless, reflect lawful psychological mechanisms that routinely function to provide meaning for subjective states, even when the true origins of these states are not known. Even in people who are not normally distressed, increased arousal is often interpreted as anxiety and is considered to be a bad thing, an index of harm, although studies dating back to Hebb's original model of 1955 have shown that, under taxing situations, moderately heightened anxiety maximally enhances learning and performance. Increased arousal is not necessarily an index of harm or a source of deterioration in functioning.

Extending these findings to the case of event-attributed distress, we can see that a state of emotional arousal will be attributed to a cause, whether this attribution is accurate or not. If the true cause is long-standing emotional fragility in a person who has also recently had a nasty life event, it is only human for the emotion to be fully misattributed to the event.

ERRORS OF JUDGMENT

Another source of mistakes in understanding causation is through errors in judgment. Under conditions of normal awareness, these errors have been extensively studied in studies comparing clinical to statistical judgments in making predictions about the behavior of clinical populations. On a general level, these errors include failing to consider alternative explanations and failing to look for additional explanations (Wedding & Faust, 1989). These normally occurring errors become compounded when clinicians see only highly biased samples consisting only of people reporting distress after an event. It seems logical to accept the attribution because the clinician is not aware of all those who experienced the event and did not develop a serious distress disorder.

Errors of judgment also contribute to misunderstandings of research relating to understanding the causes of pathological behavior. Studies of drug-taking adolescents in which subjects attribute their own use to peer influence have been criticized as overestimating peer influence because of two known sources of bias (Bauman & Ennett, 1994). First, there is evidence that the commonality of drug use among friends reflects active friendship selection favoring drug users, rather than true prevalence. Secondly, estimates of their friends' high use is known to be upwardly biased among drug-users. That is, these adolescents' own actions contributed to the factors that they then reported as causes of their drug use. In postevent distress disorders, the pre-event actions of individuals are usually considered to be irrelevant to the disorder, and this results in a loss of information which might contribute to understanding the origins of the distress.

Errors in judgments also derive from inaccurate ideas about the base rate of occurrence of a disorder, similar to the base rate problem identified by Bauman and Ennet (1994) in subjects' explanations for their drug use. In the case of chronic PTSD, the clinical literature reveals a lack of attention to base rate and dose–response data showing that most people exposed to the same toxic event do not show a significant chronic distress syndrome from it. Then, lacking this attention to base rate, and because images of a toxic event may be vivid and readily available, emotional distress can be easily attributed to a toxic exposure, with sample bias preventing either a subject or clinician from making a better judgment about the role of the event.

Other errors in judgment derive from general cognitive biases that affect memory. For example, Anthony Greenwald (1980) identified three cognitive biases that contribute to the way we construct our ideas about our self; in particular the *beneffectance* bias is the general tendency to accept responsibility for desired, but not undesired, outcomes. In constructing personal histories, normal people readily bias what is placed in memory. Such a bias has an obvious relevance for the ways in which distress is interpreted and remembered.

ERRORS OF LOGIC

Other errors in understanding the causes of behavior arise from errors in logic. These include *post hoc* reasoning and other kinds of fallacies.

Mental health professionals are trained to construct explanations after the fact to explain many kinds of observed psychopathology so that it appears to be a logical consequence of adverse experiences. These explanations derive directly from assumptions of the experience-oriented mental health models. Yet, although adverse experiences can often be found in the life histories of seriously disturbed individuals, an interesting study suggests that by using such backward reasoning, such troubled histories may be attributed causal power that is not valid. Renaud and Estes (1961) did intensive clinical interviews with 100 "above average" U.S. men to learn details of their life experiences. To the researchers' surprise, they found just as much adverse and pathological experience in these histories as they were accustomed to finding in clinical cases, but with none of the adult behavioral pathologies. Reasoning backward from evidence of distress to explanations rooted in adverse life events can thus lead to faulty conclusions about causation.

Another example of fallacious reasoning that may contribute to a neglect of individual differences in personality in explaining event-attributed distress arises from the logical error called the *pathetic fallacy* by Deutsch (1960). This is the fallacious interpretation that is made when a person is observed experiencing failure or adversity. Observers will interpret the event as a decisive devaluation experience for the person and will overvalue the harm or toxic effects to be expected. In contrast, subjects who directly experience the adverse event do not report it as being as harmful or show defensive responses to it, apparently because the subject experiences it as one small slice of experience within a lifetime of events. The observer does not have the larger context of events available as an interpretive frame.

Experimental data show that observers of extreme events tend to overestimate the magnitude and duration of the effects of adverse events upon the individuals who are directly participating (Brickman et al., 1978). Results consistent with this general phenomenon were shown in a study of war-injured men with visible injuries; they resented being helped because this implied they were being seen primarily in terms of their injury (Ladieu, Hanfmann, & Dembo, 1947).

WHEN ARE THOUGHT CONTENTS UNRELIABLE AS A MARKER OF CONDITION?

Bernard Rimland (1969) reviewed various types of fallacious cause and effect reasoning concerning pathologies of behavior, noting that clinicians often mistakenly interpret the content of a distressed person's concerns as if it were evidence of the cause of the distress. The error of this reasoning is routinely acknowledged when there are powerful biological factors such as tumors, split cerebral hemispheres, or bio-chemical disturbances that contribute to mental disorder and disturbed thought contents. It is less readily recognized as a general reasoning error that may be relevant to distress conditions when these are attrib-uted to toxic events because memories of these form the content of the distressed person's thoughts.

A powerful clinical example was provided in a description of three cases of patients suffering from intrusive obsessional images that were ascribed to flashback memories of apparently traumatic events result-ing in PTSD. When the therapeutic attention was given not to the thought content but instead to the patients' biochemical status, and serotonin reuptake antagonists were prescribed, the patients lost their intrusive traumatic images along with their obsessional and compulsive symptoms (Lipinski & Pope, 1994). Further investigation suggested none of the images corresponded with real past events. This example suggests that the content of thoughts is not necessarily a reliable source of information about the cause of distress or a necessary feature on which to focus treatment.

There is a further problem when clinicians deal with thought contents that are not readily provided by a distressed person but rather elicited through prolonged and intimate treatment procedures intended to break through repression, as in the repressed memory syndromes. We risk straying even farther away from an adequate causal understanding of a patient's distress because of the poor evidence underlying the claims for repressed memories as powerful agents of distress (Frankel, 1995). Evidence from studies of errors in memory shows that a focus on the affective features of a memory reduces the overall level of recall and, in older adults, leads to more introduced subjective elaborations along with greater confusion as to whether the recalled experience was real or imaginary (Hashtroudi & Johnson, 1994). This general phenomenon suggests that a clinical emphasis on repressed and emotional memories runs a heightened risk for error.

This evidence suggests that although thought contents may center on an experienced event and memories of it, these thought contents may represent a correlate of distress that arises from multiple sources, rather than providing proof of the cause.

We construct causal explanations and meaning around subjective experience even when it does not reflect objective reality because we find it important to believe that our experiences and actions are meaningful and reasonable. Language gives us a ready tool to use to make plausible connections. Even subjects with no clear advantage to gain from provid-ing biased reports about their adjustment may provide an account that makes sense to themselves but is in some way not reliably tapping their experience. Bereaved individuals who were asked to report on positive and negative life changes in the 4 to 7 years after their bereavement, were found to show no relation between self-reported positive life changes and personal growth with reduced presence of distress symptoms, although negative life changes were associated with increased distress (Lehman et al., 1993). This suggests that positive self-reports of growth may not be reliable indicators of what has happened.

Other studies provide us with additional mechanisms that help us understand how systematic biases in attribution operate when base rate information is lacking. Evidence shows, for example, that we expect others to feel more distress after a bad event than we expect to feel ourselves (Taylor & Brown, 1994). In parallel vein, studies of experiences of harmful discrimination among members of minority groups have shown that they typically believe there is more discrimination directed at their group than they report experiencing themselves (Taylor, Wright, Moghaddam, & Lalonde, 1990). That is, it seems that individuals customarily bias their judgments of the base rates of responses to toxic events, expecting more problems in others than they report themselves. I attribute this bias to the psychologizing of modern culture and to the exaggerated ideas of the power of environmental factors in determining distress that is the basic assumption of this culture.

Another way in which errors in attributing causes of distress has been explored is through studies of what is called *attributional shift* or the *fundamental error of attribution*. This refers to a general tendency for individuals to attribute their own behavior to situational variables and to shift this attribution to dispositional variables when considering the behavior of others (Riccio, Rabinowitz, & Axelrod, 1994). This is perfectly consistent with patients' attributing their distress to a life event, and this known bias allows us to understand that such situational attributions may be too narrow to be valid.

INDIVIDUAL AGENCY:
WHERE DOES A CAUSE BEGIN?

Another error in reasoning in the adversity–distress model is the assumption that the unit of analysis starts with an external toxic event, in that this disregards the concept of agency. Individuals initiate acts, and sometimes these acts lead to toxic events and distress outcomes.

Psychology seems to be only erratically interested in notions of personal agency, although philosophy, religion, and the law in the West have all insisted that individuals are responsible for their intentional actions and their effects since the time of the classical Greeks. Much of the power and grandeur of the Greek tragedies and Old Testament stories derived from an individual deciding to act for moral reasons in a way that would lead to great personal suffering, doing the action with this foreknowledge, and accepting the suffering as part of the human condition.

Clinical models of event-attributed distress do not make use of longer causal sequences in which actions taken by an individual can contribute to subsequent adverse life events which are then experienced as distressing. Outside professional MH practice however, the way in which people take actions to structure their own environments and then are affected by these actions has been the subject of thoughtful review within developmental and social psychology for some time (Rutter, 1986; Scarr & McCartney, 1983). In a large representative sample of families, within the approximately 12% of couples who reported spousal violence, in half the cases it was reported as mutual violence (Straus,Gelles, & Steinmetz, 1980).

Sampson and Laub (1993) examined the famous Dueck and Dueck longitudinal records of 500 delinquents and 500 controls and found that the boys' choices of friends in school, their choices of spouses, and their persistence in ensuring job stability all led to later life events that they brought about through their own actions. Each of these actions had a powerful impact on their own subsequent life experiences and behavior, for good or for ill. Unavoidable environmental factors over which they had no control, such as having delinquent siblings, were not associated with later delinquency, whereas having delinquent friends was typically associated with later delinquency. This shows that later delinquency was not simply a matter of close or prolonged exposure to other delinquents, but reflected more an adoption of delinquent values and behaviors that was active rather than passive.

This study reacquaints us with the power of personal agency, of personal actions in determining whether adverse or positive life events subsequently take place. Sampson and Laub (1993) identified key choices and actions that had significant lifelong effects. The popularized theories deriving from Freudian and behavioral theory about the dangers of intrusive life events have become increasingly established as truisms, yet Sampson and Laub say it is not as simple as this if you study lives over a long period. They found discrete life events were far less powerful in determining the trajectory of adult lives for delinquent boys than were long-term self-directed behaviors involving choices about friendships, alcohol use, and marital and work bonds. A study that looked at 900 homeless people in St. Louis found, as is predictable, that there was much violence and evidence of PTSD in the lives of these unfortunate people (North, Smith, & Spitznagel, 1994); of relevance to the question of causality, aggressive behavior was often from childhood and typically predated most problems including homelessness.

In sum, personal agency, the capacity through making active choices to select environments, events, and relationships, is important in understanding distressed individuals. Individuals initiate acts that lead to distressing outcomes, rather than simply react in response to adverse life events. Unfortunately, evidence from longitudinal studies that shows this appears to have had very limited effects on clinical thinking or practice concerning event-attributed distress disorders.

FISHER'S TWISTED PEAR

Even if there were a stronger overall correlation between toxic dose and distress response in the adversity–distress model, there is a general phenomenon in correlations involving human behavior that also contributes to errors in interpreting causation for individual cases. There is a classic distorted correlational pattern that is found on a wide range of phenomena in which there is an asymmetry of effects. In terms of the correlation between toxic dose and overall well-being, this lopsided relationship means that low-dose exposures will account very poorly for overall outcomes (which will vary from excellent to terrible), while high-dose exposures will more reliably be associated with bad outcomes. This means that finding a case with a high distress/bad outcome does not necessarily provide evidence that there has been a high-dose toxic event.

This pattern is known as Fisher's *twisted pear* (Fisher, 1959) and has been found in studies of diverse specific risk factors in relation to broad measures of well-being. When even the strongest adversity–distress correlation has a modest correlation of around .3, accounting for only about 9% of variance in distress, this asymmetry of prediction further distorts the possibility of understanding individual cases. In particular, high levels of observed distress in some individuals can be found even after low-adversity exposures, owing to the mediation of other factors.

SUMMARY: SOURCES OF ERROR IN CAUSAL EXPLANATIONS OF DISTRESS

In trying to understand the causes of distress emotions, the reasoning of patients and clinicians is vulnerable to many sources of honest error, quite apart from the cases in which deception is used. Some of these errors arise from the normal processes of the brain in attempting to create meaning and establish reasonable causal explanations, some errors arise from mistaken ideas about emotional arousal and about the base rates of distress after events. Errors in the reasoning of patients may arise from the general tendency to attribute one's own behavior to situational events. Errors among clinicians may come from backward reasoning and from making predictions about the harmful effects of events on patients that is greater than our own experience or predictions of effects on ourselves. Errors in understanding causes of distress can also arise because we incorrectly focus on thought contents as the valid guide to causation and because we tend to look at toxic events in isolation from longer chains of life and behavior. Finally, the error in assuming that high distress is evidence of a person having experienced a highly toxic event may arise from an unusual but known statistical pattern found in many examples in human behavior.

12

How Important Are Emotions as a Guide to Well-Being?

Our popular and therapeutic culture is permeated with reports and ideas about the importance of subjective emotional experience. Post-traumatic distress is but one example of the broader interest in emotions and emotional problems. This focus on subjectivity is seen in everything from the popularity of television talk shows that pursue highly emotional subjects to the proliferation of self-help groups. It is also reflected in the rise of intellectual movements such as deconstructionism/post-modernism in which the idea of objective truths is considered with disdain and individualized interpretations of the world are regarded as more important. Television programs earn their Nielson points to the extent that they are able to mobilize viewer emotions. Newscasts always ask how people feel about unusual events.

Many of the pop psychology movements of the 1970s and 1980s focused on group experiences structured to achieve maximum emotional manipulation of the participants. A major psychological industry of individual and group therapy developed to cater to this interest in emotional experience. Conventional professional therapy is devoted to examination of emotional condition and to techniques that manipulate emotional experience to create increased arousal, this being considered the means through which problems are resolved (Foa & Riggs, 1995; Watson, 1996).

This focus on emotion is a 20th-century elaboration of the European Romantic movement of the 19th century. The psychological movements triggered by Freud may be seen as quasiscientific attempts to bring these romantic notions into a more disciplined perspective. Freudian movements were not alone in arguing for the primacy of emotion in experience, for Freud's ideas were just part of the larger Romantic interest in emotion. Hitler, in *Mein Kampf*, wrote that emotions had primacy over reason in human behavior and emphasized that, for propaganda to have its greatest effects, it must be "aimed always and primarily at the emotions, and only to a certain extent to so-called reason" (p. 232). In contemporary times, the placing of emotion at the center of experience is a logical result of the psychologizing of culture that developed arising out of the Freudian emphasis on subjective emotional experience. Television has added a new immediacy and a strikingly increased frequency to our acquaintance with emotional displays. To what extent is this model of life as dominated by emotions of feeling good or bad a valid model for describing and understanding describing human experience?

ARE EMOTIONAL DISPLAYS VALID, CENTRAL MARKERS OF CONDITION?

In relation to distress emotions that are reported after toxic events, the emotion-focused model of experience assumes that the reported distress reflects profound inner experience in a way that is more true and more important than other ways of presenting the self. Because emotional distress is seen as a lawful consequence of toxic events, reports and displays of distress emotions are used in news accounts, courtrooms, in clinical practice as evidence that prior adverse experiences have occurred, even though this represents backward reasoning. The diagnostic criteria for PTSD and Acute Stress Reaction diagnoses are based on self-reports of emotion and emotion-linked images as the key evidence of disorder.

Popular psychological thinking also assumes that displays of emotionality provide a guide to the objective severity of an event. If a greater outpouring of emotional distress is observed, it is accepted as showing that a more severe event occurred. These ideas are also extended to the other end of the emotional spectrum. Just as distress emotions are believed to provide evidence of victimhood, displays of happiness emotions are assumed to provide valid evidence of self-esteem and other positive subjective inner experience.

Because, by definition, emotional distress is a report or display relating to subjective experience which cannot be objectively verified, claims for victim compensation from a toxic event on the grounds of emotional distress pose a validity problem. How valid are emotional displays as evidence of distress or well-being?

The Meaning of Emotional Displays

Across a lifetime of research in the display of emotion, Paul Ekman (1982, 1993) concluded that there are both universal, neurally determined elements in the expression of emotion, and culturally specific socially learned rules about the elicitors and display of emotion. That is, beliefs and expectations about which emotions are to be displayed in response to which situations do affect what is displayed. Emotional displays can also be affected by some kinds of major psychopathology as well as by deception. Perseverative weeping can be seen with some kinds of cerebral impairment, and this too provides no accurate guide to an inner experience of unhappiness. Emotion reports and displays, therefore, represent a combination of factors including both experienced arousal and affect, and other cultural and contextual factors, not all of which may be available in the conscious reports of the individual.

Despite decades of investigation into physiological arousal in efforts to identify specific features that might reliably signal specific "valid" emotions, the field still has not reached a point where these can be identified either by an observer or by a subject when other key information is lacking (Sinclair et al., 1994). Emotion, then, is largely an interpreted phenomenon in which arousal, immediate physical environment, and cognitive cues, in combination with long-standing perceptual dispositions all contribute to the creation of emotional meaning. What is then shown as an emotional display may be regulated to reveal or conceal other aspects of inner experience and well-being.

EMOTIONAL DISTRESS AND VIRTUE

There is an additional important feature to displays of distress, in that a positive moral valuation is typically linked with a distress status. Suffering is usually considered to be a sign that victimization has occurred, yielding, in addition, evidence of a moral or other debt owed by others. The distressed person became more worthy in some undefined sense than a person who does not report or display distress emotions. Being a victim confers a positive moral status on the person, and agencies of society are expected to respond to this as if it were a moral debt for which they must provide remedies.

These assumptions have had implications within community life, such as in the advocacy of victim impact statements in courtrooms prior to sentencing. In support of these, it is argued that justice is better served if victims of criminal activity or their relatives present an account and a display of suffering to the judge. The assumption is that this will result in a harsher sentence than would normally be provided on the basis of facts considered more objectively.

It is almost never considered that people might actively seek out situations in which they will surely expose themselves to toxic events and probable suffering. The main exception to this assumption is found in the case of the emergency response occupations concerning public safety, health, and rescue. Workers in these occupations receive particular respect and moral approval in part because they voluntarily expose themselves to toxic events for the well-being of others. For most other people, exposures to risky or toxic events are seen as unplanned and unwanted, and those who do have such exposures are considered to be victims of unwanted forces. In both cases there is a moral overlay of virtue assigned to the person exposed to such events.

Weeping, in particular, is given special status as an index to inner feelings of suffering that reflects victimhood and virtue. A weeping person is not readily judged as being an agent of deception, evil, or aggression. Whereas among the Greeks of the classical period, a moral act was seen as something done despite it predictably leading to suffering, in our modern therapeutic culture, suffering is seen as proof of moral worth through backward reasoning because it is considered almost unimaginable that people would act in a way that would cause their own distress. Suffering thus becomes proof of heroic passage through adversity.

Sympathy is readily elicited by displays of weeping, and there are probably evolutionary roots to this, possibly concerning an increased probability of survival if tears result in help and resources from others. This aroused sympathy provides an advantage to the tearful person. At the same time, we know that tears may be shown in cases where there is no suffering, no victimhood, and no moral virtue; Hitler wept very readily, as did Ivan the Terrible, and Henry VIII. Thus, weeping may represent a ready access of sentiment and emotionality without validating the additional moral status of victimhood or virtue. Weeping is not always a representation of either. This leads us to consider what has been learned about deliberate deception in distress displays that are attributed to events.

Displays of distress can be deliberately misleading. Professional actors can provide deeply touching displays of suffering through the exercise of the art of deception, and amateurs can also do this in real-life attempts to deceive. A powerful example of the latter was provided in the 1994 case of Mrs. Susan Smith of South Carolina. She wept convincingly on television as she pleaded for an abductor to return her two missing children. The weeping she displayed was, in fact, not a display of emotions of terror and fear at the mysterious loss of her children, but was impression management to establish her moral position as a victimized mother and to decoy attention away from her own actions. Eventually, the jury concluded that she murdered her children in order to clear up her domestic arrangements so as to win more commitment from a new lover, and she was convicted of the murders (McDonough, 1995).

In sum, emotional displays do not provide good evidence of distress or well-being or, by extension, experienced trauma, moral virtue, or victimhood. Instead, they can reflect individual differences in emotionality, sentimentality, cultural values, mental disorder, personal goals, and deception. All these factors are relevant to an understanding of distress reports that are attributed to life events. Clinicians must consider these contextual factors in evaluating the validity of distress reports and by extension, in evaluating claims about toxic exposures.

HAPPINESS AND SELF-ESTEEM: HOW IMPORTANT IS IT TO FEEL GOOD?

The converse of our fascination with feeling bad is the late 20th-century adoration of feeling good—and of feeling good about oneself. Every kind of social problem is analyzed as the outgrowth of low self-esteem, the lack of feeling good about oneself. Treatment programs to teach people how to love themselves are put forward as the means of raising self-esteem. It is argued that higher self-esteem will remedy everything from children's poor school achievement to poverty in the inner city and mental illness. This reflects a naive adoption of the emotion-focused model of human experience wherein it is assumed that, if the emotions can be altered in a particular way, then behavior and the full experience of life will automatically change in desirable ways. Subjective experience is thus the center of interest, while objective factors are peripheral.

This focus on the subjective experience of happiness as the core of well-being has some parallels with different kinds of Christian thought in modern U.S. life. Until recently, in American Protestant fundamentalist thought, for example, individuals were supposed to focus on their relationship with God and not to concern themselves with poverty or other social problems. These were seen as the responsibility of secular authority. Happiness and moral ease was an experience that would derive directly from a personal relationship with God. In contrast, other streams within Protestantism and within the Liberation Theology movement of the Roman Catholic Church argued that objective conditions in the larger social community were morally and theologically important and relevant. In this view, sense of meaning in life could best be achieved through doing acts of goodness that would improve conditions for others. At times, these might involve distress, but because happiness was not the goal, distress was not seen as something to be avoided necessarily. As Simone de Beauvoir wrote of her experiences in France during the German occupation, happiness was irrelevant; larger issues were at stake (de Beauvoir, 1960/1962).

What do we know about the origins of happiness? Is it an emotion that is achieved through positive life events, therapeutic exercises, or acts of moral virtue, or is it an enduring disposition representing some kind of converse to emotional distress? What is the evidence that feel-good emotions, such as those of high self-esteem, are creators or markers of deeper well-being? Because emotions are transient states that are relatively easily manipulated, and long-term subjective well-being is not, it is suggested that the relationship between emotions and well-being is not robust, causal, or meaningful.

If a goal of therapy is to increase the feel-good emotions and to manage feelings, in what sense does this represent a valid goal? The stress and coping research of the last three decades has studied emotion-focused coping in comparison with other coping tactics to see how it might function to affect distress following events. Emotion-focused coping is behavior directed to management of feelings rather than to more objectively oriented problem-solving (Folkman & Lazarus, 1980). The use of the emotion-focused coping strategies of avoidance and wishful thinking has been shown to contribute to less effective psychosocial functioning after a traumatic injury (Malia, Powell, & Torode, 1995). At the same time, the clinical goal of psychosocial well-being may not necessarily represent a profound marker of broader condition. As noted earlier, for example, among elderly nursing home residents, those who had reported higher levels of well-being were much more likely to have died within the next 30 months than those who reported low well-being (Janoff-Bulman & Marshall, 1982).

Self-Esteem and Well-Being

High self-esteem has been propounded as a key feature of well-being and achievement for some time, yet the relation of self-esteem to more objective factors of life effectiveness is not a simple one. Recent findings suggest there may be a dark side to high self-esteem. Aggression is more frequently associated with positive self-appraisals than with low self-esteem (Baumeister, Smart, & Boden, 1996). In particular, the prototype aggressor is a man whose self-appraisal is unrealistically positive.

There is evidence that unconditional parental approval given with the intention of making children feel good and enhancing their self-esteem so they will function more effectively does not yield these results when objective assessments are done. This is true even in the case of schoolwork, where criticism of a child's work is popularly seen as a negative or traumatic life event that will attack self-esteem and in turn, harm performance.

Important evidence against this popular thinking about the constructive power of positive appraisal comes from Stevenson's major cross-national studies. He and his colleagues studied the school performance of children in the United States, Japan, and Taiwan, within the context of parental support of the children's performance (Stevenson, Lee, & Stigler, 1986). They were interested both in the actual levels of competence in such basic school tasks as mathematics and in the degree to which the children's parents expressed themselves as pleased or displeased with what their children were doing. The results provide a fascinating window through which we can grasp the imbalance embedded within the contemporary emphasis on positive emotions, in which emotional satisfaction is more important than the facts. The findings show that positive emotional appraisal and parental attitudes can be strikingly discordant with objective reality. In addition, longitudinal results show that there is no causal relationship from positive emotional parental environment to competent performance in their children.

On tests of mathematical competence, the U.S. children were behind the Asian children from a very early stage in school onward. When the Asian parents were asked how satisfied they were with the performance of their children they were generally less than satisfied. In contrast, the U.S. parents were typically very pleased with their children's performance and their schooling (Stevenson, Chen, & Lee, 1993). In follow-up studies conducted 10 years after the initial report, the U.S. parents were asked if they knew the findings of the first wave of studies. If they had not already learned of them, the parents were told the results that showed that their children were doing more poorly than the children of the other countries studied. The parents were then again asked the satisfaction questions that were posed in the first wave, concerning how satisfied they were with the performance of their children.

With great consistency, the U.S. parents again showed a pattern in which a positive emotional connection to the child's work prevailed over any recognition that the objective quality of it might be improved. In addition, although the Asian children worked longer and were under more detailed parental and school supervision as to their performance, the U.S. eleventh-grade students reported themselves as being more stressed.

These data provide a striking example of the way in which the contemporary Western emphasis on feeling good operates independently of objective performance features. Further, in contrast with popular Western belief in the importance of positive emotions and feeling good, the U.S. parental behavior of unconditional positive regard for the performance of their children was actually followed by greater reports of distress in the offspring treated in this way. The parental concern with feel-good emotions did not contribute to well-being in these children concerning their performance. One might argue that the emotionally positive parental appraisals substituted for emotions of concern that would have been more appropriate to the reality, because these feeling-focused styles were actually counterproductive in the very target condition of interest to the parents, their children feeling good.

Feelings that can contribute to changes in behavior have to emerge slowly out of encounters with difficult tasks of life that do not ignore objective circumstances, but instead engage these directly with reason and effort. In the case of distress disorders, the clinical focus on exposing, examining, and working through distress feelings may be seriously misplaced. What do we know about the factors that contribute to happiness and well-being?

DO POSITIVE EVENTS CAUSE HAPPINESS?

If toxic events do not reliably lead to clinical distress, do positive life events cause happiness? This would be expected if life events substantially determine emotional condition, as professional assumptions in the adversity–distress model predict.

There is considerable evidence from longitudinal studies within psychology that happiness or the subjective experience of well-being is remarkably independent of significant life events, whether these events are positive or toxic in nature. In a recent book, social psychologist David Myers (1993) reviewed evidence and discovered that many popular ideas, such as the assumption that traumatic life events can permanently erode happiness and that highly favorable life events can significantly improve happiness, are unfounded myths. Even highly favorable life events are not predictors of long-term happiness, and happiness depends little on external factors and accomplishments. Myers concluded that it is more important that a life is given meaning through fulfillment of core values than through a search for the feeling of happiness.

Other research has shown that, in terms of absolute levels of happiness, most people rate their subjective well-being on the positive side. This is true within the general population, within minorities disadvantaged by race or income, and within groups of people who have suffered a more targeted individual toxic event sufficient to cause permanent disability (Diener & Diener, 1996). Interestingly, when independent others (both adults in the general public as well as psychology students) were asked to estimate happiness levels in the United States, both groups overestimated depression and underestimated life satisfaction ratings. It is probably this kind of general bias, in addition to biased samples, that contributes to clinicians' general tendency to see pathology in their clients' life experiences.

One theory proposed to account for the stability of positive self-report has suggested that individuals may have a *set point* or baseline emotional stance from which life events may temporarily move them away before set point processes act to return them to the baseline (Headey & Wearing, 1992). The origins of such a set point appear to lie more in genetics than in personal circumstances such as socioeconomic status, educational achievement, family income, marital status, or religious commitment, according to a study of 2,310 twins (Lykken & Tellegen, 1996). None of these factors could account for more than 3% of the variance in happiness. Longitudinal studies over 10 years in a subset of 254 of these twins suggest that the heritability of the stable component of subjective well-being is around 80%.

In sum, studies of happiness show that most people report subjective well-being that is independent of objective realities of poverty, illness, minority status, or disability, and large twin-study evidence suggests that there is a sizable genetic component to reports of happiness.

CULTURAL TRENDS IN EMOTIONALITY AND SUBJECTIVITY

The popular emphasis on the subjective experience of emotion is a general cultural trend in modern U.S. life. In the 1996 Olympics, for example, the television coverage of the events was altered by the NBC network to include a greatly expanded volume of emotional features on the personal lives of the athletes. This was done specifically to evoke emotions and was aimed at bringing in more women viewers. It succeeded in this even though these sentimental segments displaced time that would have been spent showing the world's top athletes directly performing in the events for which they were famous. This interest in the subjective and emotional aspects of life in preference to more objective features is also developing within various academic fields of cultural analysis.

Postmodernism

Postmodernism or *deconstructionism,* is a way of thinking about the world that derives from a school of literary criticism. In this approach, in considering the meaning of a text, an event, or an observation, each personal, particular, and subjective interpretation of it is considered to be equally valid, because all are nothing more than social constructions. There is scorn for the idea of objectivity and for the value of any claim that a reality independent of the human observer can be determined. All is held to be subjective and socially constructed by the participant or observer, and thus is different for each and beyond truly knowing for anyone.

Although this exaltation of subjectivity has provided considerable entertainment in the fields of literature and politics, it cannot land anyone on the moon. That is to say, it does not provide a meaningful lens through which to study the physical world, where some models are correct and some are in error. Better models explain the world meaningfully and independently of the individuals who use or propose them. In handling the tasks of everyday life, the extreme social construction view of reality is simply set aside by everyone, because anyone who really thinks that there is no way of knowing objective reality cannot navigate a car down a freeway or make a baby.

This emphasis on the subjective has been typically set aside in the experimental fields of psychology, where research usually has the goal of trying to establish general laws of behavior and function that are universally applicable across the species. In contrast, an interest in the subjective constructions of individuals has always been part of studies in psychodynamic psychology, individual differences, and development.

The new, deconstructionist version of this interest in subjective interpretation which is debated in philosophical, political, and literary theory affects debate in individual differences psychology, taking it beyond the traditional models of personality and person-centered therapy models. In the latter models, while subjective experience was always recognized as an important human phenomenon, there was typically some interest in seeking general principles and understanding general processes that will help explain subjective experience. In that search, more objective factors have been crucial.

If there are only different, but not better or worse, models of human behavior, as argued in the postmodernist view, then the entire fields of abnormal psychology and developmental psychology, for example are impossible. If there is no way of deciding whether a condition represents mental disorder, or if mental disorder is asserted to be only a socially constructed subjective concept with no knowable objective features, or if there is no reason to describe a child's functioning as representing a failure of development, and if evidence does not matter because truth is declared to be unknowable, then trying to find the error in a hypothesis about the origins of behavior using an orderly research method does not hold any value. In the postmodernist view, the findings of such an approach would be just one other subjective view among many. This perspective does not allow for the accumulation of accurate knowledge about behavior.

In this model of understanding the world, rhetoric is the basis of authority rather than more objective evidence. This means that the model fails the crucial test of allowing us to detect error within competing models. In contrast, the whole history of improving well-being in humankind has been advanced by detecting and abandoning error in models with the help of the scientific method, which seeks increasing objectivity in understanding nature. In the case of PTSD and other distress disorders, the excessive focus on events and emotional condition as put forward by patients may lead to serious clinical errors if patients' presentations of inner subjective experience are seriously flawed. Helpful alternative explanations may not be attempted under these conditions even though attention to more objectively verifiable aspects of patients' situations may be crucial to understanding their distress.

Because emotionality and subjectivity are the subject of so much popular interest, and there is an important cultural parallel from another place and time that has had lasting influence on Western culture, I would like to digress briefly to consider this phenomenon from an even broader perspective.

An Historical Perspective: Emotions in Classical Greece

Modern therapeutic activity places an emphasis on a self-oriented emotional experience of self-realization. This has been embodied in the concept of personality, which requires a narcissistic focus in therapy. Personality is most interesting to its participants (therapists and clients) and to observers, to the extent that it concerns emotionality. Accounts of the lives of individuals, even eminent scientists, diplomats, or writers, are of more interest if they reveal complex emotional problems than if they focus on more abstract or objective contributions to human culture.

It is tempting to see parallels concerning the way that displays of emotion have become central to our ideas of what is important about life, and events in ancient Greek culture. These events led away from the balance between rationality, morality, objectivity, and passion that was central to the ideas, science, and arts of the classical period toward the exaltation of emotional extremes shown in the Hellenistic period, the era of cultural decline and decay.

The culture of ancient Greece went through a number of stages, including the great classical period that provided all of Western society with spell-binding images of the human struggle for meaning, in poetry, drama, rhetoric, and sculpture. It also provided the world with enduring observational methods with which to examine the operations of the natural and social world in order to seek improved understanding. The earlier archaic period slowly evolved into the incredibly productive period of classical Athens. In turn, this culture drifted away from outstanding accomplishment into the Hellenistic era, one that was less noble and less moral in art, as well as less rigorous and scientific in studies of nature. Superstition and cults abounded, and the deteriorating culture was signaled by an increasing emphasis on emotion in all cultural productions.

The shift from an interest in ideas, acute observation, reason, and morally heroic behavior toward emotion was reflected in sculpture, drama and literature. Sculptors began going to extreme lengths to show increasingly strong emotional expressions on the faces of the figures. The figures began to be more theatrical in quality, with increasing

transparencies in the garments, showing them as increasingly tempes-
tuous, windblown, or wet. Sculptors created more intensely emotional
figures showing deformities, anger, drunkenness, old age, childhood,
and they emphasized the particularities of racial differences and of
emotion. There was a vast explosion of luxurious gravestones with
increasingly flamboyant, theatrical qualities, exaggerating the celebrity
of the lives of the deceased to a point that these eventually had to be
outlawed.

Similarly, in drama, the dignity and authority with which Aeschylus
handled powerful emotional and moral themes by combining attention
to issues of piety, justice, and passion became increasingly distorted by
later dramatists, starting with Euripedes, who worked for more extreme
emotional effects. These changes represented a deterioration in artistic
quality and a degradation of the balance between ideas of reason, justice,
and emotions. As culture drifted into the Hellenistic period, there was
a decline of written works into sensationalistic and gossip-ridden books
which were full of oddities, the fabulous, and the exotic. There were
titillating descriptions of the wonders of the world and the oddities of
strangers in such books as Callimachus' *Customs of Barbarians* (Fox,
1986); these easily parallel the modern world of daytime trash talk
shows on television. In the deteriorated culture of Hellenistic Greece,
these artistic efforts were intended to elicit emotional responses to their
novelty rather than to stimulate more productive intellectual curiosity
or disciplined investigations.

Grotesque sentimentalism reigned rather than deep passion and
concern with goodness. The culture that in its classical period had been
fascinated with virtue and tragedy, and a culture that had vigorously
challenged the received ideas of the day with rowdy debate and skepti-
cism, became increasingly bourgeois. As individuals were being enter-
tained by the increasingly histrionic and emotional theatrical
performances, they were also being urged to speak quietly and not to
upset society by leaders such as Democritus.

By the time of the library at Alexandria in the Hellenistic period, no
one was even interested in the great texts of such early scientific
thinkers as Archimedes, although there had been no subsequent science
to displace this work. A disciplined, rigorous, and skeptical curiosity
about the objective world succumbed to a passive romantic, emotional,
and sentimental taste for exotic specifics. Rigor went out of explorations
of the natural world.

The shift in Greek culture away from the balance between rationality,
morality, and passion seen in the classical period toward the exhalation
of emotional extremes in the Hellenistic period has a parallel in shifts
within modern Western culture and professional psychology. More than
2,000 years later there was a split within the cultures of the West. The
rigor of the Enlightenment, with its emphasis on reason and its attempts

to understand nature using the increasingly orderly and precise methods of empirical science, became more divorced from popular life. In contrast, the Romantic tradition, challenging this approach, had broad appeal because it required no special skills. Western popular cultures drifted into a fascination with extremes of beauty, emotion, strangeness, oddity, and grotesquerie that signified the Romantic movement in Germany and elsewhere in Europe starting in the 18th century and extending into contemporary life.

Freud's work represents an effort to tap into this romantic stream with its focus on emotion, the bizarre, and the particular, while trying to take on some of the methods and appearance of science in order to gain professional acceptance.

SUMMARY: EMOTIONS AND LIFE

Although it seems reasonable that everyone should want to feel good all the time, this comfort-oriented model is far from explaining vast areas of human behavior in which people take initiatives that they know expose themselves to danger and risk. Sometimes these initiatives are in aid of a political or religious goal, sometimes they are part of occupational choice, and sometimes they reflect a relish for excitement or a desire for ill-gotten gains.

When toxic exposures occur under these different conditions, responses will not necessarily be those of negative emotionality and distress. The rise in professional interest in postevent distress disorders reflects our culture's great interest in emotion and can be seen as part of a larger cultural style that stresses the importance of emotions. This interest does not always take into account that emotional displays and self-reports of distress are not always valid indices of well-being. Distress displays do not necessarily signify that a person experienced a toxic event.

Further, because reports and displays of distress typically elicit caring behavior from others and an interpretation of victimhood and suffering that implies injustice, postevent distress carries an additional moral value that is not typical of other mental disorders. This moralistic evaluation further contributes to the event focus in understanding distress disorders.

Popular psychology has propagated a culture that place feeling good as the central task of life, consistent with Romantic ideas arising in the 18th century, yet evidence shows that such emotions have little relationship with other very important aspects of life, such as moral qualities or achievement. Contemporary therapeutic culture also fails to consider significant evidence that happiness or subjective well-being appears to be a stable trait with a substantial genetic aspect, even though such a recognition would have important implications for treatment.

The subjectivity at the core of self-reported distress syndromes is part of a general cultural trend away from universalism and objectivity toward particularities and subjectivity, most recently represented by the postmodernist movement in the humanities. This form of analysis is actually premodern rather than postmodern and does not allow for the possibility of progress in any kind of psychological research or cure in clinical practice because progress or cure, by definition within that system of analysis, reflects only one possible interpretation. Despite this very profound problem at the heart of the model for any notions of accumulating a science of behavior, the specific idea that beliefs or attitudes are socially constructed is a useful one for understanding the phenomenon of event-attributed distress disorders.

Emotions, whether they are negative or positive in tone, are powerfully affected by social constructions of the meaning of experience, and postevent reactions represent an important example of how individual qualities, including constructed interpretations of the meaning of events, can determine responses. Given that event-attributed distress responses reflect both long-standing temperament as well as important beliefs and attributions, how effectively can professionals help relieve individuals who report these emotions?

13

Can Professional Treatments Remedy Event-Attributed Distress?

The professional mental health model is based on the assumption that event-attributed distress in individuals can be remedied with individual professional treatment. It is also based on the assumption that event-attributed distress affecting whole communities after broader disasters can be remedied with treatment directed to groups. A huge advocacy literature has developed arguing this and outlining how it should be done. In addition, we assume that professional treatment is more effective than nonprofessional or no intervention and that treatments show dose–response relations in which more is better. Finally, we assume that prevention programs can be provided to prevent event-related distress in the future, and we argue for support for our professions to provide these prevention programs.

These assumptions about treatment all have consequences in community life. Attributions arising out of the adversity–distress model of PTSD provide the basis for civil lawsuits for money for claims that typically call for provision of professional treatment resources and punitive damage awards. As the popularity of the PTSD model spreads within the general public, claims for adversity compensation are extending beyond direct victims.

In the Canadian province of British Columbia for example, there is a Criminal Injuries Compensation Act (1979) which provides public money to victims of criminal injuries to pay for their treatment, both physical and mental. Until recently, the definition of victim included family members who were dependent upon the direct victim. Then, however, the responsible legislator announced that the Act would be changed to include a far wider range of compensable victims, after he was upset to learn that some of the members of the extended family of a murdered doctor were unable to claim compensation and treatment money under the existing rules. The definition of *victim* was thus expanded and the adversity–distress model was given increased institutional support. The question of whether treatment for postevent distress is effective was entirely unattended in this legislative effort.

DOES THERAPY HELP RELIEVE
EMOTIONAL DISTRESS IN GENERAL?

From the time of Freud until the DSM–III, the distressing emotions of anxiety and depression as classically defined by neuroticism have been the prime focus of outpatient psychological treatment. Almost the entire psychoanalytic profession earned a livelihood off working with neurotics. Treatment reasoning was that individuals who could be brought to have sufficient insight into their hidden emotional conflicts from ancient traumas could achieve relief from their unhappy emotionality in turn leading to changes in behavior and well-being. Assumptions of the benefits of psychodynamic treatments of emotional distress were sturdily entrenched among the believers until the middle of the 20th century, when empirical studies of outcome began to question therapeutic efficacy.

There is now a vast literature on the effects of psychotherapy that would be inappropriate to review here, although it is necessary to note that the topic is full of controversy despite a century of varied treatments and half a century of active investigation. Psychologist Robyn Dawes (1994) wrote an important, and at times angry, book examining therapy outcome and professional claims to expertise. He concluded that there is serious doubt about professional claims of success in achieving significant improvements in well-being. Other, more sympathetic investigations of the relationship between therapeutic process and outcome also concluded that these relationships are weak—and weakest in the research of the highest quality (Shapiro et al., 1994).

Rather than concluding that this should give cause to step back from professional treatment activities, a recent review suggested that the dose–response drug metaphor should be discarded for psychotherapy, and that we should not expect the ingredients of psychotherapy to correlate with outcome (Stiles & Shapiro, 1994). Some groups within the American Psychological Association (APA; e.g., Division 12, Clinical), are aggressively seeking to identify and promulgate intervention methods that have shown effectiveness in properly controlled experiments. The enterprise, however, still has a fragile and beleaguered air about it. Other sections of the APA, such as the Practice Directorate and the monthly newsletter, more typically focus on marketing therapy services and on reports extolling expanding professional turf claims, rather than on concerns with the evidence of effectiveness.

DOES THERAPY HELP INDIVIDUALS WITH PTSD?

If the verdict is not yet clear for the benefits of psychotherapy as a general enterprise, what about the effectiveness of psychological therapy for postevent distress disorders? There are countless reports describing treatment guidelines for effective treatment of PTSD, providing rhetoric about the value of this (van der Kolk, van der Hart, & Burbridge, 1995), and describing desirable features of professional training for those who will provide this treatment (Weiss & Marmar, 1993). Recent books discussing toxic events and stress typically include several chapters on treatment, but these are usually guidelines for suggested treatments rather than impartial reviews of treatment efficacy. Treatment advocacy has expanded further into calls for specialized therapies for those reporting secondhand traumatic distress arising out of work with individuals who directly experienced an adverse event (Harris, 1995).

Arising from the event-oriented model, the task of a therapist is seen as helping an individual to alter feelings related to the intrusive external event, recent or ancient. Much effort is directed to exposure to images of the event in this process. Behavioral, cognitive, humanist, and psychodynamic treatment approaches largely ignore enduring individual differences in temperament and beliefs from consideration in treating event-attributed distress.

Dynamic treatment approaches specific to postevent distress typically follow the argument of Lindemann's (1944) classic report on the treatment of grief: Suppressing negative and difficult emotions will contribute to pathological reactions, while open confrontation of these emotions is the mechanism through which relief will occur (Horowitz, Stinson, & Field, 1991). Behavioral approaches often make use of systematic desensitization as a gentle way of successively approaching dreaded images. Although some have advocated the use of more forceful implosion exposure methods, there has been ongoing recognition that this is a high risk strategy for events such as rape (Kilpatrick & Best, 1984).

Highly specific new treatments such as Eye Movement Desensitization (EMD; Shapiro, 1995; Vaughan et al., 1994) have been proposed and aggressively marketed as proprietary products. Anecdotal reports have been published concluding that treatment programs are appreciated by patients (Brom et al., 1993), in the absence of any controlled evidence it was effective. Well-intentioned therapists publish descriptions of post-traumatic treatment programs and argue for their value (Heiney, Dunaway, & Webster, 1995; van der Kolk et al., 1995). Recent surveys suggest that specific procedures for searching for repressed memories of ancient traumatic events have become commonplace in clinical practice in both the United States and Britain (Poole, Lindsay, Memon, & Bull, 1995).

Apart from the rhetoric of PTSD treatment, what are the results from treatment studies for postevent distress using a controlled research design ? Do individuals who report distress attributed to exposure to toxic events and who are seen in professional treatment receive a benefit from this? What is the nature of effective treatments, if they exist?

When it comes to the specific issue of treatment for PTSD, reliable evidence of benefits is limited partly because of research design limitations. Research designs must be especially sensitive to controlling for the timing of treatment after a toxic event in the absence of adequate control groups, in particular concerning claims for the efficacy of procedures in the immediate period after an event. In the case of rape, for example, substantial improvement in symptoms takes place without treatment (Kilpatrick & Calhoun, 1988). From evidence concerning the natural history of changes across time in postevent symptoms, we should expect symptom decrease across time as a general rule following all toxic events if the event-focused model of PTSD has any validity.

There are other aspects of PTSD that provide complications in the evaluation of treatment effectiveness. The standard treatment focus on the primacy of the event and its necessary impact has been criticized by those who point out that severe events can have very different meanings in different cultural circumstances and that these differences have major treatment implications. Because severely toxic events are not necessarily followed by emotional distress, when the adversity–distress model calling for treatment is insisted on, individuals may end up more harmed as a result of enforced conformity to a pathology model.When an individual has been mutilated or tortured for transcendent political or religious reasons, for example, not only are there cases where there is no emotional pathology, but such individuals often actively construe their situation as positive because they have directly participated in extremely meaningful and important events. Any attempt to treat them requires pathologizing their emotional condition, which alters the meaning of their experiences (Bracken et al., 1995). In such situations, treatment creates pathology rather than remedying it.

Other problems have been identified in treatment attempting to remedy emotional distress arising out of such deliberate mistreatment. For these kinds of events, there is one strain of therapeutic argument advocating that individuals should be treated through initiating public testimony or other forms of open confrontation against those who caused their suffering (Agger & Jensen, 1993; Cienfuegos & Monelli, 1983). This is consistent with a therapeutic focus on attributions of external cause that also seeks to assign moral blame. Actual evidence is not convincing, and there are cases where this treatment approach has been actively harmful (Kozaric-Kovacic, Folnegovic-Smalc, Skrinjaric, Szajnberg, & Marusic, 1995; Watson, Tuorila, Detra, Gearhart, & Wielkiewicz, 1995).

Professional therapy models often require that survivors of toxic events should be helped to work through emotional responses such as self- blame and denial, because the prevailing personality model defines these as maladaptive. Despite this, research has begun is beginning to show that these emotional responses often function as recovery strategies that help people re-establish a sense of agency and control (Janoff-Bulman, 1992).

Reviews of PTSD Treatment Outcome

Generally, results from acceptably designed studies of conventional treatment protocols directed to postevent distress show limited effects. In one typical treatment study of U.S. Vietnam veterans that included a number of control groups, for example, 52% of patients tracked at four-week intervals stayed essentially the same (39%) or showed increases in symptoms by discharge (Hammarberg & Silver, 1994). At 1-year follow-up there was a return to pretreatment levels among those who had completed the treatment program. Treatment programs occasionally report good levels of success but contain so many different components that it is hard to identify which may be effective, such as in the brief but comprehensive early-intervention programs directed by Edna Foa (Foa, Hearst-Ikeda, & Perry, 1995). Studies often find that there is a significant decrease in symptoms across time with no treatment (Green et al., 1994) or that the passage of time is more important for recovery than treatment (Galante & Foa, 1987).

Literature reviews of the evidence of individual psychotherapy for PTSD often note that while most forms of therapy have been proposed, there is not much sophisticated outcome literature and few validated conclusions. While concluding this, McFarlane (1994) also noted that some procedures such as exposure and cognitive reworking of distressing thoughts and emotions seemed to be critical components of effective outcome, whereas simply talking about the event was not sufficient. He also found that individual differences played a significant role in outcome, beyond treatment procedure.

The effects of treatment on combat-related trauma have also been reviewed. Solomon and Shalev (1995) reviewed treatment studies and their own experience with victims of military trauma and concluded that PTSD was highly resistant to treatment, although behavioral treatments had some effects on symptoms. In their experience with the ambitious Koach project in the Israeli Defense Forces, they found that those who participated in the treatment program were worse than a control group nine months later (Z. Solomon et al., 1992). The program combined education, cognitive treatment, and behavioral exposure to stimuli and actions within a sheltered residential setting. Another review of combat-related PTSD concluded that while certain kinds of exposure methods showed benefits on the heightened emotionality symptoms in comparison with other treatments or wait-list controls, there was still need for additional treatment tactics to address the more hidden negative symptoms such avoidance and emotional numbing (Frueh, Turner, & Beidel, 1995).

Despite all the treatment advocacy, well-designed studies of treatments for PTSD are still rare. A formal, quantitative meta-analysis of PTSD treatment effects initially examined 255 studies and found that only 11 met reasonable research design criteria (S. Solomon, Gerrity, & Muff, 1992). This review found that (mostly antidepressant) drugs showed a modest but clinically meaningful effect and that behavioral treatments improved some symptoms. Interestingly, two out of the six behavioral studies focused on anxiety reduction, whereas four out of the six used anxiety induction through flooding and achieved stronger effects, although this latter method was also associated with increased risks of severe complications.

In a review of empirically validated treatments done by the Clinical Division of the American Psychological Association (Chambless et al., 1996), the best-supported treatments for PTSD (exposure, stress inoculation training) still failed to meet their criteria for "well-established," which required at least two studies meeting basic research design criteria. Instead, these treatments were graded as "probably efficacious." It appears that we are some distance from reliably being able to prescribe specific effective remedies for the emotional distress responses that people report linking with adverse events. If Headey and Wearing's (1992) set-point model of emotional stance is a good fit to data, then it may be relatively difficult to permanently change individuals' baseline levels of emotionality, although it may be useful to help individuals understand their own set-point level. In contrast, socially constructed beliefs about the meanings of toxic events should be more amenable to change.

ARE PROFESSIONALS BETTER THERAPISTS THAN NONPROFESSIONALS?

Are MH professionals better at helping people recover from postevent distress than untrained helpers? Professionals assume that their training provides skills that increase the effectiveness of treatments for events affecting individuals and even whole communities. Because of this assumption, when a community suffers from some intrusive toxic event, teams of MH professionals are commonly formed and sent in to provide professional services. What is the evidence concerning this assumption?

There is a long literature examining the relative efficacy of professional MH therapy in comparison with more informal help from nonprofessionals, and it has been hard to demonstrate the superiority of professionals. Christensen and Jacobson (1994) recently reviewed evidence concerning the efficacy of nonprofessional therapists, examining many large previous reviews. They concluded that "up to now the evidence strongly suggests that under many if not most conditions, paraprofessionals or professionals with limited experience perform as well as or better than professionally trained psychotherapists. Professional training and clinical experience may not add to the efficacy of psychotherapy" (p. 10). When they reviewed studies of self-administered treatment, they found that the outcome achieved was comparable in effect sizes to that achieved with professional treatments. They concluded that future psychotherapy research should explicitly address comparisons of professional and nonprofessional treatments. In particular, they noted that there is a key difference in the principle underlying nonprofessional, self-administered treatments, which posits that helping another person also helps the helper achieve an increased sense of autonomy and empowerment. By definition, this is different from the process in which an expert is consulted.

Professionals Versus Nonprofessionals and PTSD Treatment

In the case of the treatment of postevent distress disorders, a similar issue was raised by John McKnight, Director of the Urban Affairs and Policy Research Institute at Northwestern University in Chicago (1994). As an example of the problem he saw in the use of professionals for treatments following distressing life events, he described a Master's degree program at the University of Minnesota designed to train and certify professional bereavement counselors. The promoters of the training program apparently made the argument that there are a number of recognized stages bereaved individuals must experience in order to complete a successful bereavement process. They argued that, without specialized professional help, most bereaved individuals do not complete all of these necessary stages and remain in a condition of postbereavement distress. This proved that it was necessary to have specialized workers who could go to the newly bereaved and help them successfully complete the passage of all the proper stages. On the basis of this argument the university program was created, and the state of Minnesota accepted the credentials generated by the program as the appropriate certificate for "certified bereavement counselors."

McKnight observed that the freshly invented bereavement professionals saw their proper role as inserting themselves into the lives of newly bereaved. He argued against this, with the view that this was not only not helpful or simply neutral in its consequences, but actively harmful for several reasons. The intrusion of strangers actively destroyed the normal human experience in which the bereaved reconnect with family and friends. Bereavement represented a life event that could have been the basis of much mutual support and aid, as well as the basis of an intensified experience of community and social support from those close to the bereaved. Instead, it was turned into a more impersonal situation regulated by a stranger. McKnight noted that professionals come with different values, and these may be actively discordant and intrusive, rather than simply useless.

Another problem with the bereavement counselor plan was that the argument was based on the poorly validated model of human emotional experience derived from observations by Elizabeth Kübler-Ross (1969). This stage model, initially about the stages of dying, was picked up in New Age popular psychology and turned into an industry asserting that certain kinds of professionally assisted grief work are necessary in order for individuals to recover from high-grief deaths (e.g., unanticipated deaths; Lindemann, 1944), to avoid the risk of suffering prolonged morbid grief. Other theorists have applied similar stage models to other adverse events, such as disasters, outlining the stages of a disaster and the stages of human emotional response to it (Shader & Schwartz, 1966).

This continues a tradition of stage models in psychology, including Piaget's developmental studies of cognition (Iinhelder & Piaget, 1964) and Kohlberg's stage model of the development of moral thinking (Kohlberg, 1981). Such stage models have been subjected to much empirical testing and, in the domains of adult social behavior, do not appear to have led to any consensus as to their validity. Of specific relevance to postevent distress, careful examination of the evidence underlying stage theory assumptions about responses to loss has shown that these are not supported, and responses to loss events are highly variable (Wortman & Silver, 1987). Stage models thus appear to be ill-matched to the data of postevent distress, and there is little evidence that the event-focused PTSD model provides any better basis for effective treatments.

HOW EFFECTIVE ARE MENTAL HEALTH PROFESSIONALS AFTER COMMUNITY DISASTERS ?

Some years ago, when the professionalization of community disasters was in its early stages, Brenton (1975) complained about government response to disaster. Government agencies providing direct concrete assistance pulled out after 6 to 8 weeks, and all that the community was left with was "buck-passing" once the bureaucracy took over, with increasing complaints. He recommended that there should be psychological first-aid teams immediately after a disaster. Since Brenton's time, formal training programs in community mental health first aid have developed, a disaster response network has been established within psychology, and there is a now sizable literature on community-oriented mental health counseling after disasters.

At the community level it is now assumed that when disaster strikes a community, specialized teams of professionals must be brought in to help all survivors, who are "in danger of developing extremely severe post-traumatic stress disorder" (De Clercq, 1995, p. 19). The disaster literature is replete with calls for more disaster training of mental health personnel, creation of disaster counseling services, rhetoric outlining desirable features of postevent debriefing (Everly, 1995), and professional turf claims over which MH profession is best suited for this kind of work (Bell, 1995). Recommendations for the provision of disaster counseling often appear as the final element in articles reporting studies of the aftermath of disasters (Canino et al., 1990; Rosser et al., 1991). The actual provision of such services, at times, reaches extravagant proportions as in the case of 18 survivors of a sea collision in the U.S. Coast Guard. They, along with family members and friends, were provided with 264 treatment meetings over 12 days in the aftermath of the event (McCaughey, 1984).

Countless examples of professional mental health intervention into communities following adverse events can be read in the daily newspapers. Recent examples of this intervention at work in my home province of British Columbia have been demonstrated following a natural disaster, the discovery of a pedophile school teacher, and the violent death of a teenager. A few years ago, the government sent in a professional counseling team for a whole town in the mountains after it was established that a popular school principal had made sexual use of the children under his care. In another case, a teenage girl died a violent death in a suburb; once the nature of her death was clearly established the provincial government again rushed in a group of professionals to help counsel her schoolmates, her teachers, and the parents of her schoolmates, to help them work through their emotions. Interviews with weeping students were put on prime-time TV news, and, in these interviews, the events were construed in such a way that florid emotional displays were expected and were reliably elicited. In focusing on these emotional outpourings, the television coverage implicitly suggested that these were normal responses and implied that professional help was needed to help the children and adults recover to a better emotional condition.

In another example, in the winter of 1994, eight Inuit (Eskimo) hunters known for their expertise in Arctic waters were lost at sea, and their small community was devastated by their loss. Immediately, the government of the Northwest Territories packed up a planeload of mental health professionals from more southerly urban centers to help the community work through its grief. If a government refused to initiate these kinds of professional treatments, popular opinion would decry this as cruel, unfeeling, and irresponsible.

In the United States, both the American Psychological Association and the American Red Cross have encouraged the states to develop networks of psychologists trained to provide short-term services at the scene of a disaster, both to disaster victims and relief workers. As of 1993, 41 states and provinces had begun to do this (Vernberg & Vogel, 1993).

This popular professional treatment model generated some additional critical appraisal from John McKnight. He examined the assumptions underlying professional community-directed response programs after community-wide toxic events from a rational and observational perspective (McKnight, 1994). He concluded that professional management of adversity is not helpful, but rather is actively harming community well-being. He argued that, as a result of the professional perspective, individuals in a community lose their chances to struggle and help each other, lose their sense of community and sense of involvement, and the extremely important social bonds essential for community life become loosened. The presence of strangers weakens the capacity of the community to grapple with its problems, and diminishes the likelihood that members of the community will develop leadership or new skills. The insertion of professionals gives a deep message that the community is incapable of helping itself and that only outsiders have the skills to deal with the aroused feelings. In sum, McKnight argued that the rush to pump strangers—who are there because they are professionals—into a community when difficulties arise, can be actively harmful to the community.

In light of the powerful popular and clinical rhetoric about the importance or harmfulness of professional MH interventions following community disasters, what does the evidence show? Because a toxic life event will cause emotional disorder of a clinical magnitude only within a small subset of exposed individuals, it appears that recovery of well-being typically occurs without professional interventions. How does this compare to the effectiveness of formal professional therapy, which, as noted earlier, has not yet identified a treatment of choice for postevent distress disorders?

There is evidence that professional interventions may be less productive than self-generated recovery processes, which more often center on topics quite different from the emotion-focus of MH therapy. In describing the most important part of the recovery of Ugandan women from rape in war, for example, observers found that the women were most interested in organizing group meetings that focused on economic development projects, not on their experiences of rape (Bracken et al., 1995). In a report concerning the effects of political repression on children in South Africa and the role of MH professionals, Swartz and Levett (1989) concluded that "progressive professionals are generally not interested in reproducing the elite and alienating excess of a mental health industry which is based on assumptions of the type that people respond to hardship with psychopathology, which, in turn, needs to be treated by experts" (p. 741).

When treatment studies are well-designed to include no-treatment controls, the evidence suggests that natural recovery leads to outcomes equally beneficial as well-run professional treatments. In a treatment study reported at the 1996 meetings of the American Psychological Association, Australian psychologist Brett McDermott described an energetic, creative, and rational treatment program provided to children whose lives had been severely disrupted by the massive bushfires of 1994 in New South Wales (McDermott, 1996). Of importance, it was done as an experiment with random assignment of children to active and control conditions. All schools did critical incident debriefing; after 6 months, children were screened to identify those most in need of help. Over the next 8 months, half of these children received active treatment including the use of an innovative workbook that the younger children could complete with the help of their parents. At the conclusion of the treatment program, 90% of the parents expressed satisfaction with it, and 78% of the children reported it helped them a little or a lot. Nevertheless, when compared with the untreated control group, there were no differences on symptom rates for any aspects of anxiety or depression, which were very low. McDermott concluded that he was not actually surprised by the results because the students did not have much risk based on pre-event characteristics. This was a beautifully conducted piece of treatment research, with children randomly assigned to the two groups, careful measurements, and well-designed treatments, yet treatment provided no advantage. Instead, pre-existing attributes of the children accounted for natural recovery to the low rates of distress that were seen 14 months after the fire.

What about help from nonprofessionals? Support from the individual's own social network greatly aids when disaster strikes (Boman, 1979). A study of tornado victims in 1975 in Nebraska found that those who handled the event best preferred to use informal support structures rather than government services (Bell, 1978). Similarly, a study of the survivors of a massive flood in South Dakota in 1972 found that the best outcome was found in survivors who made high use of kinship ties; the only beneficial effects associated with government services was in the concrete matter of housing (Bolin, 1976).

In the Australian bush fires of 1983, where professional mental health disaster workers used a crisis intervention approach and a grief model for treatment (focusing on the meaning of the event), fire victims apparently found this professional attention aversive enough to lead to premature terminations of contact even when distress was present and increasing (McFarlane, 1990). McFarlane noted that people preferred to use their normal primary health network, and recommended that mental health professionals might best direct their efforts to educating front-line workers and the general public rather than to treatment.

It appears that family and friends perform other functions in a way superior to professional services as well. For example, in a massive flood in Denver, Colorado in 1965, people did not attend to government warnings until they heard confirmatory information from friends and family, then the families evacuated as whole units, mostly to homes of relatives and friends rather than to government-established disaster shelters (Drabek & Boggs, 1968). Other disasters have similarly shown that psychological support was provided far more usefully through linkages with family and friends than with professional helpers. Victims of a tornado in Kansas in 1966 reported strengthening their relationships with relatives as a result of the disaster, and these nonprofessional interactions were associated with recovery (Drabek, Key, Erickson, & Crowe, 1975).

When a community is hit by a disaster, such as an earthquake, flood, or fire, what is both normal and truly remarkable is the ability of the survivors to create order from chaos. Arvidson (1969) studied the Alaskan earthquake of 1964 and descriptions of behavior following the San Francisco earthquake of 1906 and observed the almost universal equanimity of the response of individuals to the effects of the earthquakes. Similarly, after the great Johnstown flood near Pittsburgh at the turn of the century, the most striking aspect of the period after the flood was the calmness and efficiency with which the survivors responded. The entire town, including homes and steel mills, was destroyed, with great loss of life and property, yet within hours the survivors had organized work teams and begun the dreadful business of dealing with the dead, with the pollution, and the wreckage. These teams set about re-establishing order, attending to the injured, and rebuilding the community. There were no outside helpers or specialists, just survivors working with each other in a great communal struggle to recreate their village through exercise of an integrated community of spirit and effort.

These examples do not directly compare the efficacy of professional and nonprofessional recovery methods but they do provide examples that show that remarkable recovery can occur in the absence of professional efforts. The examples also suggest there are meaningful reasons why nonprofessional remedies may be superior in influencing well-being after disaster strikes a community. Evidence supporting this was reviewed in a recent book about disasters (Ursano, McCaughey, & Fuller-ton, 1994). The authors concluded that self-help groups are probably the most important means of community recovery because they represent a known social structure. If enduring individual adaptive skills are significant determinants of emotional condition, it may be that most individuals emerge from toxic community events in better general condition if they are not put into the constraints of a passive condition of waiting for resources to be provided by external agents.

IS THERE A DOSE–RESPONSE EFFECT FOR THERAPY IN WHICH MORE IS BETTER?

The psychoanalytic model of therapy that has encompassed the Western world across most of this century has been based on an assumption that there is no particular limit to the time required for benefits. By midcentury it was common for affluent urban individuals to enter into dynamic therapy that continued for years. Film personalities Woody Allen and Mia Farrow have each been in therapy for much of their adult lifetimes, and several of their children started therapy long before they were of school age. A senior psychotherapist recently urged ongoing personal therapy for dealing with "personal crud, forever," in addressing aspiring therapists (Maher, 1995).

This assumption is based on a dose–response model in which, if a little is good, then more is obviously better. It fails, however, to pay attention to the ancient dictum from Paracelsus in the Middle Ages: "It's the dose that makes the poison." He understood clearly that any agent that has genuine effects may heal in one dose but harm if more is given. Although this principle is still not accepted in Chinese traditional medicine (which incorrectly asserts that even if a medicine does not work it can do no harm), in fact Paracelsus' principle holds true for virtually every kind of biologically active exposure that organisms can encounter. It holds true for medicines, radiation, and for every kind of food and drink. Even water can kill if the dose is too high, and there are documented cases of psychiatric patients who were dipsomaniacs for water, dying of the electrolyte imbalance created by their excessive water intake. The assumption that more and longer therapy is better than less defies this principle every bit as much as Chinese traditional medicine does; nevertheless it has been pervasive with MH professionals with a psychodynamic orientation. Is there any evidence showing that more therapy is better than less?

There is a growing literature suggesting that the dose–response model may be inappropriate when applied to psychotherapy for distress disorders. Most outpatient therapy is done for conditions that represent negative emotionality of the type that is at the heart of event-attributed distress disorders, thus general therapy outcome studies have some degree of relevance for postevent symptoms. Years ago, a very interesting study was reported by English psychiatrists, analyzing positive psychodynamic changes reported in neurotic patients who had not received any treatment after an initial screening interview (Malan, Heath, Bacal, & Balfour, 1975). They discovered that the single screening interview led to significant positive changes in this population. Possibly because this contradicted the professional beliefs of the day, this report quickly vanished into obscurity.

Of eight psychotherapy studies examined for duration effects in a famous early review, five found no differences in efficacy comparing time-limited or time-unlimited, two found better results with time-limited, and only one found better results with time-unlimited psychotherapy (Luborsky, Singer, & Luborsky, 1975). By the early 1980s, additional evidence began to accumulate from more well-controlled studies that brief therapy could not only prove effective in reducing medical utilization, it was even better than long-term and more frequent treatment for a specific group of interminable patients (Cummings & VandenBos, 1981).

During the 1980s, meta-analyses of collections of studies of psychotherapy outcome began to be published, as statistical treatments for managing these developed, and duration effects were studied. The first major meta-analysis of psychotherapy found only a weak curvilinear correlation between treatment effect sizes and the duration of therapy (Smith, Glass, & Miller, 1980). There were two time periods that showed better outcome (Week 8 and, to a lesser degree, Week 20), but, in general, as treatments moved beyond Week 8 to Week 12, the size of treatment effects was cut in half. Shapiro and Shapiro (1982) did a meta-analysis of 143 treatment outcome studies and found no significant linear relation between duration and effect. A more recent single study found no differences in outcome comparing 8-week to 16-week treatments (Shapiro & Barkham, 1990).

In a recent review of duration and outcome in psychotherapy, Steenbarger (1994) concluded that "meaningful and enduring change can occur within the context of brief—and sometimes very brief—interventions" (p. 111). He found that relatively few studies had directly addressed the issue of duration of treatment. Of those that had, these "generally failed to demonstrate the incremental efficacy of lengthier, time-unlimited treatments" (p. 111). If there is any benefit from professional therapy, it seems likely that an inverse-U curve describes the relationship between duration of therapy and outcome, just as we would expect from Parcelsus' ancient law.

Despite the mounting evidence questioning the assumption that more therapy is better than less, U.S. dynamic therapists showed very little interest in time-limited therapy until very recent times. It is not clear if this shift is based on outcome evidence or new principles, or if it has arisen from changes in payment accessibility under the emerging intrusion of insurance companies into managing profits in U.S. health care. (A key feature of these financial arrangements is that interminable therapy will not be paid for, whereas short-term therapy will be.)

In association with this sudden economic change, the American Psychological Association newsletter, the Monitor, now frequently includes articles concerning how to get in on managed care reimbursement programs through creating brief therapy programs. Psychologists are being sold books describing how to document the effects of therapy so that bureaucrats in the big insurance companies can be persuaded that investing in therapy services will actually provide a cost benefit in improved functioning. New books are emerging on brief therapy, and a new journal has just been started, called *Crisis Intervention and Time-Limited Treatment*. The advertising blurb states, "Crisis intervention and time-limited treatment have become the treatment of choice in a large number of human service, criminal justice, health and mental health settings." It is worth noting that they did not say "in private practice settings," suggesting that it is mainly economic pressures that are driving the shift to briefer treatment, rather than evidence from studies of treatment outcome.

Although it is true that not all psychodynamic therapists ignored briefer kinds of therapy, and there have always been a few individuals within the paradigm who have advocated and experimented with brief therapy, these were always the outliers and the mavericks rather than the mainstream. It appears that the mainstream is changing now only because of the possible losses of income from traditional sources and because of the possibility of fresh sources of income. The evidence from clinical research has long suggested some value for various kinds of brief therapy.

ARE PREVENTION PROGRAMS EFFECTIVE FOR LATER TOXIC EVENTS?

In light of the fragile evidence of treatment effectiveness for distressed emotional condition, can professionals perform a more reliably useful service by providing prevention programs that will be effective in mitigating later effects of toxic events?

By the mid 1980s, the concept of *stress inoculation training* was recommended within the behavioral literature, as a parallel with medical immunizations. The idea was to increase hardiness as a preventive against future distress from adverse events or as a treatment following an adverse event such as rape (Kilpatrick, Veronen, & Resick, 1982). There is also a literature advocating the use of stress during training as a preventative against war-induced posttraumatic stress disorder

(Armfield, 1994). This inoculation concept is directly contrary to the standard professional model of a dose–response relationship between adversity exposure and distress, which would predict increasing distress with increasing exposure. In contrast, it is consistent with a more biological model of habituation, which would predict that repeated exposures to alarming stimuli should lead to decreases in responsivity. To the extent that prevention programs attempt to replicate the dreaded event with many repetitions so as to decrease arousal, they could provide a test of the biological model, but I am not aware of any prevention programs that do this.

The usual professional approach to prevention emphasizes a more educational approach in which possible events are discussed and effective responses are rehearsed. An example of this was provided in a retrospective analysis reviewing a professional lifetime observing humans under high stress conditions of war and natural disasters. Researchers (Minkowski, Morisseau, Marciano, & Hurau, 1993) observed that the behavior of children in war-torn Vietnam was highly different depending on whether the children were living in the North where elaborate protective drills were constantly practiced and mental health was excellent, or in the South where no orderly prevention was practiced and where profound mental distress was extremely frequent. What is the evidence about the value of prevention programs, either through deliberate toxic exposures or through general education directed to responses, when it is studied in a more controlled manner?

One kind of possible preparation for toxic events is the experience of having had the same event previously. In the case of MH professionals, the limited evidence about pre-event experience with similar events suggests it is not very helpful. Lundin and Bodegard (1993) studied Swedish emergency earthquake workers recruited on short notice to help in the Armenian earthquake. They found that professionals who had a past experience of disaster work reported significantly more unpleasant feelings during their first week on site than inexperienced volunteers. Although this effect was reversed at nine months, the inexperienced group did not show any rise in unpleasant symptoms at the later date, and actual symptom reports of professionals and nonprofessionals did not differ in the end.

Another kind of prevention programming consists of educational efforts directed to the general public. A study of the effects of predisaster education on adults after Hurricane Hugo in comparison with untrained controls found that disaster education experience was associated with increased levels of stress, as measured both by psychophysiological and psychological criteria (Faupel & Styles, 1993). A prediction of an earthquake disaster to schoolchildren as a means of helping them prepare for it contributed to increased emotional distress (widespread appearance of PTSD symptoms), rather than to increased feelings of competence

(Kiser et al., 1993). Nor do MH prevention programs for children concerning sexual abuse show any convincing evidence of efficacy (Reppucci & Haugaard, 1989).

On a much more long-term basis, a longitudinal study of the effects of preventative treatments on a large mixed group of young boys including those at high risk for delinquency, all living in a difficult urban environment, found that preventative interventions had no beneficial effects over a 30-year period (McCord, 1978). Further, it found considerable evidence of negative effects. Men in the treatment and control groups (totaling 506) did not show differences in disorders often linked to stressful life events, such as juvenile and adult crime rates, treatment for alcoholism, or premature death. Similarly, they showed no significant differences on outcomes reflecting well-being, such as marriage rates, parenting rates, occupational achievements, and work satisfaction (if they were professionals). Moreover, these rates were similar for boys within each group whether they had early been identified as being difficult and at high risk or as being average.

Unfortunately, the boys in the treatment group did show worse outcomes on a number of important indicators. They were more likely to commit a second crime, meet criteria for alcoholism, have stress-related diseases, have serious mental illness, die younger, have occupations with lower prestige, and report their work was not satisfying if they were blue-collar workers. All those in the treatment condition had received five years of biweekly meetings, more than half received additional academic tutoring, about half received medical or psychiatric attention, and sizable proportions were sent to summer camps and other active community programs for boys. Of those who remembered their participation 30 years later, nearly all remembered it favorably. Had these subjective evaluations been the sole form of scrutiny, the program would have been judged as a success. Not only was this not the case when more objective data were studied, but, in subsequent analyses of additional data, it became clear that the treated group was still worse off on a number of additional important indicators (McCord, 1979).

SUMMARY: EFFECTS OF TREATMENT

Professional psychotherapy for long-term or event-attributed emotional distress does not appear to have reliable or powerful effects. There is little good evidence that professionals achieve better outcome than others, either in the treatment of individuals or in helping communities. There is little replicated evidence that specific treatments for PTSD have reached a stage in which therapists will be effective if they follow specified procedures. There is little support for the professional assumption that therapy of a longer duration achieves better outcomes than brief therapy. Prevention programs, whether focused on stress exposure or on response training, appear to have highly variable effects, and there is not yet an established method that will reliably and significantly improve the responses of individuals who confront toxic events. Overall, most of the professional mental health assumptions about the value of psychotherapy in general, or about the value of prevention or treatment of postevent distress disorders in particular, are not well supported by evidence.

14

Conclusion and Implications

The prevailing model used by clinical psychologists, psychiatrists, and other MH professionals predicts that toxic events will normally trigger clinically significant distress symptoms in a dose–response manner. This event-focused model is very poorly supported by the evidence. When prospective and representative samples are followed, most people do not respond to toxic events with serious and long-term distress disorders in the way that is assumed to be a normal, traumatic response in both professional and popular models. Toxic events occur in very high frequencies even in civilian life in peacetime, yet this high prevalence is not matched by high prevalence rates for event-attributed distress disorders such as Acute Stress Disorder and PTSD. The lifetime prevalence of PTSD symptoms and fresh incidence rates of PTSD after a toxic event are both quite low and do not represent a majority response. When we study large samples exposed to common adversity, distress reports of clinical magnitude are not predictable and normative, but instead represent minority responses. Various intensities of exposure to toxic events do not reliably show the central features of a dose–response relationship, in that most exposed individuals do not report significant acute or chronic or delayed distress condition, while some individuals with minimal or even vicarious exposure do report significant distress that is ascribed to events.

It appears that adversity dose of toxic life experiences typically accounts for something less than 10% of the subjective symptoms of emotional distress (Byrne, 1984; McFarlane, 1987; Miller & Ingham, 1979). People respond to acute events with great individual variability which arises mostly from individual differences in long-standing qualities. The most important of these are long-standing traits of emotionality and general belief systems. Most people show short-lived distress that is not clinically significant, then recover, showing resilience and adaptation. A small percentage show event-attributed distress syndromes of clinical magnitude, a different small proportion show highly idiosyncratic responses including exhilaration or gains in confidence, and some show event-attributed distress syndromes in the absence of any significant exposure. These individual differences mean that postevent symptom reports need to be understood more in the context of long-standing features of temperament and individual beliefs than is provided for in the event-oriented model.

The gap between the prevalence of toxic exposures and the prevalence and incidence of clinically significant distress disorder is customarily studied in the stress and coping literature and in the health psychology literature through moderator variables including personality traits, coping, and social support. The role of beliefs or attributions in affecting thoughts and behavior has been examined within social psychology in the 1970s and the 1980s. The important ways in which individuals differ in major pre-event psychological characteristics have been intensively studied in personality research. The genetic contributions to long-tern negative emotionality have been studied in twin studies. These literatures have had little impact upon the thinking of mental health professionals in clinical practice for postevent distress disorders.

In contrast to the poor evidence in support of an event-oriented model, there is considerable evidence that long-standing individual differences in important psychological characteristics determine most of the response after exposure to a toxic event. When both event and pre-event individual factors are included in studying postevent responses, individual difference account for more of the variance in response than event features do. These individual characteristics include past behavior, disorders, acts, emotionality, cognitive competency, beliefs, and values.

WHY IS THE EVENT-FOCUSED MODEL
SO PERSISTENT?

The persistence of the idea that a toxic event is the main factor accounting for the development of distress syndromes can be explained through a number of factors. One is the obvious fact that distress arises after an event and another is the ready availability of images of the event in the thoughts of the person. But these obvious features conceal a much more complex event that requires more explanation, for most people do not develop the clinical syndrome of PTSD after a toxic exposure.

The greatest source of the erroneous popular and professional emphasis on toxic events arises from long-standing models that were developed from biased samples using the fallacious reasoning described as the *availability bias* (Dawes, 1994). In this, the features found in a sample of cases that are conveniently clinically available are erroneously taken to represent features that will also be typical of the general population. In the case of the event–distress model of PTSD, the availability bias means that because distressed people seeking treatment may often report a definable toxic event as the origin of their distress, through fallacious backward reasoning it is concluded that it did cause the symptoms and that these symptoms are to be expected in everyone facing the same event.

A recent study concerning war-attributed distress syndromes provides an example of this biased base rate problem. PTSD was "found in high prevalence in all subgroups" (Sutker & Allain, 1996, p. 18). The sample consisted of volunteer veterans who were explicitly targeted for evaluations arising out of POW experience and of volunteers solicited to a project studying the impact of military trauma. The authors commented in two short sentences on the possibility of sample bias yet went on to stress their findings of "increased rates of mental disorder and PTSD, reflecting war trauma residuals" (p. 24). Measures of premilitary individual differences in cognitive competence, behavior, or personality were not examined, and the bias of the sample was apparently discounted without further concern. The high rates, however, do not represent the basic combat and POW population.

Cognitive social psychologists Tversky and Kahneman (1974) have found that the availability bias is especially quick to operate if a problem matches a stereotype. People do have stereotypes about the significant harm that is to be expected when others encounter adversity, and the predicted harm is greater than their own past or expected responses. In the case of PTSD, not only is there a powerful stereotype, but major theories of behavior further justify biased stereotypical generalizations of significant harm.

The event-focused model also persists because of biases and errors in attribution which are found alike in clinical and popular thinking. Finally, the model persists because of political pressures arising from groups of individuals who attribute their difficulties with life to specific events for which others can be blamed. In turn, these pressures are compatible with professional guild interests. At times, this political power factor is part of a quest for compensation, and this raises the question of the validity of attributions.

IMPLICATIONS FOR ASSESSMENT AND TREATMENT

The flawed emphasis upon the event in the adversity–distress model contributes to a set of false beliefs in which florid emotional disarray and long-term disorder is increasingly regarded as a normal human response to adversity. This idea represents a social construction that exaggerates the meaning and power of life events. To the extent that this assumption is incorrect, it impairs the ability of clinicians to help individuals who seek treatment for distress disorders. Recognition of the importance of individual differences in contributing to postevent distress reactions has implications for the roles of MH professionals in postevent distress. It also has implications for the diagnostic criteria in general, as well as in the diagnosis and treatment of individual cases.

Professional Intervention and Toxic Events

Mental health professions gain power if they are successful within the wider community in constructing a model of experience that calls for their services. A recent book described the way in which the profession of social work in the United States gained power by constructing a certain view of unwed mothers across the first half of this century (Kunzel, 1994). McKnight's (1994) thesis about the risks of profession-alizing community life is a challenging one because it goes counter to the major modern trend about the role of mental health professionals in North American life.

This trend toward gaining professional power has been accompanied and aided by an increasingly entrenched family of assumptions about human behavior. These assumptions directly contribute to the advance-ment of MH professional interests that risk becoming market oriented rather than service oriented. Apart from the increasing evidence of commercial fraud and abuse arising within the professions from this market orientation (Ulicny, 1994), the more basic questioning of the assumptions that lie underneath even very well-intentioned profes-sional activities is rarely addressed. An event-oriented model of postevent distress contributes to rhetoric calling for more professional mental health services to deal with these distress reports. The enlarged customer base for professional clinicians arising from this includes both mental health clinical services and expert witness testimony in large civil damage lawsuits and insurance cases.

Professionals need to understand the way the adversity–distress model might create biased belief systems in patients that will contribute to an increased incidence of emotional problems. There is a serious risk in accepting a flawed model, and there are specific clinical implications of the flaws in the current model.

Diagnostic Implications

Long-standing traits and beliefs provide resilience or vulnerability to life events. Therefore, the diagnostic criteria of PTSD appear to contain a significantly incorrect emphasis on a target event or experience. Those people who respond with clinical levels of impairment will be better understood if important individual pre-event behavior and traits are incorporated into diagnostic evaluations and criteria.

The classical diathesis–stress model needs to be taken more seriously in understanding the development of event-attributed syndromes. Using a metaphor from medicine adapted from a suggestion by a colleague, it may be useful to think of two individuals exposed to malaria. The person who has sickle-cell anemia as a genetic inheritance has resistance and is less likely to develop the disease, whereas the person without the sickle-cell gene will have a greater likelihood of becoming infected. Although both are exposed, only one person becomes a clinical case, and caseness requires an enduring, pre-event attribute of the individual in interaction with an exposure. Once the syndrome is developed in a subset of the vulnerable, its main features are predictable. In diagnosing individual caseness, it is important to understand that this person is part of a subset of individuals whose enduring qualities predisposed them to respond with disorder. It is important to identify both the contribution of enduring traits and the exposure.

PTSD Criteria. We need to rethink the diagnosis of posttraumatic stress disorder, with a view to recognizing that the causal factors are far broader than the toxic life event which is currently featured as the core criterion. Breslau and Davis (1987) criticized the original DSM–III assumption for defining a special class of events as "extraordinary" stressors causing PTSD, noting that the "potential effects of individual differences on the responsiveness to stressors are obliterated by the overwhelming impact of the stressor. Despite its plausibility, this assumption has little empirical support" (p. 261). Since then, the evidence continues to suggest that the apparent symptoms of distress reflect a combination of powerful long-standing individual and group characteristics triggered into life by visible and proximal adverse life events that are quickly invested with powerful etiological attributes, with the help of belief systems.

The DSM diagnosis for PTSD would match nature better if the diagnosis gave greater prominence to the role of individual features of emotionality, resilience, and beliefs as well as if it identified life events only as one possible concomitant of the distress behavior. A toxic event could even be optional, while symptom criteria might include a small number of additional features such as anger, and obsessional beliefs about blame. This broader approach to diagnosis should be used even where a toxic event is clearly identified as a component of thoughts. The data also suggest that well-intentioned arguments in support of a proposed new event-focused diagnostic category (e.g., disorders of extreme stress; Newman, Orsillo, Herman, Niles, & Litz, 1995) may be ill advised in light of the poor relationship between event toxicity and distress response.

There is an additional problem with the PTSD criteria as they stand. Requiring a specific event as cause adds a moral overlay to the condition. An event means that someone or something external is the responsible agent of suffering, and often there is a highly visible someone or something. Whenever possible, then, some external agency owes a moral debt for the suffering. This seems to be unique among the mental disorders, and lends a complex feature to PTSD that confounds rather than helps understand the distress. If this feature led to more effective remedies, it might be justifiable, but the evidence suggests that a distressed person who focuses on issues of blame is actually hampered from recovering. Removing the event from the diagnostic criteria would remove the issue of attribution as a central feature and would allow the suffering person to work more productively in understanding the ways in which beliefs and emotions can be more successfully regulated.

Treatment Implications

The defects in the current diagnostic formulation of PTSD also have implications for treatment, providing some clues as to why treatment has not been more effective and suggesting directions that might lead to better outcomes. An interactional model that incorporates individual differences in the postevent distress disorders does not deny reports of distress nor does it negate the possibility that treatment may alleviate distress. What it does alter is the understanding of the disorder's origins to more clearly recognize the role of long-standing emotionality and beliefs in contributing to distress, and this has treatment implications. Making use of this idea are treatment proposals and efforts aimed at changing the meaning assigned to events (e.g., Foa, Hearst-Ikeda, & Perry, 1995; Kreitler & Kreitler, 1988). In addition, it would seem that treatment that moves beyond an event focus to include broader long-standing features of negative emotionality and problematical belief systems should provide advantages because these factors are important in the distress syndrome.

WHY ARE POSTEVENT DISTRESS REPORTS RESISTANT TO TREATMENT?

Treatment research programs have not yet identified a reliable method of reducing PTSD and related distress syndromes. Part of the problem lies in the way that PTSD is explicitly attributed to an event. People readily invoke the counterfactual fallacy both to account for their distress ("If this event hadn't happened, then I wouldn't have been distressed"), and, as Dawes (1994) noted, to account for their recovery after therapy ("If I hadn't had this therapy, then I wouldn't be better"). Despite its attractiveness as an explanation, it represents a logical fallacy and not evidence.

An event-dominated model of PTSD treatment would seem to require intervention therapy that confronted, sued, or punished those responsible for the event where that is feasible, yet there is evidence that this approach can do harm. In addition, for the future well-being of patients, treatment would require their removal from environments where there would be life events with potentially stressful features. A treatment method that focuses on events runs the risk of sustaining a model of life that stresses the dangers of life events and of creating further emotional disorder when there are future toxic exposures, rather than supporting a model of life that builds a sense of competency in handling events.

The move away from inner defined anxiety to externally defined stress as a central paradigm directing research and clinical practice arose in the 1960s as behaviorism began to make significant inroads into the professional hegemony of psychotherapists who used psychodynamic models. The 1967 attempt by Holmes and Rahe to measure external stressful life events came just at a time when clinical practice was moving from an etiological model focusing on distal, childhood experience, to a cognitive-behavioral model that emphasized proximal stimulus events.

Although it has been traditional to view these models as largely antithetical, both identify the causes of emotional distress in external events. The limitations in treatment effectiveness of both dynamic and cognitive-behavioral treatments, however, may relate to their common emphasis on the event, although therapists in both models are concerned with the typical emotional responses and the thoughts associated with them. To that extent, both are consistent with an individual differences model.

Therapy models tend to presume that any personality or behavioral quality such as temperament or neuroticism that has a significant genetic component will be inaccessible to remedies. That assumption is far from necessary in treating all kinds of physical disorders, and there is no reason to believe that psychological treatment approaches could not also be developed to deal with problematic emotionality even while accepting that it has deep roots in genetically moderated temperament. An individual-differences model of postevent distress does not mean that therapy can be of no benefit when individuals report distress after an event. Rather than assuming that emotional disarray represents only a logical and predictable response to life events, treatment clinicians can, for example, help individuals recognize long-standing excessive emotionality.

This is not the same thing as blaming the victim, for no moral evaluation is implied. The issue has nothing to do with responsibility or moral blame. Just as one person is born with flat feet and therefore cannot run well, whereas another wins the Olympics, recognition of individual emotional dispositions allows realistic programs to enhance function without expecting miracles. The flat-footed person will not win top races, but will run better if his particular needs are identified and remedied than if he is simply forced to run.

Longer-term resilience might be enhanced if therapy educated individuals in the ways in which their characteristic thought and reaction styles can contribute to prolonged distress. This may provide individuals with a better framework with which to interpret and manage their responses to future life events. Constitutionally vulnerable individuals could be taught to recognize when excessive arousal is affecting their thoughts so that they can learn to use tactics to develop a more distanced perspective on their emotionality. Helping individuals to understand that blaming an external event for their emotional condition will not contribute to long-term well-being might be also part of a useful approach. These approaches make full use of the recognition that changes in the way an individual thinks about events and about their emotions and thoughts will be at the core of effective treatment.

There are other treatment implications of a more accurate model of postevent behavior. These relate to larger social units such as rapid-deployment trauma teams or disaster teams. These response services are also based on the assumption it will be normal for event-exposed individuals to need treatment. These treatment programs should be understood in a more humble, exploratory, and investigatory framework, rather than advocated or marketed as demonstrably valid interventions that are required by most people. Little effective evaluation of these is reported.

ALTERNATIVE LIFE-EVENT MODELS

Rather than defining life events as stressors and as the source of risk and danger, it seems useful to consider life events as elements in long sequences that may, in part, arise from individual choices and acts. Even objectively toxic events are often described by participants as a mixture of risks and benefits, and these qualities derive from the ways in which individuals interpret their experience. Some research, for example, has suggested that toxic life events may have positive psychological features. Because all events are interpreted through an active process, extreme events often result in individuals developing new perspectives that are helpful to them. Some people rediscover long-neglected religious faith, the meaning of family connections, or a commitment to a cause. People often discover new competencies during extreme toxic events.

What are the mechanisms through which this might be true? Physiological analogies provide one way of thinking about this. Limited exposure to some kinds of physical stressors helps enhance the body's resistance to later stress exposures, a principle long used in biochemical immunization. In addition, general physical effort contributes to strength and hardiness. Top athletes use this principle to train, putting their bodies through increasingly taxing events to provide both stress and mastery experiences.

The physiological principle of adaptation represents another kind of learned-resistance model in which an organism responds with less reactivity following repeated exposures to a stimulus that is normally arousing. The model was used in early psychophysical studies of physiological changes to stimulation thresholds and in studies of responses to sensory stimuli as an index of learning. It has been adapted into other areas, such as developmental studies of language learning in infants. In these studies, sucking responses diminish across repeated exposures to a language sound that is recognized, then reappear if the infant detects minor changes in the sound, providing evidence that the infant has learned to discriminate the sounds. Learning through repeated exposure thus raises the threshold for the perception of the stimulus and reduces the response of the individual.

Exposure to events that elicit arousal has been studied to determine the effects of aroused anxiety on performance on complex tasks. Results have shown there is an inverted-U relationship between efficacy on complex performance tasks and anxiety. Low emotional arousal is not associated with maximal functioning on complex tasks, which instead is best found under conditions that elicit moderate anxiety. These well-understood relations raise the possibility that many kinds of exposures to moderately taxing environmental events might yield learning and show a similar inverted-U relationship with well-being. Of special importance, aroused anxiety is not necessarily a bad thing.

Mixed evidence of the effects of repeated toxic exposures comes from studies of the effects of severe floods in South Africa. Repeated exposure led to depleted internal coping mechanisms, but to more effective "external" coping (Burger, 1992). Other evidence suggests that prolonged and continuous exposure to horrific stimuli results in lower levels of distress in comparison with brief exposures to the same stimuli, suggesting a learning effect that contributed to a positive adaptation (Mitchell, personal communication, 1995). The experience of rescue and police in other settings also supports this general finding.

It is probable that some of this effect is through the beliefs that these workers have about the world and their place in it, whether these beliefs are long-standing or are developed through experience on the job. Toxic life events can be interpreted in many ways, and individual differences in these interpretations have an impact on emotional responses. Toxic events may be seen as stressors that lead to increased sensitization and heightened emotional response (Friedman, 1994), as experiences that can lead to familiarity, habituation, and adaptation, or even as experiences that can result in stress inoculation that will reduce negative emotional responsiveness to future toxic events.

In addition to understanding individual variations in construing the meaning of events and responses to them, it is necessary to consider that adverse life events may provide learning experiences in which an individual develops skills. March (1990) reviewed the construct of PTSD and concluded that the disorder represents a failure of real-life habituation in that patients fail to lose their distress response despite repeated exposures through the phenomenon of re-experiencing.

In an interactional model that takes full recognition of personal characteristics, individual ways of interpreting the meaning of events can interact with events to yield a more effective and less disturbed emotional condition. It seems that this model is a better fit to reality than the adversity–distress model of PTSD. Therapy focused on the event as the causative agent is not expected contribute as positively to future mental health as a broader model that includes serious incorporation of long-standing individual differences.

CONCLUSION

This book has been an attempt to identify and examine major assumptions about the power of toxic life events. These assumptions support professional clinical interventions in the lives of individuals who have been exposed to such events. I asked if these assumptions exaggerate individual expectations of psychological malfunctioning and distress as a response to adverse life events and concluded that this is the case. A key factor that defines the prototypical adversity disorder of PTSD is the event, and this diagnostic emphasis is not justified by examination of prevalence or incidence rates. Other evidence shows significant dissociations between dose and response, further revealing problems with the model. I also examined expectations of the effectiveness of professional interventions and concluded these are yet to be shown reliably effective, in part, because treatments are based on a faulty set of assumptions about causation.

A more interactional model is proposed for understanding the relations between adversity and distress, in which toxic life events have different power depending on the way in which they are construed, by individuals who vary in emotionality and beliefs. This model matches the evidence better, and suggests ways of improving diagnostic understanding and treatment for individuals whose lives are seriously disrupted by distressing emotions that persist long after toxic events.

Most people have been part of events in which they have "experienced, witnessed, or (were) confronted with an event or events that involved actual or threatened death or serious injury, or a threat to the physical integrity of self or others" and in which their response involved "intense fear, helplessness, or horror" (American Psychiatric Association, 1994, pp. 427–428). Despite these experiences, only a minute fraction of people goes on to develop the chronic syndrome of persisting fears and life impairment that is defined as the posttraumatic stress disorder. Most people traverse these events with resilience after a period of initial distress, owing to combinations of personal factors that are significantly unacknowledged in the clinical literature concerning diagnosis and treatment. This resilience often reveals heroic moral attributes, but its normality is also an important fact of nature. It is important for clinicians to understand this as they try to help those who are unable to navigate toxic exposures without persisting and significant distress.

References

Agger, I., & Jensen, S. B. (1993). The psychosexual trauma of torture. In J. P. Wilson & B. Raphael (Eds.), *International handbook of traumatic stress syndromes* (pp. 684–702). New York: Plenum Press.

Aldwin, C. M., Levenson M. R., Spiro, A, III, & Bossé, R. (1989). Does emotionality predict stress? Findings from the Normative Aging Study. *Journal of Personality and Social Psychology, 56*(4), 618–624.

Alexander, D. A. (1993). Stress among police body handlers: A long-term follow-up. *British Journal of Psychiatry, 163*, 806–808.

Allodi, F. A. (1994). Post-traumatic stress disorder in hostages and victims of torture. *Psychiatric Clinics of North America, 17*(2), 279–288.

Alter-Reid, K., Gibbs, M. S., Lachenmeyer, J. R., Sigal, J., & Massoth, N. A. (1986). Sexual abuse of children: A review of the empirical findings. *Clinical Psychology Review, 6*, 249–266.

American Psychiatric Association. (1980). *Diagnostic and statistical manual of mental disorders* (3rd ed.). Washington, DC: Author

American Psychiatric Association. (1987). *Diagnostic and statistical manual of mental disorders* (3rd ed., Rev.). Washington, DC Author.

American Psychiatric Association. (1994). *Diagnostic and statistical manual of mental disorders* (4th ed.). Washington, DC: Author.

Amick-McMullan, A., Kilpatrick, D. G., & Resnick, H. S. (1991). Homicide as a risk factor for PTSD among surviving family members. *Behavior Modification, 15*(4), 545–559.

Andrews, G., Tennant, C., Hewson, D. M., & Vaillant, G. E. (1978). Life event stress, social support, coping style, and risk of psychological impairment. *Journal of Nervous and Mental Disease, 166*(5), 307–316.

Antonovsky, A. (1979). *Health, stress, and coping.* San Francisco: Jossey-Bass.

Antonovsky, A. (1987). *Unravelling the mystery of health: How people manage stress and stay well.* San Francisco: Jossey–Bass.

Aptekar, L. (1990). A comparison of the bicoastal disasters of 1989. *Behavior Science Research, 24*(1–4), 73–104.

Armfield, F. (1994). Center for the family in transition. *Military Medicine, 159* (12), 739–746.

Arnett, J. (1991). Still crazy after all these years: Reckless behavior among young adults aged 23–27. *Personality and Individual Differences, 12*, 1305–1313.

Arvidson, R. (1969). On some mental effects of earthquakes. *American Psychologist, 24*(6), 605–606.

Atkinson, B., Henderson, J. B., Sparr, B. W., & Deale, R. (1982). Assessment of Vietnam veterans for post-traumatic stress disorder in veteran administration disability claims. *American Journal of Psychiatry, 139*, 9.

146

Basoglu, M. (Ed.). (1992). *Torture and its consequences: Current treatment approaches.* New York: Cambridge University Press.

Basoglu, M., & Paker, M. (1995). Severity of trauma as predictor of long-term psychological status in survivors of torture. *Journal of Anxiety Disorders, 9*(4), 339–353.

Baum, A., O'Keefe, M. K., & Davidson, L. M. (1990). Acute stressors and chronic response: The case of traumatic stress. *Journal of Applied Social Psychology, 20,* 1643–1654.

Bauman, K. E., & Ennett, S. T. (1994). Peer influence on adolescent drug use. *American Psychologist, 49*(9), 820–822.

Baumeister, R. F., Smart, L., & Boden, J. M. (1996). Relation of threatened egotism to violence and aggression: The dark side of high self-esteem. *Psychological Review, 103,* 5–33.

Beaton, R. D., & Murphy, S. A. (1995). Working with people in crisis: Research implications. In C. R. Figley (Ed.), *Compassion fatigue: Coping with secondary traumatic stress disorder in those who treat the traumatized* (pp. 51–81). New York: Brunner/Mazel.

Belferman, M. (1996, February 8). For children in crisis, a sanctuary. *The Washington Post,* pp. Md.1.

Bell, B. D. (1978). Disaster impact and response: Overcoming the thousand natural shocks. *The Gerontologist, 18*(6), 531–540.

Bell, B. D., Kara, G., & Batterson, C. (1978). Service utilization and adjustment patterns of elderly tornado victims in an American disaster. *Mass Emergencies, 3*(2/3), 71–81.

Bell, J. L. (1995). Traumatic event debriefing: Service delivery designs and the role of social work. *Social Work, 40*(1), 36–43.

Belter, R. W., Dunn, S. E., & Jeney, P. (1991). The psychological impact of Hurricane Hugo on children: A needs assessment. *Advances in Behaviour Research and Therapy, 13*(3), 155–161.

Berg, G. E., Watson, C. G., Nugent, B., Gearhart, L. P., & Juba, M. (1994). A comparison of combat's effects on PTSD scores in veterans with high and low moral development. *Journal of Clinical Psychology, 50*(5), 669–676.

Blanc, C. S. (1994). *Urban children in distress: Global predicaments and innovative strategies.* Geneva: Gordon and Breach.

Blanchard, E. B., Hickling, E. J., Mitnick, N., & Taylor, A. E. (1995). The impact of severity of physical injury and perception of life threat in the development of post-traumatic stress disorder in motor vehicle accident victims. *Behaviour Research and Therapy, 33*(5), 529–534.

Blanchard, E. B., Hickling, E. J., Taylor, A. E., & Loos, W. (1995). Psychiatric morbidity associated with motor vehicle accidents. *Journal of Nervous and Mental Disease, 183*(8), 495–504.

Blanchard, E. B., Hickling, E. J., Taylor, A. E., Loos, W. R., & Gerardi, R. J. (1994). Psychological morbidity associated with motor vehicle accidents. *Behaviour Research and Therapy, 32*(3), 283–290.

Blanchard, E. B., Hickling, E. J., Vollmer, A. J., Loos, W. R., Buckley, T. C., & Jaccard, J. (1995). Short-term follow-up of post-traumatic stress symptoms in motor vehicle accident victims. *Behaviour Research and Therapy, 33*(4), 369–377.

Bland, L. C., & Sowa, C. J. (1994). An overview of resilience in gifted children. *Roeper Review, 17*(2), 77–80.

Bledin, K. (1994). Post-traumatic stress disorder "once removed": A case report. *British Journal of Medical Psychology, 67*(2), 125–1299.

Block, J. (1993). Studying personality the long way. In D. Funder, R. Parke, C. Tomlinson-Keasy, & K. Widaman (Eds.), *Studying lives through time: Approaches to personality and development* (pp. 9–41). Washington, DC: American Psychological Association.

Bolin, R. C. (1976). Family recovery from natural disaster: A preliminary model. *Mass Emergencies, 1*(4), 267–277.

Boman, B. (1979). Behavioural observations on the Granville train disaster and the significance of stress for psychiatry. *Social Science and Medicine, 13*(4), 463–471.

Bornstein, R. A., Miller, H. B., & van Schoor, T. (1988). Emotional adjustment in compensated head injury patients. *Neurosurgery, 23*(5), 622–627.

Bouchard, T. J., Lykken, D. T., McGue, M., Segal, N. L., & Tellegen, A. (1990). Sources of human psychological differences: The Minnesota study of twins reared apart. *Science, 250*, 223–228.

Boyce, T. W., Chesterman, E. A., Martin, N., & Folkman, S. (1993). Immunologic changes occurring at kindergarten entry predict respiratory illnesses after the Loma Prieta earthquake. *Journal of Developmental and Behavioral Pediatrics, 14*(5), 296–303.

Bracken, P. J., Giller, J. E., & Summerfield, D. (1995). Psychological responses to war and atrocity: The limitations of current concepts. *Social Science and Medicine, 40*(8), 1073–1082.

Bradburn, I. S. (1991). After the earth shook: Children's stress symptoms 6–8 months after a disaster. *Advances in Behaviour Research and Therapy, 13*(3), 173–179.

Brandon, N. (1969). *The psychology of self-esteem*. New York: Bantam.

Bremner, J. D., Randall, P., Scott, T. M., Bronen, R. A., Seibyl, J. P., Southwick, S. M., Delaney, R. C., McCarthy, G., Charney, D. S., & Innis, R. B. (1995). MRI-based measurement of hippocampal volume in patients with combat-related posttraumatic stress disorder. *American Journal of Psychiatry, 152*(7), 973–981.

Bremner, J. D., Southwick, S. M., Johnson, D. R., Yehuda, R., & Charney, D. S. (1993). Childhood physical abuse and combat-related posttraumatic stress disorder in Vietnam veterans. *American Journal of Psychiatry, 150*(2), 235–239.

Brenton, M. (1975). Studies in the aftermath. *Human Behavior, 4*(5), 56–61.

Breslau, N., & Davis, G. C. (1987). Posttraumatic stress disorder. *Journal of Nervous and Mental Disease, 175*(5), 256–264.

Breslau, N., Davis, G. C., Andreski, P., & Peterson, E. (1991). Traumatic events and posttraumatic stress disorder in an urban population of young adults. *Archives of General Psychiatry, 48*, 216–222.

Brickman, P., Coates, D., & Janoff–Bulman, R. (1978). Lottery winners and accident victims: Is happiness relative? *Journal of Personality and Social Psychology, 36*(8), 917–927.

Brickman, P., Rabinowitz, V. C., Karuza, J., Coates, D., Cohn, E., & Kidder, L. (1982). Models of helping and coping. *American Psychologist, 37*(4), 368–384.

Brom, D., Kleber, R. J., & Hofman, M. C. (1993). Victims of traffic accidents: Incidence and prevention of post-traumatic stress disorder. *Journal of Clinical Psychology, 49*(2), 131–140.

Brooks, B. (1985). Sexually abused children and adolescent identity development. *American Journal of Psychotherapy, 39*(3), 401–410.

Brown, G. R., & Anderson, B. (1991). Psychiatric morbidity in adult patients with childhood histories of sexual and physical abuse. *American Journal of Psychiatry, 148*(1), 55–61.

Bulman, R. J., & Wortman, C. B. (1977). Attributions of blame and coping in the "real world": Severe accident victims react to their lot. *Journal of Personality and Social Psychology, 35*(5), 351–363.

Burger, L. (1992). *Coping with repetitive natural disasters: A study of the Ladysmith floods* (Vol. 26, pp. 1–22). Pretoria, South Africa: Psychology Department, University of South Africa.

Burger, L., Van-Staden, F., & Nieuwoudt, J. (1989). The Free-State floods: A case study. *South African Journal of Psychology, 19*(4), 205–209.

Burgess, J. A., & Dworkin, S. F. (1993). Litigation and post-traumatic TMD: How patients report treatment outcome. *Journal of the American Dental Association, 124*(6), 105–110.

Burke, J. D., Borus, J. F., Burns, B. J., Millstein, K. H., & Beasley, M. C. (1982). Changes in children's behavior after a natural disaster. *American Journal of Psychiatry, 139*(8), 1010–1014.

Burkholder, B. T., & Toole, M. J. (1995). Evolution of complex disasters. *The Lancet, 346,* 1012–1015.

Burns, M. O., & Seligman, M. E. P. (1989). Explanatory style across the life span: Evidence for stability over 52 years. *Journal of Personality and Social Psychology, 56*(3), 471–477.

Burstein, A. (1985). How common is delayed stress disorder? *American Journal of Psychiatry, 142*(7), 887.

Byrne, D. G. (1984). Personal assessments of life-event stress and the near future onset of psychological symptoms. *British Journal of Medical Psychology, 57,* 241–248.

Canino, G. J., Bravo, M., Rubio-Stipec, M., & Woodbury, M. (1990). The impact of disaster on mental health: Prospective and retrospective analyses. *International Journal of Mental Health, 19*(1), 51–69.

Casella, L., & Motta, R. W. (1990). Comparison of characteristics of Vietnam veterans with and without Posttraumatic Stress Disorder. *Psychological Reports, 67*(2), 595–605.

Cassileth, B. R., Lusk, E., Miller, D. S., Brown, L. L., & Miller, C. (1985). Psychosocial correlates of survival in advanced malignant disease? *New England Journal of Medicine, 312*(24), 1551–1555.

Cederblad, M., & Dahlin, L. (1994). Salutogenic childhood factors reported by middle-aged individuals: Follow-up of the children from the Lundby Study grown up in families experiencing three or more childhood psychiatric risk factors. *European Archives of Psychiatry & Clinical Neuroscience, 244*(1), 1–11.

Chambless, D. L., Sanderson, W. C., Shoham, V., Johnson, S. B., Pope, K. S., Crits-Christoph, P., Baker, M., Johnson, B., Woody, S. R., Sue, S., Beutler, L., Williams, D. A., & McCurry, S. (1996). An update on empirically validated therapies. *The Clinical Psychologist, 49*(2), 5–18.

Champion, L. A., Goodall, G., & Rutter, M. (1995). Behaviour problems in childhood and stressors in early adult life: I. A 20 year follow-up of London school children. *Psychological Medicine, 25*(2), 231–246.

Chess, T. A. (1977). *Temperament and development.* New York: Brunner/Mazel.

Chew, P. K., Phoon, W. H., & Mae-Lim, H. A. (1976). Epidemic hysteria among some factory workers in Singapore. *Singapore Medical Journal, 17*(1), 10–15.

Chibnall, J. T., & Duckro, P. N. (1994). Post-traumatic stress disorder in chronic post-traumatic headache patients. *Headache, 34*(6), 357–361.

Christensen, A., & Jacobson, N. S. (1994). Who (or what) can do psychotherapy: The status and challenge of nonprofessional therapies. *Psychological Science, 5*(1), 8–14.

Cicchetti, D., & Garmezy, N. (1993). Prospects and promises in study of resilience. *Development and Psychopathology, 5*(4), 497–502.

Cienfuegos, A. J., & Monelli, C. (1983). The testimony of political repression as a therapeutic instrument. *American Journal of Orthopsychiatry, 53,* 43.

Clarke, K. M. (1996). Change processes in a creation of meaning event. *Journal of Consulting and Clinical Psychology, 64*(3), 465–470.

Cleiren, M., Diekstra, R. F., Kerkhof, A. J., & van der Wal, J. (1994). Mode of death and kinship in bereavement: Focusing on "who" rather than "how." *Crisis, 15*(1), 22–36.

Cohen, F., & Lazarus, R. S. (1973). Active coping processes, coping dispositions, and recovery from surgery. *Psychosomatic Medicine, 35,* 375–389.

Cohen, S., & Williamson, G. M. (1991). Stress and infectious disease in humans. *Psychological Bulletin, 109,* 5–23.

Cohen, S. I. (1994). Persistent post-traumatic stress disorder: Role of alcohol ignored. *British Medical Journal, 309*(6958), 873.

Colvin, C., & Block, J. (1994). Do positive illusions foster mental health? An examination of the Taylor and Brown formulation. *Psychological Bulletin, 116*(1), 3–20.

Conley, J. J. (1984). Longitudinal consistency of adult personality: Self-reported psychological characteristics across 45 years. *Journal of Personality and Social Psychology, 47*(6), 1325–1333.

Cordray, S. M., Polk, K. R., & Britton, B. M. (1992). Premilitary antecedents of post-traumatic stress disorder in an Oregon cohort. *Journal of Clinical Psychology, 48*, 271–280.

Costa, P. T., & McCrae, R. R. (1986). Personality stability and its implications for clinical psychology. *Clinical Psychology Review, 6*, 407–423.

Costa, P. T., McCrae, R. R., & Zonderman, A. B. (1987). Environmental and dispositional influences on well-being: Longitudinal follow-up of an American longitudinal sample. *British Journal of Psychology, 78*, 299–306.

Costa, P. T., & Metter, E. J. (1994). Personality stability and its contribution to successful aging. *Journal of Geriatric Psychiatry, 27*(1), 41–59.

Cottler, L. B., Compton, W. M., Mager, D., Spitznagel, E. L., & Janca, A. (1992). Post-traumatic stress disorder among substance users from the general population. *American Journal of Psychiatry, 149*, 664–670.

Cousins, N. (1979). *Anatomy of an illness.* New York: W. W. Norton.

Crandall, C. S. (1992). Psychophysical scaling of stressful life events. *Psychological Science, 3*(4), 256–258.

Criminal Injuries Compensation Act, R. S. B. C. (1979). c. 83.

Cronbach, L. J. (1957). The two disciplines of scientific psychology. *American Psychologist, 12*, 671–684.

Cummings, N., & VandenBos, G. R. (1981). The general practice of psychology. *International Review of Applied Psychology, 30*(3), 355–375.

Curran, P. S. (1988). Psychiatric aspects of terrorist violence: Northern Ireland 1969–1987. *British Journal of Psychiatry, 153*, 470.

D'Andrea, L. M. (1994). Cluster analysis of adult children of alcoholics. *International Journal of Addictions, 29*, 565–582.

Davis, C. G., Lehman, D. R., Wortman, C. B., Silver, R. C., & Thompson, S. C. (1995). The undoing of traumatic life events. *Personality and Social Psychology Bulletin, 21*(2), 109–124.

Davis, G. C., & Breslau, N. (1994). Post-traumatic stress disorder in victims of civilian trauma and criminal violence. *Psychiatric Clinics of North America, 17*(2), 289–299.

Dawes, R. M. (1994). *House of cards: Psychology and psychotherapy built on myth.* New York: The Free Press.

de Berniéres, L. (1996, January). Legends of the fall. *Harper's Magazine,* 78–81.

de Beauvoir, S. (1962). *The prime of life* (P. Green, Trans.). Harmondsworth, UK: Penguin. (Original work published 1960)

De Clercq, M. (1995). Disasters and families. *New Trends in Experimental and Clinical Psychiatry, 11*(1), 19–24.

de la Fuente, R. (1990). The mental health consequences of the 1985 earthquakes in Mexico. *International Journal of Mental Health, 19*(2), 21–29.

DeLongis, A., Folkman, S., & Lazarus, R. S. (1988). The impact of daily stressors on health and mood: Psychological and social measures as mediators. *Journal of Personality and Social Psychology, 54*, 486–495.

Depue, R. A., & Monroe, S. M. (1986). Conceptualization and measurement of human disorder in life stress research: The problem of chronic disturbance. *Psychological Bulletin, 99*, 36–51.

Deryugin, Y. I. (1989) Some psychological problems in the aftermath of the earthquake in Armenia [On-line]. *Psikologicheskii-Zhurnal, 10,* 129–134. Abstract from: PsycLIT Item: AN: 28-70658

Desjarlais, R., Eisenberg, L., Good, B., & Kleinman, A. (1995). *World mental health: Problems and priorities in low-income countries.* New York: Oxford University Press.

Deutsch, M. (1960). The pathetic fallacy: An observer error in social perception. *Journal of Personality, 28,* 317–332.

Diener, E., & Diener, C. (1996). Most people are happy. *Psychological Science, 7*(3), 181–185.

Diener, E., & Fujita, F. (1995). Resources, personal strivings, and subjective well-being: A nomothetic and idiographic approach. *Journal of Personality and Social Psychology, 68*(5), 926–935.

Dixon, P., Rehling, G., & Shiwach, R. (1993). Peripheral victims of the Herald of Free Enterprise disaster. *British Journal of Medical Psychology, 66,* 150–165.

Dohrenwend, B. S., & Dohrenwend, B. P. (1978). Some issues in research on stressful life events. *Journal of Nervous and Mental Disease, 153,* 207–234.

Downey, G., Silver, R. C., & Wortman, C. B. (1990). Reconsidering the attribution–adjustment relation following a major negative event: Coping with the loss of a child. *Journal of Personality and Social Psychology, 59*(5), 925–940.

Drabek, T. E., & Boggs, K. S. (1968). Families in disaster: Reactions and relatives. *Journal of Marriage and the Family, 30*(3), 443–451.

Drabek, T. E., Key, W. H., Erickson, P. E., & Crowe, J. L. (1975). The impact of disaster on kin relationships. *Journal of Marriage and the Family, 37*(3), 481–494.

Durkin, M. S., Khan, N., Davidson, L. L., Zaman, S. S., & Stein, Z. A. (1993). The effects of a natural disaster on child behavior: Evidence for posttraumatic stress. *American Journal of Public Health, 83*(11), 1549–1553.

Dutton, M. A., & Rubenstein, F. L. (1995). Working with people with PTSD: Research implications. In C. R. Figley (Ed.), *Compassion fatigue: coping with secondary traumatic stress disorder in those who treat the traumatized* (pp. 82–100). New York: Brunner/Mazel.

Dynes, R. R., & Quarantelli, E. L. (1976). The family and community context of individual reactions to disaster. In H. J. Parad, H. L. P. Resnik, & L. G. Parad (Eds.), *Emergency and Disaster Management: A mental health source book* (pp. 231–244). Bowie, MD: Charles Press.

Eaton, W. W., Sigal, J. J., & Weinfeld, M. (1982). Impairment in Holocaust survivors after 33 years: Data from an unbiased community sample. *American Journal of Psychiatry, 139*(6), 773–777.

Ekman, P. (1982). *Emotion in the human face.* (2nd ed.). New York: Academic.

Ekman, P. (1993). Facial expression and emotion. *American Psychologist, 48*(4), 384–392.

Elder, G. J., & Clipp, E. (1989). Combat experience and emotional health: Impairment and resilience in later life. *Journal of Personality, 57*(2), 311–314.

Erikson, E. H. (1963). *Childhood and society* (2nd ed.). New York: Norton.

Everly, G. S. (1995). The role of the Critical Incident Stress Debriefing (CISD) process in disaster counseling. *Journal of Mental Health Counseling, 17*(3), 278–290.

Eysenck, H. J. (1994). Neuroticism and the illusion of mental health. *American Psychologist, 49*(11), 971–972.

Fairbank, J. A., Fitterling, J. M., & Hansen, D. J. (1991). Patterns of appraisal and coping across different stressor conditions among former prisoners of war with and without posttraumatic stress disorder. *Journal of Consulting and Clinical Psychology, 59*(2), 274–281.

Fairbank, J. A., McCaffrey, R. J., & Keane, T. M. (1985). Psychometric detection of fabricated symptoms of posttraumatic stress disorder. *American Journal of Psychiatry, 142*(4), 501–503.

Falsetti, S. A., & Resick, P. A. (1995). Causal attributions, depression, and post-traumatic stress disorder in victims of crime. *Journal of Applied Social Psychology, 25*(12), 1027–1042.

Famularo, R., Kinscherff, R., & Fenton, T. (1991). Posttraumatic stress disorder among children clinically diagnosed as borderline personality disorder. *Journal of Nervous and Mental Disease, 179*(7), 428–431.

Farmer, J. E., & Peterson, L. (1995). Injury risk factors in children with attention deficit hyperactivity disorder. *Health Psychology, 14,* 325–332.

Faupel, C. E., & Styles, S. P. (1993). Disaster education, household preparedness, and stress responses following Hurricane Hugo. *Environment and Behavior, 25*(2), 228–249.

Feinstein, A., & Dolan, R. (1991). Predictors of post-traumatic stress disorder following physical trauma: An examination of the stressor criterion. *Psychological Medicine, 21,* 85–91.

Figley, C. F. (1978). *Stress disorder among Vietnam veterans.* New York: Brunner/Mazel.

Figley, C. R. (Ed.). (1995). *Compassion fatigue: Coping with secondary traumatic stress disorder in those who treat the traumatized.* New York: Brunner/Mazel.

Finkbeiner, A. K. (1996). *After the death of a child.* New York: The Free Press.

Finkelhor, D. (1990). Sexual abuse in a national survey of adult men and women: Prevalence, characteristics, and risk factors. *Child Abuse and Neglect, 14,* 19–28.

Finn, S. E. (1986). Stability of personality self-ratings over 30 years: Evidence for an age/cohort interaction. *Journal of Personality and Social Psychology, 50,* 813–818.

Fisher, J. (1959). The twisted pear and the prediction of behavior. *Journal of Consulting Psychology, 23,* 400–405.

Flagler, S. L. (1987). Recurrent poisoning in children: A review. *Journal of Pediatric Psychology, 12,* 631–641.

Foa, E. B., Hearst-Ikeda, D., & Perry, K. J. (1995). Evaluation of a brief cognitive-behavioral program for the prevention of chronic PTSD in recent assault victims. *Journal of Consulting and Clinical Psychology, 63*(6), 948–955.

Foa, E. B., & Riggs, D. S. (1995). Posttraumatic stress disorder following assault: Theoretical considerations and empirical findings. *Current Directions in Psychological Science, 4*(2), 61–65.

Fogelman, C. W., & Parenton, V. J. (1959). Disaster and aftermath: Selected aspects of individual and group behavior in critical situations. *Social Forces, 38*(2), 129–135.

Folkman, S., & Lazarus, R. S. (1980). An analysis of coping in a middle-aged community sample. *Journal of Health and Social Behavior, 21,* 219–239.

Fox, B. H. (1995). The role of psychological factors in cancer incidence and prognosis. *Oncology (Huntington), 9*(3), 245–253.

Fox, N. A. (1994). Dynamic cerebral processes underlying emotion regulation. *Monographs of the Society for Research in Child Development, 59*(2–3), 152–166, 250–283.

Fox, R. L. (1986). Hellenistic culture and literature. In J. Boardman, J. Griffin, & O. Murray (Eds.), *The Oxford history of the classical world* (pp. 338–364). Oxford: Oxford University Press.

Frankel, F. H. (1993). Adult reconstruction of childhood events in the multiple personality literature. *American Journal of Psychiatry, 150,* 954–958.

Frankel, F. H. (1995). Discovering new memories in psychotherapy: Childhood revisited, fantasy, or both? *New England Journal of Medicine, 333*(9), 591–594.

Fraser, G. (1996, April 6). Land of the free, home of the sound bite. *The Globe and Mail,* p. D4.

Freedy, J., Saladin, M., Kilpatrick, D. G., Resnick, H. S., & Saunders, B. E. (1994). Understanding acute psychological distress following natural disaster. *Journal of Traumatic Stress, 7*(2), 257–273.

Freedy, J. R., & Donkervoet, J. C. (1995). Traumatic stress: An overview of the field. In J. R. Freedy & S. E. Hobfoll (Eds.), *Traumatic stress: From theory to practice* (pp. 3–28). New York: Plenum.

Freedy, J. R., & Hobfoll, S. E. (1995). Preface. In J. R. Freedy & S. E. Hobfoll (Eds.), *Traumatic stress: From theory to practice* (pp. ix–xi). New York: Plenum.

Freedy, J. R., Shaw, D. L., Jarrell, M. P., & Masters, C. R. (1992). Towards an understanding of the psychological impact of natural disasters: An application of the conservation stress model. *Journal of Traumatic Stress, 5*(3), 441–454.

Frenkel, E., Kugelmass, S., Nathan, M., & Ingraham, L. J. (1995). Locus of control and mental health in adolescence and adulthood. *Schizophrenia Bulletin, 21*(2), 219–226.

Frese, M. (1992). A plea for realistic pessimism: On objective reality, coping with stress, and psychological dysfunction. In L. Montada, S. H. Filipp, & M. Lerner (Eds.), *Life crises and experiences of loss in adulthood* (pp. 81–94). Hillsdale, NJ: Lawrence Erlbaum Associates.

Friedman, H. S. (Ed.). (1991). *Hostility, coping, and health.* Washington, DC: American Psychological Association.

Friedman, H. S., & Tucker, J. S. (1993). Does childhood personality predict longevity? *Journal of Personality and Social Psychology, 65*(1), 176–185.

Friedman, H. S., Tucker, J. S., Schwartz, J. E., Tomlinson–Keasey, C., Martin, L. R., Wingard, D. L., & Criqui, M. H. (1995). Psychosocial and behavioral predictors of longevity. *American Psychologist, 50*(2), 69–78.

Friedman, H. S., & VandenBos, G. R. (1992). Disease-prone and self-healing personalities. *Hospital & Community Psychiatry, 43*(12), 1177–1179.

Friedman, J. S., & Booth–Kewley, S. (1987). The "disease-prone personality": A meta-analytic view of the construct. *American Psychologist, 42*(6), 539–555.

Friedman, M. J. (1994). Neurobiological sensitization models of post-traumatic stress disorder: Their possible relevance to multiple chemical sensitivity syndrome. *Toxicology and Industrial Health, 10*(4–5), 449–462.

Friedman, M. J., Schnurr, P. P., & McDonagh, C. A. (1994). Post-traumatic stress disorder in the military veteran. *Psychiatric Clinics of North America, 17*(2), 265–277.

Frueh, B. C., Turner, S. M., & Beidel, D. C. (1995). Exposure therapy for combat-related PTSD: A critical review. *Clinical Psychology Review, 15*(8), 799–817.

Galante, R., & Foa, D. (1987). An epidemiological study of psychic trauma and treatment effectiveness for children after a natural disaster. *Journal of the American Academy of Child Psychiatry, 25*(3), 357–363.

Garmezy, N. (1971). Vulnerability research and the issue of primary prevention. *American Journal of Orthopsychiatry, 41*, 101–116.

Garmezy, N. (1991). Resilience and vulnerability to adverse developmental outcomes associated with poverty. *American Behavioral Scientist, 34*(4), 416–430.

Garmezy, N. (1993). Children in poverty: Resilience despite risk. *Psychiatry: Interpersonal and Biological Processes, 56*(1), 127–136.

Garmezy, N., & Masten, A. S. (1986). Stress, competence, and resilience: Common frontiers for therapist and psychopathologist. *Behavior Therapy, 17*, 500–521.

Garrison, C. Z., Weinrich, M. W., Hardin, S. B., Weinrich, S., & Wang, L. (1993). Post-traumatic stress disorder in adolescents after a hurricane. *American Journal of Epidemiology, 138*(7), 522–530.

Gazzaniga, M. S., & LeDoux, J. E. (1978). *The integrated mind.* New York: Plenum.

Gervais, A. (1934). *A surgeon's China* (V. Sheean, Trans.). London: Hamish Hamilton.

Goenjian, A. (1993). A mental health relief programme in Armenia after the 1988 earthquake. *British Journal of Psychiatry, 163*, 230–239.

Goldsteen, R., & Schorr, J. K. (1982). The long-term impact of a man-made disaster: An examination of a small town in the aftermath of the Three Mile Island nuclear reactor accident. *Disasters, 6*(1), 10–19.

Goleman, D. (1994, April 17). Those who stay calm in disasters face psychological risk, studies say. *The New York Times*, p. 20.

Goreta, M. (1994). Posttraumatic stress disorder resulting from war traumas and its forensic-psychiatric meaning. *Journal of Psychiatry & Law, 22*(4), 505–525.

Grassi, L., Rosti, G., LaSalvia, A., & Marangolo, M. (1993). Psychosocial variables associated with mental adjustment to cancer. *Psycho-Oncology, 2*, 11–20.

Green, B. L. (1990). Defining trauma: Terminology and generic stressor dimensions. *Journal of Applied and Social Psychology, 20*, 1632–1642.

Green, B. L., Grace, M. C., & Gleser, G. C. (1985). Identifying survivors at risk: Long-term impairment following the Beverly Hills supper club fire. *Journal of Consulting and Clinical Psychology, 53*(5), 672–678.

Green, B. L., Grace, M. C., Lindy, J. D., Gleser, G. C., & Leonard, A. (1990). Risk factors for PTSD and other diagnoses in a general sample of Vietnam veterans. *American Journal of Psychiatry, 147*(6), 729–733.

Green, B. L., Grace, M. C., Vary, M. G., Kramer, T. L., Gleser, G. C., & Leonard, A. C. (1994). Children of disaster in the second decade: A 17-year follow-up of Buffalo Creek survivors. *Journal of the American Academy of Child and Adolescent Psychiatry, 33*(1), 71–79.

Green, B. L., Korol, M., Grace, M. C., & Vary, M. G. (1991). Children and disaster: Age, gender and parental effects on PTSD symptoms. *Journal of the American Academy of Child and Adolescent Psychiatry, 30*(6), 945–951.

Green, B. L., Lindy, J., D., Grace, M. C., & Gleser, G. C. (1990). Buffalo Creek survivors in the second decade: Stability of stress symptoms. *American Journal of Orthopsychiatry, 60*(1), 43–54.

Green, B. L., & Solomon, S. D. (1995). The mental health impact of natural and technological disasters. In J. R. Freedy & S. E. Hobfoll (Eds.), *Traumatic stress: From theory to practice* (pp. 163–180). New York: Plenum.

Green, B. L., Lindy, J. D., Grace, M. C., & Leonard, A. C. (1992). Chronic posttraumatic stress disorder and diagnostic comorbidity in a disaster sample. *Journal of Nervous and Mental Disease, 180*(12), 760–766.

Green, M. M., McFarlane, A. C., Hunter, C. E., & Griggs, W. M. (1993). Undiagnosed post-traumatic stress disorder following motor vehicle accidents. *Medical Journal of Australia, 159*(8), 529–534.

Greenwald, A. G. (1980). The totalitarian ego: Fabrication and revision of personal history. *American Psychologist, 35*(7), 603–618.

Greenwald, H. P. (1995). *Who survives cancer?* Berkeley, CA: University of California Press.

Greer, S., Morris, T., & Pettingale, K. W. (1979). Psychological response to breast cancer: Effect on outcome. *Lancet, ii*(8146), 785–787.

Grinker, K., & Spiegel, S. (1945). *Men under stress*. Philadelphia: Blakiston.

Gross, J. L., & Munoz, R. F. (1995). Emotion regulation and mental health. *Clinical Psychology: Science and Practice, 2*(2), 151–164.

Gunderson, J. G., & Sabo, A. N. (1993). The phenomenological and conceptual interface between borderline personality disorder and PTSD. *American Journal of Psychiatry, 150*(1), 19–27.

Hammarberg, M., & Silver, S. M. (1994). Outcome of treatment for posttraumatic stress disorder in a primary care unit serving Vietnam veterans. *Journal of Traumatic Stress, 7*(2), 195–216.

Hardin, S. B., Carbaugh, L., Weinrich, S., Pesut, D., & Carbaugh, C. (1992). Stressors and coping in adolescents exposed to Hurricane Hugo. *Issues in Mental Health Nursing, 13,* 191–205.

Harkness, A. R., Tellegen, A., & Waller, N. (1995). Differential convergence of self-report and informant data for multidimensional personality questionnaire traits: Implications of the construct of negative emotionality. *Journal of Personality Assessment, 64*(1), 185–204.

Harris, C. J. (1995). Sensory-based therapy for crisis counselors. In C. R. Figley (Ed.), *Compassion fatigue: Coping with secondary traumatic stress disorder in those who treat the traumatized* (pp. 101–114). New York: Brunner/Mazel.

Hashtroudi, S., & Johnson, M. K. (1994). Aging and the effects of affective and factual focus on source monitoring and recall. *Psychology & Aging, 9*(1), 160–170.

Headey, B., & Wearing, A. (1992). *Understanding happiness: A theory of subjective well-being.* Melbourne, Australia: Longman Cheshire.

Hebb, D. O. (1955). Drives and the C.N.S. (conceptual nervous system). *Psychological Review, 62,* 243–254.

Hefez, A. (1985). The role of the press and the medical community in the epidemic of "mysterious gas poisoning" in the Jordan West Bank. *American Journal of Psychiatry, 142*(7), 833–837.

Heiney, S. P., Dunaway, N. C., & Webster, J. (1995). Good grieving: An intervention program for grieving children. *Oncology Nursing Forum, 22 (4),* 649–655.

Helzer, J. E., Robins, L. N., & McEvoy, L. (1987). Post-traumatic stress disorder in the general population. *The New England Journal of Medicine, 317*(26), 1630–1634.

Henderson, A. S., Byrne, D. G., & Duncan-Jones, P. (1981). *Neurosis and the social environment.* Sydney, Australia: Academic Press.

Henderson, N. D. (1982). Human behavior genetics. *Annual Review of Psychology, 33,* 403–440.

Hendin, H., & Haas, A. P. (1984). Combat adaptations in Vietnam veterans without posttraumatic stress disorders. *American Journal of Psychiatry, 141,* 956–960.

Herbert, T. B., & Cohen, S. (1993). Stress and immunity in humans: A meta-analytic review. *Psychosomatic Medicine, 55,* 364–379.

Herman, E. (1995). *The romance of American psychology.* Berkeley, CA: University of California Press.

Herman, J. L. (1996). *Trauma and recovery.* New York: Basic Books.

Hersey, J. (1980). *Hiroshima.* New York: Knopf.

Higgins, G. O. C. (1994). *Resilient adults: Overcoming a cruel past.* San Francisco: Jossey-Bass.

Hillary, B. E., & Schare, M. L. (1993). Sexually and physically abused adolescents: An empirical search for PTSD. *Journal of Clinical Psychology, 49*(2), 161–165.

Hitler, A. (1939). *Mein kampf.* New York: Reynal & Hitchcock.

Hoiberg, A. (1980). Military effectiveness of navy men during and after Vietnam. *Armed Forces & Society, 6*(2), 232–246.

Holden, C. (1996). Whistleblower woes. *Science, 271,* 35.

Holmes, T. H., & Rahe, R. H. (1967). The social readjustment rating scale. *Journal of Psychiatric Research, 11,* 213–218.

Horowitz, M. J. (1986). *Stress response syndromes.* New York: Jason Aronson.

Horowitz, M. J., Stinson, C., & Field, N. (1991). Natural disasters and stress response syndromes. *Psychiatric Annals, 21*(9), 556–562.

Hyer, L., Boudewyns, P. A., O'Leary, W. C., & Harrison, W. R. (1987). Key determinants of the MMPI-PTSD subscale: Treatment considerations. *Journal of Clinical Psychology, 43*(3), 337–340.

Hyer, L., Braswell, L., Albrecht, B., Boyd, S., Boudewyns, P., & Talbert, S. (1994). Relationship of NEO-PI to personality styles and severity of trauma in chronic PTSD victims. *Journal of Clinical Psychology, 50*(5), 699–707.

Hyer, L., Woods, M. G., & Boudewyns, P. A. (1989). Early recollections of Vietnam veterans with PTSD. *Individual Psychology: Journal of Adlerian Theory, Research & Practice, 45*(3), 300–312.

Hyer, L., Woods, M. G., & Boudewyns, P. A. (1991). A three tier evaluation of PTSD among Vietnam combat veterans. *Journal of Traumatic Stress, 4*(2), 165–194.

Hyer, L. A., Woods, M., Harrison, W. R., & Boudewyns, P. A. (1989). MMPI F-K index among hospitalized Vietnam veterans. *Journal of Clinical Psychology, 45*(2), 250–254.

Inhelder, B., & Piaget, J. (1964). *Early growth of logic in the child: Classification and seriation.* London: Routledge & Paul.

Ironson, G., Taylor, C. B., Boltwood, M., Bartzokis, T., Dennis, C., Chesney, M., Spitzer, S., & Segall, G. M. (1992). Effects of anger on left ventricular ejection fraction in coronary artery disease. *American Journal of Cardiology, 70*(3), 281–285.

Janoff-Bulman, R. (1989a). Assumptive worlds and the stress of traumatic events: Applications of the schema construct. *Social Cognition, 7*(2), 113–136.

Janoff-Bulman, R. (1989b). The benefits of illusions, the threat of disillusionment, and the limitations of inaccuracy. *Journal of Social and Clinical Psychology, 8*(2), 158–175.

Janoff-Bulman, R. (1992). *Shattered assumptions: Towards a new psychology of trauma.* New York: Free Press.

Janoff-Bulman, R., & Brickman, P. (1982). Expectations and what people learn from failure. In N. T. Feather (Ed.), *Expectations and actions* (pp. 207–237). Hillsdale, NJ: Lawrence Erlbaum Associates.

Janoff-Bulman, R., & Marshall, G. (1982). Mortality, well-being, and control: A study of a population of institutionalized aged. *Personality & Social Psychology Bulletin, 8*(4), 691–698.

Johnson, P. (1995). Cheer up, Prince William: History may well prove on your side. *The Spectator* (Vol. 275, No. 8733), 34.

Johnson, W. B. (1995). Narcissistic personality as a mediating variable in manifestations of post-traumatic stress disorder. *Military Medicine, 160*(1), 40–41.

Jones, F. D. (1967). Experiences of a division psychiatrist in Vietnam. *Military Medicine, 132*(12), 1003–1008.

Joseph, S. A., Brewin, C. R., Yule, W., & Williams, R. (1993). Causal attributions and post-traumatic stress in adolescents. *Journal of Child Psychology and Psychiatry, 34*(2), 247–253.

Joseph, S. A., Yule, W., Williams, R., & Hodgkinson, P. (1994). Correlates of post-traumatic stress at 30 months: The Herald of Free Enterprise disaster. *Behaviour Research and Therapy, 32*(5), 521–524.

Kagan, J. (1989). Temperamental contributions to social behavior. *American Psychologist, 44*(4), 668–674.

Kagan, J. (1994). *Galen's prophecy: Temperament in human nature.* New York: Basic Books.

Kamen, L. P., & Seligman, M. E. (1987). Explanatory style and health. *Current Psychology: Research & Reviews, 6*(3), 207–218.

Kaminer, W. (1992). *I'm dysfunctional, you're dysfunctional.* Reading, MA: Addison-Wesley.

Kanner, A. D., Coyne, J. C., Schaefer, C., & Lazarus, R. S. (1981). Comparison of two modes of stress measurement: Daily hassles and uplifts versus major life events. *Journal of Behavioral Medicine, 4*, 1–39.

Kaylor, J., King, D., & King, L. (1987). Psychological effects of military service in Vietnam: A meta-analysis. *Psychological Bulletin, 102*(2), 257–271.

Keane, T. M., & Wolfe, J. (1990). Comorbidity in post-traumatic stress disorder: An analysis of community and clinical studies. *Journal of Applied Social Psychology, 20*(21, pt. 1), 1776–1788.

Kendler, K. S., Kessler, R. C., Walters, E. E., MacLean, C., Neale, M. C., Heath, A. C., & Eaves, L. J. (1995). Stressful life events, genetic liability, and onset of an episode of Major Depression in women. *American Journal of Psychiatry, 152*(6), 833–842.

Khoosal, D. I., Broad, J. A., & Smith, R. J. (1987). A one-year psychological follow-up of the most severely burned victims of the Bradford fire. *Burns, 13*(5), 411–415.

Kidson, M. A. (1993). Post-traumatic stress disorder in Australian World War II veterans attending a psychiatric outpatient clinic. *Medical Journal of Australia, 158*(8), 563–566.

Kilpatrick, D. G., & Best, C. L. (1984). Some cautionary remarks on treating sexual assault victims with implosion. *Behavior Therapy, 15*(4), 421–423.

Kilpatrick, D. G., & Calhoun, K. S. (1988). Early behavioral treatment for rape trauma: Efficacy or artifact? *Behavior Therapy, 19*(3), 421–427.

Kilpatrick, D. G., Veronen, L. J., & Resick, P. A. (1982). Psychological sequelae to rape: Assessment and treatment strategies. In D. M. Doleys, R. L. Meredith, & A. R. Ciminero (Eds.), *Behavioral medicine: Assessment and treatment strategies* (pp. 473–497). New York: Plenum.

King, D. W., King, L. A., Foy, D. W., & Gudanowski, D. M. (1996). Prewar factors in combat-related posttraumatic stress disorder: Structural equation modeling with a national sample of female and male Vietnam veterans. *Journal of Consulting and Clinical Psychology, 64*(3), 520–531.

Kiser, L., Heston, J., Hickerson, S., & Millsap, P. (1993). Anticipatory stress in children and adolescents. *American Journal of Psychiatry, 150*(1), 87–92.

Kleinmen, A., & Eisenberg, L. (1995). Mental health in low-income countries. *Nature Medicine, 1*(7), 630–631.

Kobasa, S., Hilker, R., & Maddi, S. (1979). Who stays healthy under stress? *Journal of Occupational Medicine, 21*, 595–598.

Kobasa, S. C., Maddi, S. R., Puccetti, M. C., & Zola, M. A. (1985). Effectiveness of hardiness, exercise and social support as resources against illness. *Journal of Psychosomatic Research, 29*(5), 525–533.

Kobasa, S. C., & Puccetti, M. C. (1983). Personality and social resources in stress resistance. *Journal of Personality and Social Psychology, 45*(4), 839–850.

Kohlberg, L. (1981). *The meaning and measurement of moral development.* Worcester, MA: Clark University Press.

Kohn, P. M., Lafreniere, K., & Gurevich, M. (1991). Hassles, health, and personality. *Journal of Personality and Social Psychology, 61*(3), 478–482.

Konkov, F. E. (1991). Primary psychological intervention with families of earthquake survivors in Armenia. *American Journal of Family Therapy, 19*(1), 54–59.

Koopman, C., Classen, C., & Spiegel, D. (1994). Predictors of posttraumatic stress symptoms among survivors of the Oakland/Berkeley, California firestorm. *American Journal of Psychiatry, 151*(6), 888–894.

Korgeski, G. P., & Leon, G. (1983). Correlates of self-reported and objectively determined exposure to Agent Orange. *American Journal of Psychiatry, 140*, 1443–1449.

Kozaric-Kovacic, D., Folnegovic-Smalc, V., Skrinjaric, J., Szajnberg, N. M., & Marusic, A. (1995). Rape, torture, and traumatization of Bosnian and Croatian women: Psychological sequelae. *American Journal of Orthopsychiatry, 65*(3), 428–433.

Kreitler, S., & Kreitler, H. (1988). Trauma and anxiety: The cognitive approach. *Journal of Traumatic Stress, 1*(1), 35–36.

Kreitler, S., Kreitler, H., & Carasso, R. (1987). Cognitive orientation as predictor of pain relief following acupuncture. *Pain, 28*(3), 323–241.

Kübler-Ross, E. (1969). *On death and dying.* London: Macmillan.

Kudler, H. S. (1993). Borderline personality disorder and PTSD. *American Journal of Psychiatry, 150*(12), 1906.

Kuhne, A., Orr, S. P., & Barage, E. (1993). Psychometric evaluation of post-traumatic stress disorder: The Multidimensional Personality Questionnaire as an adjunct to the MMPI. *Journal of Clinical Psychology, 49*(2), 218–225.

Kunzel, R. G. (1994). *Fallen women, problem girls.* New Haven, CT: Yale University Press.

Ladieu, G., Hanfmann, E., & Dembo, T. (1947). Studies in adjustment to visible injuries: Evaluation of help by the injured. *Journal of Abnormal and Social Psychology, 42,* 169–192.

Laufer, R. S., Gallops, M. D., & Frey-Wouters, E. (1984). War stress and trauma: The Vietnam experience. *Journal of Health and Social Behavior, 25,* 65–85.

Lazarus, R. S. (1966). *Psychological stress and the coping process.* New York: McGraw-Hill.

Lee, K. A., Vaillant, G. E., Torrey, W. C., & Elder, G. H. (1995). A 50-year prospective study of the psychological sequelae of World War II combat. *American Journal of Psychiatry, 152*(4), 516–522.

Lees-Haley, P. R., & Dunn, J. T. (1994). The ability of naive subjects to report symptoms of mild brain injury, post-traumatic stress disorder, major depression, and generalized anxiety disorder. *Journal of Clinical Psychology, 50*(2), 252–256.

Leff, J., & Vaughn, C. (1985). *Expressed emotion in families: Its significance for mental illness.* New York: Guilford Press.

Lehman, D. R., Davis, C. G., DeLongis, A., Wortman, C. B., Bluck, S., Mandel, D. R., & Ellard, J. H. (1993). Positive and negative life changes following bereavement and their relations to adjustment. *Journal of Social and Clinical Psychology, 12*(1), 90–112.

Lehman, D. R., Wortman, C. B., & Williams, A. F. (1987). Long-term effects of losing a spouse or child in a motor vehicle crash. *Journal of Personality and Social Psychology, 52*(1), 218–231.

Leor, J., Poole, W. K., & Kloner, R. A. (1996). Sudden cardiac death triggered by an earthquake. *New England Journal of Medicine, 334*(7), 413–419.

Levy, S., Herberman, R. B., Maluish, A. M., Schlien, B., & Lippman, M. (1985). Prognostic risk assessment in primary breast cancer by behavioral and immunological parameters. *Health Psychology, 4,* 99–113.

Lima, B. R., & Pai, S. (1993). Response to the psychological consequences of disasters in Latin America. *International Journal of Mental Health, 21*(4), 59–71.

Lindal, E., & Stefansson, J. G. (1993). The lifetime prevalence of anxiety disorders in Iceland as estimated by the National Institute of Mental Health Diagnostic Interview Schedule. *Acta Psychiatrica Scandinavica, 88*(1), 29–34.

Lindemann, E. (1944). Symptomatology and management of acute grief. *American Journal of Psychiatry, 101*(2), 141–148.

Lipinski, J. F., & Pope, H. G. (1994). Do "flashbacks" represent obsessional imagery? *Comprehensive Psychiatry, 35*(4), 245–247.

Livingston, H. M., Livingston, M. G., & Fell, S. (1994). The Lockerbie disaster: A 3-year follow-up of elderly victims. *International Journal of Geriatric Psychiatry, 9*(12), 989–994.

Livingston, R., Lawson, L., & Jones, J. G. (1993). Predictors of self-reported psychopathology in children abused repeatedly by a parent. *Journal of the American Academy of Child and Adolescent Psychiatry, 32*(5), 948–953.

Loehlin, J. C. (1989). Partitioning environmental and genetic contributions to behavioral development. *American Psychologist, 443,* 1285–1292.

Loftus, E. F., Garry, M., & Feldman, J. (1994). Forgetting sexual trauma: What does it mean when 38% forget? *Journal of Consulting and Clinical Psychology, 62*(6), 1177–1181.

Lonigan, C. J., Shannon, M. P., Finch, A. J., & Daugherty, T. K. (1991). Children's reactions to a natural disaster: Symptom severity and degree of exposure. *Advances in Behaviour Research and Therapy, 13*(3), 135–154.

Lonigan, C. J., Shannon, M. P., Taylor, C. M., Finch, A. J., & Sallee, F. R. (1994). Children exposed to disaster: II. Risk factors for the development of post-traumatic symptomatology. *Journal of the American Academy of Child and Adolescent Psychiatry, 33*(1), 94–105.

Luborsky, L., Singer, B., & Luborsky, L. (1975). Comparative studies of psychotherapies: Is it true that "everyone has won and all must have prizes"? *Archives of General Psychiatry, 32*, 995–1008.

Lucas, R. A. (1969). *Men in crisis: A study of a mine disaster.* New York: Basic Books.

Lund, M., Foy, D., Sipprelle, C., & Strachan, A. (1984). The Combat Exposure Scale: A systematic assessment of trauma in the Vietnam War. *Journal of Clinical Psychology, 40*(6), 1323–1328.

Lundin, T., & Bodegard, M. (1993). The psychological impact of an earthquake on rescue workers: A follow-up study of the Swedish group of rescue workers in Armenia, 1988. *Journal of Traumatic Stress, 6*(1), 129–139.

Luthar, S. S. (1991). Vulnerability and resilience: A study of high-risk adolescents. *Child Development, 62*, 600–616.

Lykken, D., & Tellegen, A. (1996). Happiness is a stochastic phenomenon. *Psychological Science, 7*(3), 186–189.

Lynn, E. J., & Belze, M. (1984). Factitious posttraumatic stress disorder: The veteran who never got to Vietnam. *Hospital and Community Psychiatry, 35*(7), 697–701.

Lyon, E. (1993). Hospital staff reactions to accounts by survivors of childhood abuse. *American Journal of Orthopsychiatry, 63*(3), 410–416.

Maher, A. (1995, August). *Lasting lessons from a lifetime of conducting and researching psychotherapy.* Paper presented at the meeting of the American Psychological Association, New York.

Maier, S. F., Watkins, L. R., & Fleschner, M. (1994). Psychoneuroimmunology: The interface between behavior, brain and immunity. *American Psychologist, 49*(12), 1004–1017.

Malan, D. H., Heath, E. S., Bacal, H. A., & Balfour, F. H. (1975). Psychodynamic changes in untreated neurotic patients. *Archives of General Psychiatry, 32*, 110–126.

Malia, K., Powell, G., & Torode, S. (1995). Coping and psychosocial function after brain injury. *Brain Injury, 9*(6), 607–618.

Malt, U. (1988). The long-term psychiatric consequences of accidental injury: A longitudinal study of 107 adults. *British Journal of Psychiatry, 153*, 810–818.

Manrique, Fr. S. (1927/1967). *Travels of Fray Sebastien Manrique 1629–1643* (C. E. Luard, Fr. H. Hosten, Trans.). Nendeln, Liechtenstein: Kraus Reprint Limited. (Original translated work published 1927)

March, J. S. (1990). The nosology of posttraumatic stress disorder. *Journal of Anxiety Disorders, 4*, 61–82.

Masten, A. S., & Best, K. M. (1990). Resilience and development: Contributions from the study of children who overcome adversity. *Development & Psychopathology, 2*(4), 425–444.

Mayou, R., Bryant, B., & Duthie, R. (1993). Psychiatric consequences of road traffic accidents. *British Medical Journal, 307*(6905), 647–651.

Maziade, M., Caron, C., Coté, R., Mérette, C., Bernier, H., Laplante, B., Boutin, P., & Thivierge, J. (1990). Psychiatric status of adolescents who had extreme temperaments at age 7. *American Journal of Psychiatry, 147*(11), 1531–1536.

McCarren, M., Janes, G. R., Goldberg, J., Eisen, S. A., True, W. R., & Henderson, W. G. (1995). A twin study of the association of post-traumatic stress disorder and combat exposure with long-term socioeconomic status in Vietnam veterans. *Journal of Traumatic Stress, 8*(1), 111–24.

McCarroll, J. E., Ursano, R. J., & Fullerton, C. S. (1995). Symptoms of PTSD following recovery of war dead: 13–15-month follow-up. *American Journal of Psychiatry, 152*(6), 939–941.

McCaughey, B. G. (1984). U.S. Coast Guard collision at sea. *U.S. Naval Health Research Center Report, 84*(20), 1–8.

McCord, J. (1978). A thirty-year follow-up of treatment effects. *American Psychologist, 33*(3), 284–289.

McCord, J. (1979). Following up on Cambridge–Somerville: Response to Paul Wortman. *American Psychologist, 34*(8), 727.

McCormick, R. A., Taber, J. I., & Kruedelback, N. (1989). The relationship between attributional style and post-traumatic stress disorder in addicted patients. *Journal of Traumatic Stress, 2*(4), 477–487.

McCrae, R. R., & Costa, P. T. J. (1987). Validation of the five-factor model of personality across instruments and observers. *Journal of Personality and Social Psychology, 52*(1), 81–90.

McDermott, B. (1996, August 11). *Sutherland Bushfire trauma project: A randomized controlled treatment trial*. Paper presented at the meeting of the American Psychological Association, Toronto.

McDonough, M. (1995, July 29). Susan Smith gets life in prison. *The Herald-Journal of Spartanburg, SC*, p. 1.

McFarlane, A. C. (1987). Life events and psychiatric disorder: The role of a natural disaster. *British Journal of Psychiatry, 151*, 362–67.

McFarlane, A. C. (1988a). The longitudinal course of posttraumatic morbidity: The range of outcomes and their predictions. *Journal of Nervous and Mental Disease, 176*(11), 30–39.

McFarlane, A. C. (1988b). Relationship between psychiatric impairment and a natural disaster: The role of distress. *Psychological Medicine, 18*, 129–139.

McFarlane, A. C. (1990). An Australian disaster: The 1983 bushfires. *International Journal of Mental Health, 19*(2), 36–47.

McFarlane, A. C. (1992). Avoidance and intrusion in posttraumatic stress disorder. *Journal of Nervous and Mental Disease, 180*(7), 439–445.

McFarlane, A. C. (1994). Individual psychotherapy for posttraumatic stress disorder. *Psychiatric Clinics of North America, 17*(2), 393–408.

McFarlane, A. C., & Papay, P. (1992). Multiple diagnoses in posttraumatic stress disorder in the victims of a natural disaster. *Journal of Nervous and Mental Disease, 180*(8), 498–504.

McFarlane, A. C., Policansky, S. K., & Irwin, C. (1987). A longitudinal study of the psychological morbidity in children due to a natural disaster. *Psychological Medicine, 17*, 727–738.

McIntosh, D. N., Cohen, R., & Wortman, C. B. (1993). Religion's role in adjustment to a negative life event: Coping with the loss of a child. *Journal of Personality and Social Psychology, 65*(4), 812–821.

McKnight, J. (1994). *Community and its counterfeits* [Radio broadcast, Canadian Broadcasting Corporation]. Toronto: Canadian Broadcasting Corporation RadioWorks.

McNally, R. J., & Shin, L. M. (1995). Association of intelligence with severity of posttraumatic stress disorder symptoms in Vietnam combat veterans. *American Journal of Psychiatry, 152*(6), 936–938.

McSherry, W. C., & Holm, J. E. (1994). Sense of coherence: Its effects on psychological and physiological processes prior to, during, and after a stressful situation. *Journal of Clinical Psychology, 50*(4), 476–487.

Mecca, A. M., Smelser, N. J., & Vasconsellos, J. (1989). *The social importance of self-esteem*. Berkeley, CA: University of California Press.

Merry, S. N., & Andrews, L. K. (1994). Psychiatric status of sexually abused children 12 months after disclosure of abuse. *Journal of American Child and Adolescent Psychiatry, 33*(7), 939–944.

Meyer, T. J., & Mark, M. M. (1995). Effects of psychosocial interventions with adult cancer patients: A meta-analysis of randomized experiments. *Health Psychology, 14*(2), 101–108.

Micale, M. (1994). Charcot and les nèvroses traumatiques: Historical and scientific reflections. *Revue Neurologique (Paris), 150*(8–9), 498–505.

Milgram, R. M., & Milgram, N. A. (1976). The effect of the Yom Kippur War on anxiety level in Israeli children. *Journal of Psychology, 94,* 107–113.

Miller, D. T., & Turnbull, W. (1992). The counterfactual fallacy: Confusing what might have been with what ought to have been. In L. Montada, S. H. Filipp, & M. Lerner (Eds.), *Life crises and experiences of loss in adulthood* (pp. 179–193). Hillsdale, NJ: Lawrence Erlbaum Associates.

Miller, P. M., & Ingham, J. G. (1979). Reflections on the life-events-to-illness link with some preliminary findings. In I. Sarason & C. Spielberger (Eds.), *Stress and anxiety* (Vol. 6, pp. 313–336). New York: John Wiley.

Miller, S. M. (1992). Monitoring and blunting in the face of threat: Implications for adaptation and health. In L. Montada, S. H. Filipp, & M. Lerner (Eds.), *Life crises and experiences of loss in adulthood* (pp. 255–273). Hillsdale, NJ: Lawrence Erlbaum Associates.

Minkowski, A., Morisseau, L., Marciano, P., & Hurau, R. (1993). Mental stress on children exposed to war and natural disaster. *Infant Mental Health Journal, 14*(4), 273–282.

Miranda, J., Perez-Stable, E. J., Munoz, R. F., Hargreaves, W., & Henke, C. J. (1991). Somatization, psychiatric disorder, and stress in utilization of ambulatory medical services. *Health Psychology, 10*(1), 46–51.

Mo, G. M., Chen, G. Q., Li, L. Z., & Tseng, W. S. (1995). Koro epidemics in Southern China. In T. Y. Lin, W. S. Tseng, & E. K. Yeh (Eds.), *Chinese societies and mental health* (pp. 231–246). Hong Kong: Oxford University Press.

Morens, D. M. (1995). Mass fainting at medieval rock concerts. *New England Journal of Medicine, 333*(20), 1361.

Morgan, C. A., Grillon, C., Southwick, S. M., & Nagy, L. M. (1995). Yohimbine facilitated acoustic startle in combat veterans with post-traumatic stress disorder. *Psychopharmacology, 117*(4), 466–471.

Morgan, H. J., & Janoff-Bulman, R. (1994). Positive and negative self-complexity: Patterns of adjustment following traumatic versus nontraumatic life experiences. *Journal of Social and Clinical Psychology, 13*(1), 63–85.

Munroe, J. F., Shay, J., Fisher, L., Makary, C., Rapperport, K., & Zimering, R. (1995). Preventing compassion fatigue: A team treatment model. In C. R. Figley (Ed.), *Compassion fatigue: Coping with secondary traumatic stress disorder in those who treat the traumatized* (pp. 209-231). New York: Brunner/Mazel.

Murphy, S. A. (1984). After Mount St. Helens: Disaster stress research. *Journal of Psychosocial Nursing and Mental Health Services, 22*(7), 9–18.

Myers, D. G. (1993). *The pursuit of happiness: Who is happy—and why.* New York: Avon.

Myers, D. G., & Diener, E. (1995). Who is happy? *Psychological Science, 6*(1), 10–19.

Nader, K., Pynoos, R., Fairbanks, L., & Frederick, C. (1990). Children's PTSD reactions one year after a sniper attack at their school. *American Journal of Psychiatry, 147*(11), 1526–1530.

Nader, K. O., Pynoos, R. S., Fairbanks, L. A., al Ajeel, M., & al Asfour, A. (1993). A preliminary study of PTSD and grief among the children of Kuwait following the Gulf Crisis. *British Journal of Psychology, 32*(3), 407–416.

Newman, B. (1980, March 7). Malaysian malady: When the spirit hits, a scapegoat suffers. *The Wall Street Journal,* pp. 1, 24.

Newman, E., Orsillo, S. M., Herman, D. S., Niles, B. L., & Litz, B. T. (1995). Clinical presentation of disorders of extreme stress in combat veterans. *Journal of Nervous and Mental Disease, 183*(10), 628–632.

Nolen-Hoeksema, S., & Morrow, J. (1991). A prospective study of depression and posttraumatic stress symptoms after a natural disaster: The 1989 Loma Prieta earthquake. *Journal of Personality and Social Psychology, 61*(1), 115–121.

Norris, F. (1990). Screening for traumatic stress: A scale for use in the general population. *Journal of Applied Social Psychology, 20*, 1704–1718.

Norris, F. H. (1992). Epidemiology of trauma: Frequency and impact of different potentially traumatic events in different demographic groups. *Journal of Consulting and Clinical Psychology, 60*(3), 409–418.

Norris, F. H., & Gary, A. (1993). Chronic stress as a mediator of acute stress: The case of Hurricane Hugo. *Journal of Applied Social Psychology, 23*, 1263–1284.

North, C. S., Smith, E. M., McCool, R. E., & Lightcap, P. (1989). Acute postdisaster coping and adjustment. *Journal of Traumatic Stress, 2*(3), 353–360.

North, C. S., Smith, E. M., & Spitznagel, E. L. (1994). Violence and the homeless: An epidemiological study of victimization and aggression. *Journal of Traumatic Stress, 7*(1), 95–110.

Norton, G. R., Goszer, L., Strub, H., & Man, S. C. (1984). The effects of belief on acupuncture analgesia. *Canadian Journal of Behavioural Science, 16*(1), 22–29.

Ormel, J., & Wohlfarth, T. (1991). How neuroticism, long-term difficulties, and life situation change influence psychological distress: A longitudinal model. *Journal of Personality and Social Psychology, 60*(5), 744–755.

Packer, I. K. (1983). Post-traumatic stress disorder and the insanity defense: A critical analysis. *Journal of Psychiatry and Law, 11*(2), 125–136.

Patterson, T. L., Shaw, W. S., Semple, S. J., Cherner, M., McCutchan, J. A., Atkinson, J. H., Grant, I., Nannis, E., & HIV Group. (1996). Relationship of psychosocial factors to HIV disease progression. *Annals of Behavioral Medicine, 18*(1), 30–39.

Pearlin, L. I., & Schooler, C. (1978). The structure of coping. *Journal of Health and Social Behavior, 19*, 2–21.

Pearlman, L. A., & MacIan, P. S. (1995). Vicarious traumatization: An empirical study of the effects of trauma work on trauma therapists. *Professional Psychology: Research and Practice, 26*, 558–565.

Peterson, C., Seligman, M., & Vaillant, G. E. (1988). Pessimistic explanatory style is a risk factor for physical illness: A thirty-five-year longitudinal study. *Journal of Personality and Social Psychology, 55*(1), 23–27.

Peterson, C., & Seligman, M. E. (1983). Learned helplessness and victimization. *Journal of Social Issues, 39*(2), 103–116.

Peterson, C., & Seligman, M. E. (1984). Causal explanations as a risk factor for depression: Theory and evidence. *Psychological Review, 91*(3), 347–374.

Petrie, K., Moss–Morris, R., & Weinman, J. (1995). The impact of catastrophic beliefs on functioning in chronic fatigue syndrome. *Journal of Psychosomatic Research, 39*(1), 31–37.

Pickens, J., Field, T., Prodromidis, M., & Pelaez-Nogueras, M. (1995). Posttraumatic stress, depression and social support among college students after Hurricane Andrew. *Journal of College Student Development, 36*(2), 152–161.

Pillemer, K. A. (1986). Risk factors in elder abuse: Results from a case-control study. In K. A. Pillemer & R. S. Wolf (Eds.), *Elder abuse: Conflict in the family* (pp. 239–265). Dover, MA: Auburn House.

Pitman, R. K., & Orr, S. P. (1993). Psychophysiologic testing for post-traumatic stress disorder: Forensic psychiatry application. *Bulletin of the American Academy of Psychiatry and Law, 21*, 37–52.

Platt, J. J., & Husband, S. D. (1986). Post-traumatic stress disorder in forensic practice. *America Journal of Forensic Psychology, 4*(1), 29–56.

Plomin, R. (1989). Environment and genes. *American Psychologist, 44*(2), 105–111.

Pogrebin, R. (1996, January 28). Anatomy of a murder scene. *The New York Times Magazine*, pp. 42–48.

Poole, D. A., Lindsay, D. S., Memon, A., & Bull, R. (1995). Psychotherapy and the recovery of memories of childhood sexual abuse: U.S. and British practitioners' opinions, practices, and experiences. *Journal of Consulting and Clinical Psychology, 63*, 426–437.

Potts, M. K. (1994). Long-term effects of trauma: Post-traumatic stress among civilian internees of the Japanese during World War II. *Journal of Clinical Psychology, 50*(5), 681–698.

Powers, P. S., Cruse, C. W., Daniels, S., & Stevens, B. (1994). Posttraumatic stress disorder in patients with burns. *Journal of Burn Care Rehabilitation, 15*(2), 147–53.

Pozgain, I., Filakovic, P., & Perekovic, V. (1992). Posttraumatic stress disorder in Croatian soldiers at east Slavonian front [On-line]. *Psychologische Beitrafe, 34*, 258–263. (Abstract from: PsycINFO Item: 82-37134)

Pynoos, R. S., Goenjian, A., Tashjian, M., Karakashian, M., Manjikian, R., Manoukian, G., Steinberg, A. M., & Fairbanks, L. A. (1993). Post-traumatic stress reactions in children after the 1988 Armenian earthquake. *British Journal of Psychiatry, 163*, 239–247.

Pyszczynski, T. (1989). Depression, self-focused attention, and the negative memory bias. *Journal of Personality and Social Psychology, 57*, 351–357.

Quarantelli, E. L. (1985). An assessment of conflicting views on mental health: The consequences of traumatic events. In C. R. Figley (Ed.), *Trauma and its wake* (pp. 173–215). New York: Brunner/Mazel.

Quirk, G. J., & Casco, L. (1994). Stress disorders of families of the disappeared: A controlled study in Honduras. *Social Science and Medicine, 39*(12), 1675–1979.

Rabkin, J. G., & Struening, E. L. (1976). Life events, stress and illness. *Science, 194*, 1013–1020.

Rabkin, J. G., Wagner, G., & Rabkin, R. (1996). Treatment of depression in HIV+ men: Literature review and report of an ongoing study of testosterone replacement therapy. *Annals of Behavioral Medicine, 18*(1), 24–29.

Ravella, P. C. (1995). A survey of U.S. Air Force flight nurses' adaptation to service in Vietnam. *Aviation and Space Environmental Medicine, 66*(1), 80–83.

Reinherz, H. Z., Giaconia, R. M., Lefkowitz, E. S., Pakiz, B., & Frost, A. K. (1993). Prevalence of psychiatric disorders in a community population of older adolescents. *Journal of the American Academy of Child and Adolescent Psychiatry, 32*(2), 369–377.

Renaud, H., & Estes, F. (1961). Life history interviews with one hundred normal American males: "Pathogenicity" of childhood. *American Journal of Orthopsychiatry, 31*, 786–802.

Reppucci, N. D., & Haugaard, J. J. (1989). Prevention of child sexual abuse. *American Psychologist, 44*(10), 1266–1275.

Resnick, H. S., Kilpatrick, D. G., Best, C. L., & Kramer, T. L. (1992). Vulnerability–stress factors in development of posttraumatic stress disorder. *Journal of Nervous and Mental Disease, 180*(7), 424–430.

Resnick, H. S., Kilpatrick, D. G., Dansky, B. S., Saunders, B. E., & Best, C. L. (1993). Prevalence of civilian trauma and posttraumatic stress disorder in a representative national sample of women. *Journal of Consulting and Clinical Psychology, 61*(6), 984–991.

Riccio, D. C., Rabinowitz, V. C., & Axelrod, S. (1994). Memory: When less is more. *American Psychologist, 49*(11), 917–926.

Rich, V. (1994, November 26). Armenia's poor health. *The Lancet, 344*, 1496.

Riggs, D. S., Rothman, B. O., & Foa, E. B. (1995). A prospective examination of symptoms of posttraumatic stress disorder in victims of nonsexual assault. *Journal of Interpersonal Violence, 10*(2), 210–214.

Rimland, B. (1969). Psychogenesis versus biogenesis: The issues and the evidence. In S. C. Plog & R. B. Edgerton (Eds.), *Changing perspectives in mental illness* (pp. 702–735). New York: Holt, Rinehart and Winston.

Rittenberg, S., & Bennett, A. (1993). *The man who stayed behind*. New York: Simon & Schuster.

Roca, R. P., Spence, R. J., & Munster, A. M. (1992). Posttraumatic adaptation and distress among adult burn survivors. *American Journal of Psychiatry, 149*(9), 1234–1238.

Rosen, G. R. (1995). The Aleutian Enterprise sinking and posttraumatic stress disorder: Misdiagnosis in clinical and forensic settings. *Professional Psychology: Research and Practice, 26*(1), 82–87.

Rosser, R., Dewar, S., & Thompson, J. (1991). Psychiatric aspects of disaster. *Journal of the Royal Society of Medicine, 84*(1), 4–8.

Rotter, J. B. (1966). Generalized expectancies for internal vs. external control of reinforcement. *Psychological Monographs: General and Applied, 80*(1/609), 1–28.

Rubonis, A., & Bickman, L. (1991). Psychological impairment in the wake of disaster: The disaster–psychopathology relationship. *Psychological Bulletin, 109*, 384–399.

Ruijs, M. B., Gabreels, F. J., & Keyser, A. (1993). The relation between neurological trauma parameters and long-term outcome in children with closed head injury. *European Journal of Pediatrics, 152*(10), 844–847.

Rutter, M. (1986). Meyerian psychobiology, personality development, and the role of life experiences. *American Journal of Psychiatry, 143*(9), 1077–1087.

Rutter, M. (1989). Pathways from childhood to adult life. *Journal of Child Psychology and Psychiatry, 30*, 23–51.

Rutter, M. (1994). Beyond longitudinal data: Causes, consequences, changes, and continuity. *Journal of Consulting and Clinical Psychology, 62*(5), 928–940.

Sack, W. H., Clarke, G., Him, C., Dickason, D., Goff, B., Lanham, K., & Kinzie, J. D. (1993). A 6-year follow-up study of Cambodian refugee adolescents traumatized as children. *Journal of the American Academy of Child and Adolescent Psychiatry, 32*(2), 431–437.

Saigh, P. A. (1988). Anxiety, depression, and assertion across alternating intervals of stress. *Journal of Abnormal Psychology, 97*(3), 338–341.

Sampson, R. J., & Laub, J. H. (1993). *Crime in the making: Pathways and turning points through life*. Cambridge, MA: Harvard University Press.

Sarason, B. R., Sarason, I. G., & Pierce, G. R. (Eds.). (1990). *Social support: An interactional view*. New York: John Wiley & Sons.

Scarr, S., & McCartney, K. (1983). How people make their own environments: A theory of genotype–environment effects. *Child Development, 54*, 424–435.

Schachter, S., & Singer, J. E. (1962). Cognitive, social and physiological determinants of emotional state. *Psychological Review, 69*, 379–399.

Schauben, L. J., & Frazier, P. A. (1995). Vicarious trauma: The effects on female counselors of working with sexual violence survivors. *Psychology of Women Quarterly, 19*, 49–64.

Scheier, M. F., & Carver, C. S. (1992). Effects of optimism on psychological and physical well-being: Theoretical overview and empirical update. *Cognitive Therapy and Research, 16*, 201–228.

Schnurr, P. P., Friedman, M. J., & Rosenberg, S. D. (1993). Premilitary MMPI scores as predictors of combat-related PTSD symptoms. *American Journal of Psychiatry, 150*, 479–483.

Schottenfield, R. S., & Cullen, M. R. (1995). Occupation-induced post-traumatic stress disorders. *American Journal of Psychiatry, 142*, 198–202.

Schwartzberg, S. S., & Janoff-Bulman, R. (1991). Grief and the search for meaning: Exploring the assumptive worlds of bereaved college students. *Journal of Social and Clinical Psychology, 10*(3), 270–288.

Schwarz, E. D., & Kowalski, J. M. (1992). Personality characteristics and posttraumatic stress symptoms after a school shooting. *Journal of Nervous and Mental Disease, 180*(11), 735–737.

Schwarz, E. D., & Kowalski, J. M. (1993). Malignant memories: Effect of a shooting in the workplace on school personnel's attitudes. *Journal of Interpersonal Violence, 8*(4), 468–485.

Scott, J. (1991, September 21). It was mass hysteria—and the cause remains unknown. *The Vancouver Sun* (reprinted from the *Los Angeles Times*), p. B7

Scott, R. B., Brooks, N., & McKinlay, W. (1995). Post-traumatic morbidity in a civilian community of litigants: A follow-up at 3 years. *Journal of Traumatic Stress, 8*(3), 403–417.

Segal, S. A., & Figley, C. R. (1988). Stressful events. *Hospital and Community Psychiatry, 39*(9), 998.

Seligman, M. E. P., & Buchanan, G. (1995, August). *Learned optimism: Prevention of depression and of ill health.* Paper presented at the meeting of the American Psychological Association, New York.

Seligman, M. E. P., Kamen, L. P., & Nolen-Hoeksma, S. (1988). Explanatory style across the lifespan: Achievement and health. In R. M. Lerner, E. M. Hetherington, & M. Perlmutter (Eds.), *Child development in lifespan perspective* (pp. 91–114). Hillsdale, NJ: Lawrence Erlbaum Associates.

Shader, R. I., & Schwartz, A. J. (1966). Management of reactions to disaster. *Social Work, 11*(2), 99–104.

Shannon, M. P., Lonigan, C. J., Finch, A. J., & Taylor, C. M. (1994). Children exposed to disaster: I. Epidemiology of post-traumatic symptoms and symptom profiles. *Journal of the American Academy of Child and Adolescent Psychiatry, 33*(1), 80–93.

Shapiro, D. A., & Barkham, M. (1990). The second Sheffield psychotherapy project: Rationale, design and preliminary outcome data. *British Journal of Medical Psychology, 63*(2), 97–108.

Shapiro, D. A., Harper, H., Startup, M. J., Reynolds, S., Bird, D., & Suokas, A. (1994). The high watermark of the drug metaphor. In R. L. Russell (Ed.), *Reassessing psychotherapy research* (pp. 1–35). New York: Guilford Press.

Shapiro, D. A., & Shapiro, D. (1982). Meta-analysis of comparative therapy outcome research: Descriptive statistics on 143 studies. *Catalog of Selected Documents in Psychology, 12*(4), 46–47.

Shapiro, F. (1995). *Eye movement desensitization and reprocessing: Basic principles, protocols, and procedures.* New York: Guilford Press.

Shedler, J., Mayman, M., & Manis, M. (1993). The illusion of mental health. *American Psychologist, 48*(11), 1117–1131.

Sherwood, R. J., Funari, D. J., & Piekarski, A. M. (1990). Adapted characters styles of Vietnam veterans with Posttraumatic Stress Disorder. *Psychological Reports, 66*(2), 623–631.

Shontz, F. C. (1975). *The psychological aspects of physical illness and disability.* New York: Macmillan.

Shore, J. H., Vollmer, W. M., & Tatum, E. L. (1989). Community patterns of posttraumatic stress disorders. *Journal of Nervous and Mental Disease, 177*(11), 681–685.

Sigal, J. J., & Weinfeld, M. (1985). Stability of coping style 33 years after prolonged exposure to extreme stress. *Acta Psychiatrica Scandinavica, 71*(6), 559–566.

Sigal, J. J., & Weinfeld, M. (1989). *Trauma and rebirth: Intergenerational effects of the Holocaust.* New York: Praeger.

Silk, K. R., Westen, D., Lohr, N. E., & Ogata, S. N. (1991). "Dissociation, borderline personality disorder, and childhood trauma": Reply. *American Journal of Psychiatry, 148*(6), 812–813.

Silsby, H. D., & Jones, F. D. (1985). The etiologies of Vietnam posttraumatic stress syndrome. *Military Medicine, 150*, 6–7.

Silver, R., Wortman, C. B., & Crofton, C. (1990). The role of coping in support provision: The self presentational dilemma of victims of life crisis. In B. R. Sarason, I. G. Sarason, & G. R. Pierce (Eds.), *Social support: An interactional view* (pp. 397–426). New York: Wiley.

Sinclair, R. C., Hoffman, C., Mark, M. M., Martin, L. L., & Pickering, T. L. (1994). Construct accessibility and the misattribution of arousal: Schachter and Singer revisited. *Psychological Science, 5*(1), 15–19.

Skre, I., Onstad, S., Torgersen, S., Lygren, S., & Kringlen, E. (1993). A twin study of DSM–III–R anxiety disorders. *Acta Psychiatrica Scandinavica, 88*(2), 85–92.

Skuse, D. (1984). Extreme deprivation in early childhood. *Journal of Child Psychology and Psychiatry, 25*(4), 523–573.

Slagle, D. A., Reichman, M., Rodenhauser, P., Knoedler, D., & Davis, C. L. (1990). Community psychological effects following a non-fatal aircraft accident. *Aviation, Space, and Environmental Medicine, 61*(10), 879–886.

Sloan, P. (1988). Post-traumatic stress in survivors of an airplane crash-landing: A clinical and exploratory research intervention. *Journal of Traumatic Stress, 1*(2), 211–229.

Small, G. W., Propper, M. W. (1991). Mass hysteria among student performers: Social relationships as a symptom predicator. *American Journal of Psychiatry, 148*, 1200–1205.

Smith, D. W., & Frueh, B. C. (1996). Compensation seeking, comorbidity, and apparent exaggeration of PTSD symptoms among Vietnam combat veterans. *Psychological Assessment, 8*(1), 3–6.

Smith, E. M., Robins, L. M., Przubeck, T. R., Goldrig, E., & Solomon, S. (1986). Psychosocial consequences of a disaster. In J. Shore & L. Robins (Eds.), *Psychosocial disaster stress studies: New methods and findings* (pp. 49–76). Washington, DC: American Psychiatric Press.

Smith, M. L., Glass, G. V., & Miller, T. I. (1980). *The benefits of psychotherapy.* Baltimore, MD: Johns Hopkins University Press.

Solomon, A., & Shalev, A. Y. (1995). Helping victims of military trauma. In J. R. Freedy & S. E. Hobfoll (Eds.), *Traumatic stress: From theory to practice* (pp. 241–261). New York: Plenum.

Solomon, S. D., Gerrity, E. T., & Muff, A. M. (1992). Efficacy of treatments for posttraumatic stress disorder. *Journal of the American Medical Association, 268*(5), 633–638.

Solomon, Z., Shalev, A., Spiro, S. E., Dolev, A., Bleich, A., Waysman, M., & Cooper, S. (1992). Negative psychometric outcomes: Self-report measures and a follow-up telephone survey. *Journal of Traumatic Stress, 5*, 225–246.

Southwick, S. M., Morgan, A., Nagy, L. M., Bremner, D., Nicolaou, A. L., Johnson, D. R., Rosenheck, R., & Charney, D. S. (1993). Trauma-related symptoms in veterans of Operation Desert Storm: A preliminary report. *American Journal of Psychiatry, 150*(10), 1524–1528.

Southwick, S. M., Yehuda, R., & Giller, E. L. (1993). Personality disorders in treatment-seeking combat veterans with posttraumatic stress disorder. *American Journal of Psychiatry, 150*(7), 1020–1023.

Sparr, L. F. (1995). Post-traumatic stress disorder: Does it exist? *Neurologic Clinics, 13*(2), 413–429.

Spiegel, D., & Sands, S. H. (1989). Psychological influences on metastatic disease progression. *Cancer Growth and Progression, 8*, 282–288.

Spurrell, M. T., & McFarlane, A. C. (1993). Post-traumatic stress disorder and coping after a natural disaster. *Social Psychiatry and Psychiatric Epidemiology, 28*(4), 194–200.

Steele, G. P., Henderson, S., & Duncan-Jones, P. (1980). The reliability of reporting adverse experiences. *Psychological Medicine, 10*, 301–306.

Steenbarger, B. N. (1994). Duration and outcome in psychotherapy: An integrative review. *Professional Psychology: Research and Practice, 25*(2), 111–119.

Steinglass, P., & Gerrity, E. (1990). Natural disasters and posttraumatic stress disorder: Short-term versus long-term recovery in two disaster-affected communities. *Journal of Applied Social Psychology, 20*(1), 1746–1765.

Stevenson, H. W., Chen, C. S., & Lee, S. Y. (1993). Mathematics achievement of Chinese, Japanese, and American children: Ten years later. *Science, 259*(5091), 53–58.

Stevenson, H. W., Lee, S. Y., & Stigler, J. W. (1986). Mathematics achievement of Chinese, Japanese, and American children. *Science, 231*(4739), 693–699.

Stiles, W. B., & Shapiro, D. (1994). Disabuse of the drug metaphor: Psychotherapy process–outcome correlations. *Journal of Consulting and Clinical Psychology, 62*, 942–948.

Stout, C. E., & Knight, T. (1990). Impact of a natural disaster on a psychiatric inpatient population: Clinical observations. *Psychiatric Hospital, 21*(3), 129–135.

Strachan, A. (1994, November 18). Attention to students way to break cycle of violence. *The Vancouver Sun,* p. B9.

Stratton, J. G., Parker, D. A., & Snibbe, J. R. (1984). Post-traumatic stress: Study of police officers involved in shootings. *Psychological Reports, 55*(1), 127–131.

Strelau, J. (1995). Temperament risk factor: The contribution of temperament to the consequences of the state of stress. In S. E. Hobfoll & M. W. de Vries (Eds.), *Extreme stress and communities: Impact and intervention* (pp. 63–81). Dordrecht, the Netherlands: Kluwer Academic.

Summers, G. M., & Cowan, M. L. (1991). Mental health issues related to the development of a natural disaster response system. *Military Medicine, 156*(1), 30–32.

Sutker, P. B., & Allain, A. N. (1995). Psychological assessment of aviators captured in World War II. *Psychological Assessment, 7*(1), 66–68.

Sutker, P. B., & Allain, A. N. (1996). Assessment of PTSD and other mental disorders in World War II and Korean conflict POW survivors and combat veterans. *Psychological Assessment, 8*(1), 18–25.

Sutker, P. B., Davis, J. M., Uddo, M., & Ditta, S. R. (1995). War zone stress, personal resources, and PTSD in Persian Gulf War returnees. *Journal of Abnormal Psychology, 104*(3), 444–452.

Sutker, P. B., Uddo, M., Brailey, K., Allain, A. N., & Errera, P. (1994). Psychological symptoms and psychiatric diagnoses in Operation Desert Storm troops serving Graves registration duty. *Journal of Traumatic Stress, 7*(2), 159–71.

Swanson, G. S., & Blount, J. (1990). Comprehensive System Rorschach data on Vietnam combat veterans. *Journal of Personality Assessment, 54*(1–2), 160–169.

Swartz, L., & Levett, A. (1989). Political repression and children in South Africa: The social construction of damaging effects. *Social Science & Medicine, 28*, 741.

Talbert, F. S., Albrecht, N. N., Albrecht, J. W., Boudewyns, P. A., Hyer, L. A., Touzé, J. H., & Lemmon, C. R. (1994). MMPI profiles in PTSD as a function of comorbidity. *Journal of Clinical Psychology, 504*(4), 529–536.

Talbert, F. S., Braswell, L. C., Albrecht, J. W., Hyer, L. A., & Boudewyns, P. A. (1993). NEO-PI profiles in PTSD as a function of trauma level. *Journal of Clinical Psychology, 49*(5), 663–669.

Taubes, G. (1995). Epidemiology faces its limits. *Science, 269*, 164–169.

Taylor, D. M., Wright, S. C., Moghaddam, F. M., & Lalonde, R. N. (1990). The personal/group discrimination discrepancy: Perceiving my group, but not myself, to be a target for discrimination. *Personality and Social Psychology Bulletin, 16,* 254–262.

Taylor, S. E., & Brown, J. D. (1988). Illusion and well-being: A social psychological perspective on mental health. *Psychological Bulletin, 103,* 193–210.

Taylor, S. E., & Brown, J. D. (1994). "Illusion" of mental health does not explain positive illusions. *American Psychologist, 49*(11), 972–973.

Team, C. N. F. I. (1995). Epidemic optic neuropathy in Cuba: Clinical characterization and risk factors. *New England Journal of Medicine, 333*(18), 1176–1182.

Tellegen, A., Lykken, D. T., Bouchard, T. J., Wilcox, K. J., Segal, N. C., & Rich, S. (1988). Personality similarity in twins reared apart and together. *Journal of Personality and Social Psychology, 54*(6), 1031–1039.

Terr, L. C. (1981). Psychic trauma in children: Observations following the Chowchilla school-bus kidnapping. *American Journal of Psychiatry, 138*(1), 14–19.

Tranah, T., & Farmer, R. D. (1994). Psychological reactions of drivers to railway suicide. *Social Science and Medicine, 38*(3), 459–469.

Tversky, A., & Kahneman, D. (1974). Judgments under uncertainty: Heuristics and biases. *Science, 185,* 1124–1131.

Ulicny, G. R. (1994). Marketing brain injury rehabilitation services: Toward a more ethical approach. *Journal of Head Trauma and Rehabilitation, 9*(4), 73–76.

Ullman, S. E. (1995). Adult trauma survivors and post-traumatic stress sequelae: An analysis of reexperiencing, avoidance, and arousal criteria. *Journal of Traumatic Stress, 8*(1), 179–188.

Ursano, R. J., McCaughey, B. G., & Fullerton, C. S. (Eds.). (1994). *Individual and community responses to trauma and disaster: The structure of human chaos.* Cambridge, UK: Cambridge University Press.

Usala, P. D., & Hertzog, C. (1991). Evidence of differential stability of state and trait anxiety in adults. *Journal of Personality and Social Psychology, 60*(3), 471–479.

van der Kolk, B. A., van der Hart, O., & Burbridge, J. (1995). The treatment of post traumatic stress disorder. In S. E. Hobfoll & M. W. deVries (Eds.), *Extreme stress and communities: Impact and intervention* (pp. 421–443). Dordrecht, Netherlands: Kluwer Academic.

van Driel, R. C., & Op den Velde, W. (1995). Myocardial infarction and post-traumatic stress disorder. *Journal of Traumatic Stress, 8*(1), 151–159.

Vaughan, K., Armstrong, M. S., Gold, R., O'Connor, H., Jenneke, W., & Tarrier, N. (1994). A trial of eye movement desensitization compared to image habituation training and applied muscle relaxation in post-traumatic stress disorder. *Journal of Behavioral Therapy and Experimental Psychiatry, 25*(4), 283–291.

Vernberg, E. M., & Vogel, J. M. (1993). Interventions with children after disasters. *Journal of Clinical Child Psychology, 22,* 485–498.

Vrana, S., & Lauterbach, D. (1994). Prevalence of traumatic events and posttraumatic psychological symptoms in a nonclinical sample of college students. *Journal of Traumatic Stress, 7*(2), 289–302.

Waller, N. G., & Shaver, P. R. (1994). The importance of nongenetic influences on romantic love styles: A twin-family study. *American Psychological Society, 5*(5), 268–274.

Watson, C. G., Tuorila, J., Detra, E., Gearhart, L. P., & Wielkiewicz, R. M. (1995). Effects of a Vietnam War memorial pilgrimage on veterans with posttraumatic stress disorder. *Journal of Nervous and Mental Disease, 183*(5), 315–319.

Watson, D., & Tellegen, A. (1985). Toward a consensual structure of mood. *Psychological Bulletin, 98*(2), 219–235.

Watson, J. C. (1996). The relationship between vivid description, emotional arousal, and in-session resolution of problematic reactions. *Journal of Consulting and Clinical Psychology, 64*(3), 459–464.

Watson, P. B. (1989). A tormented mind: Clinical and theoretical implications of overwhelming life events. *Australian & New Zealand Journal of Psychiatry, 23*(1), 97–102.

Weaver, T. L., & Clum, G. A. (1995). Psychological distress associated with interpersonal violence: A meta-analysis. *Clinical Psychology Review, 15*(2), 115–140.

Wedding, D., & Faust, D. (1989). Clinical judgment and decision making in neuropsychology. *Archives of Clinical Neuropsychology, 4*(3), 233–265.

Weisenberg, M., Schwarzwald, J., Waysman, M., Solomon, Z., & Klingman, A. (1993). Coping of school-age children in the sealed room during SCUD missile bombardment and postwar stress reactions. *Journal of Consulting and Clinical Psychology, 61*(3), 462–467.

Weiss, D. S., & Marmar, C. R. (1993). Teaching time-limited dynamic psychotherapy for post-traumatic stress disorder and pathological grief. *Psychotherapy, 30*(4), 587–591.

Werner, E. E. (1993). Risk, resilience, and recovery: Perspectives from the Kauai Longitudinal Study. *Development and Psychopathology, 5*(4), 503–515.

Wessely, S. (1987). Mass hysteria: Two syndromes? *Psychological Medicine, 17,* 109–120.

Weston, W. A., & Dalby, J. T. (1991). A case of pseudologia fantastica with antisocial personality disorder. *Canadian Journal of Psychiatry, 36*(8), 612–614.

Wetter, M. W., & Deitsch, S. E. (1996). Faking specific disorders and temporal response consistency on the MMPI-2. *Psychological Assessment, 8*(1), 39–47.

Wilde, G. J. S. (1982). The theory of risk homeostasis: Implications for safety and health. *Risk Analysis, 2,* 209–225.

Williams, L. M. (1994). Recall of childhood trauma: A prospective study of women's memories of child sexual abuse. *Journal of Consulting and Clinical Psychology, 62*(6), 1167–1176.

Wilson, J. P. (1994). The historical evolution of PTSD diagnostic criteria. *Journal of Traumatic Stress, 7*(4), 681–698.

Wolfe, J., Keane, T., Kaloupek, D., Mora, C., & Wine, P. (1993). Patterns of positive readjustment in Vietnam combat veterans. *Journal of Traumatic Stress, 6*(2), 179–193.

World Bank. (1993). *World development report 1993: Investing in health.* New York: Oxford University Press.

Wortman, C. B. (1976). Causal attributions and personal control. In J. H. Harvey, W. J. Ickes, & R. F. Kidd (Eds.), *New directions in attributional research* (pp. 23-52). Hillsdale, New Jersey: Lawrence Erlbaum Associates.

Wortman, C. B., Sheedy, C., Gluhoski, V., & Kessler, R. C. (1992). Stress, coping, and health: Conceptual issues and directions for future research. In H. S. Friedman (Ed.), *Hostility, coping, & health* (pp. 227–256). Washington, DC: American Psychological Association.

Wortman, C. B., & Silver, R. C. (1987). Coping with irrevocable loss. In G. VandenBos & B. K. Bryant (Eds.), *Cataclysms, crises, and catastrophes: Psychology in action* (pp. 185–235). Washington, DC: American Psychological Association.

Wortman, C. B., & Silver, R. C. (1992). Reconsidering assumptions about coping with loss: An overview of current research. In L. Montada, S. H. Filipp, & M. Lerner (Eds.), *Life crises and experiences of loss in adulthood* (pp. 341–365). Hillsdale, NJ: Lawrence Erlbaum Associates.

Wortman, C. B., Silver, R. C., & Kessler, R. C. (1993). The meaning of loss and adjustment to bereavement. In M. S. Stroebe, W. Stroebe, & R. O. Hansson (Eds.), *Handbook of bereavement: Theory, research, and intervention* (pp. 349–366). New York: Cambridge University Press.

Wyman, P. A., & Cowen, E. L. (1993). The role of children's future expectations in self-esteem functioning and adjustment to life stress: A prospective study of urban at-risk children. *Development and Psychopathology, 5*(4), 649–661.

Yehuda, R., Boisoneau, D., Lowy, M. T., & Giller, E. L. (1995). Dose–response changes in plasma cortisol and lymphocyte glucocorticoid receptors following dexamethasone administration in combat veterans with and without posttraumatic stress disorder. *Archives of General Psychiatry, 52*(7), 583–593.

Zaidi, L. Y., & Foy, D. W. (1994). Childhood abuse experiences and combat-related PTSD. *Journal of Traumatic Stress, 7*, 33–42.

Zborowski, M. (1969). *People in pain*. San Francisco: Jossey-Bass.

Ziegler, P. (1995). *London at war*. New York: Alfred Knopf.

Ziv, A., & Israeli, R. (1973). Effects of bombardment on the manifest anxiety level of children living in kibbutzim. *Journal of Consulting and Clinical Psychology, 40*(2), 287–291.

Zuckerman, M. (1971). Dimensions of sensation seeking. *Journal of Consulting and Clinical Psychology, 28*, 477–482.

Zuckerman, M., Kolin, A., Price, L., & Zoob, J. (1964). The development and validation of a sensation-seeking scale. *Journal of Consulting and Clinical Psychology, 28*, 477–482.

Author Index

Subject Index